Cafe Indiana

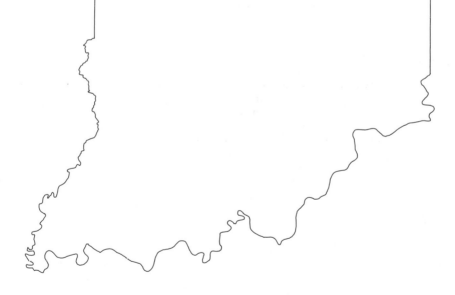

Cafe Indiana

A Guide to Indiana's Down-Home Cafes

Joanne Raetz Stuttgen

The University of Wisconsin Press

The University of Wisconsin Press
1930 Monroe Street
Madison, Wisconsin 53711

www.wisc.edu/wisconsinpress/

3 Henrietta Street
London WC2E 8LU, England

Printed in the United States of America

Library of Congress Cataloging-in-Publication Data

Stuttgen, Joanne Raetz, 1961–
Cafe Indiana : a guide to Indiana's down-home cafes / Joanne Raetz Stuttgen.
p.   cm.
Includes index.
ISBN 0-299-22494-5 (alk. paper)
1. Restaurants—Indiana—Guidebooks. 2. Indiana—Guidebooks. I. Title.
TX907.3.I35S88   2007
647.95772—dc22   2007011948

Book layout and composition: Alcorn Publication Design

Dedicated to
Josie and Larry Montgomery,
Lapel Family Restaurant, Lapel,
and
JoAnn Phillips and the Spartan Group,
Spartan Inn, Wingate,
whose cafes were destroyed by fire during the writing of this book.
And to the memory of John E. Hurt Sr., a native of Hall, Indiana,
who loved country-fried steak with milk gravy

Contents

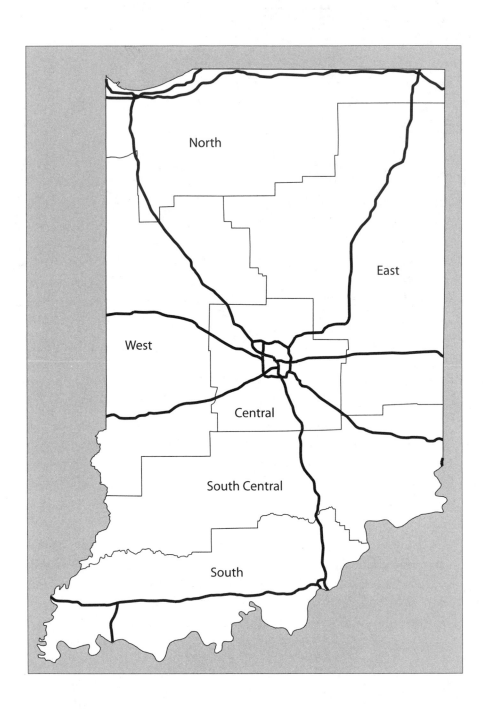

North

East

West

Central

South Central

South

Preface

Getting Started

Welcome to *Cafe Indiana*.

Cafe Indiana is my third book on small town cafes. It follows two editions of *Cafe Wisconsin* (1993, 2004). Now and again I had contemplated a Hoosier version, so when the University of Wisconsin Press agreed, I pulled out my Indiana road map and began plotting my next statewide food foray.

A great way to learn about Indiana is to learn what it is not. Certainly there are many similarities between Wisconsin and Indiana cafes, but it is the differences that are most striking. I grew up in Minnesota, lived in Wisconsin, and came to Indiana in 1990. For the past seventeen years I have lived in Martinsville, but *Cafe Indiana* taught me that all these years I haven't really been a Hoosier at all. I knew nothing about what Hoosiers like to eat or, for that matter, what goes on in Hoosier cafes. I thought I was an expert on cafe food and culture, but my education was just beginning.

Come on. Let's go out to eat.

The inspiration for the cafe books comes from my bicycling friends in Eau Claire, Wisconsin, who joined me for countless Sunday morning pie rides in search of the ultimate cafe.

As the sun rose above the wooded hills, we'd roll out of town. Some thirty or forty miles later, we'd lean our bikes against the front of a small town cafe, where we'd refuel on pie, cinnamon rolls, toast, and coffee for the return trip home.

In this way we came to know the highways running through neighboring counties, the small towns sprinkled in the valleys and cut into the hills. By the lure of good food we came to feel a sense of place and the lingering of the past in the present, and we came to appreciate the power of rootedness and belonging that merges individuals into community.

As a folklorist, I am interested in cultural traditions that maintain a familiar sameness despite change over time and across regions. This is the sort of change that produces the all-American apple pie and its countless variations: mock apple pie, dutch or french apple pie, apple crisp, apple cobbler, apple pan dowdy. By considering objects that are created by human hands—apple pie—or performances by individuals in social settings, such as joke telling or card playing, folklorists explore cultural patterns that give form and meaning to human lives, both in the vanished past and in the present.

During my research for both *Cafe Indiana* and *Cafe Wisconsin*, I sought historical and regional connections between small town, main street, and back street eateries by considering food traditions, architecture and ornamentation, ownership and patronage, and social groups (sometimes called Liars Clubs or Roundtables). I wanted to discover what roles cafes play in small towns and in the lives of individuals, and why cafes have survived—in some cases even thrived—in Indiana across time and space.

Other writers have attempted to translate food and eating into a cultural experience. In *Blue Highways* (1982), William Least Heat-Moon deliberately sought out "Ma in her beanery and Pap over his barbecue pit, both still serving slow food from the same place they did thirty years ago." Perhaps best remembered for his "calendar method" of rating cafes, in which a no-calendar cafe is little better than an "interstate pit stop" and a seven-calendar cafe is a golden legend from the past, Heat-Moon whetted the appetites of adventure eaters throughout the country for the deliberately prepared, regionally diverse "slow food" found in obscure eateries along remote byways.

Nearly fifty years before Heat-Moon left his Missouri home for cafes unknown, Duncan Hines's *Adventures in Good Eating,* first published in 1936, was being thumbed by travelers and businessmen the country over. Annually for the next twenty-six years, Hines updated his pocket-sized guide to restaurants serving genuine home-cooked food. His selections leaned more toward glamorous hotel and resort dining rooms in larger cities than unpretentious small town, main street eateries. In Indiana, he heartily endorsed the Greystone Hotel on the square in Bedford ("one of my favorites in this section of Indiana"), Mangas Cafeteria in Elwood, and Little White Kitchen in Lewisville. All are scarcely memories today.

Until they ceased in 1962, the yearly volumes of *Adventures in Good Eating* were regarded by Hines and his thousands of readers as indispensable companions on any trip, whether across the country or across the city. Although Hines's perspective is genteel, his sentiment is practical and earthy. Hines wrote of his mission in 1942: "How hard it is to find simple dishes finely prepared. Cornbread, fried potatoes, codfish cakes, baked beans, eggs, etc. And when the hungry tourist does find them, how he shouts the glad news to all his friends."

Hines was lucky. He didn't have to contend with preprocessed and frozen foods, such as instant mashed potato flakes (and now, preservative-laced real mashed potatoes air-sealed in a plastic bag) and frozen "home-baked" (not homemade) pies that frustrate today's adventure eaters.

In her essay "The Great American Pie Expedition" (1989, 1995), Sue Hubbell argues that the use of frozen pie crusts is a sure sign of an inadequate cook and "probably a mercy, because if left to their own devices they would make worse." Leaving Washington, D.C., with her dog, Tazzie, Hubbell trekked through the Northeast, the Ozarks, and on into Oklahoma in search of perfect pie. She followed three rules devised during her travels: 85 percent of cafes located between two businesses will have good pie. Good pie is often found near places where meadowlarks sing. Never eat pie within one mile of an interstate highway. I know little about meadowlarks, but I do know about squeeze-in cafes versus off-the-highway truck stops. At the former, you're likely to find from-scratch, fresh-apple pie and at the second, premade, flash-frozen pie assembled at a manufacturing plant hundreds of miles away and "home baked" in the restaurant kitchen.

Jane and Michael Stern's *Roadfood* (first edition 1977, latest edition 2005) is a paperback compendium of humble eateries that serve outstanding regional fare, ranging from catfish and chili dogs to Chicago-style pizza, chitterlings, and corn chowder. For three years, the Sterns traveled with truckers along interstates and major highways, discovering "the essence of America" by sampling its varied roadside tastes. In Indiana, the Sterns ate coconut custard pie at the Remington Cafe in Remington, praised the fried chicken and cherry pecan torte at the Fiesta Restaurant in Madison, and breakfasted on buckwheat pancakes at the Courtesy Coffee Shop in Winchester. The Fiesta and Courtesy Coffee Shop no longer exist.

The Remington Cafe has been reinvented as Peppin's Cafe, now The Lovely Cafe, which is featured in this book.

Several Hoosiers before me have offered their own takes on the state's dining experience. Reid Duffy is well known for *Duffy's Diner* on Indianapolis's WRTV Channel 6, and his *Indiana's Favorite Restaurants* (2001, 2006) is a "gastronomic Who's Who of the Hoosier state." *Dining Secrets of Indiana* (fifth edition, no date), a paperback guide produced by Poole Publishing, covers a "wide variety of unique and interesting dining experiences" found primarily in the state's larger cities. A third book is Wendell Trogdon's *Main Street Diners* (2001), a basic, nostalgic directory to small town eateries "where Hoosiers begin their day." What makes *Cafe Indiana* different is its deep focus on Hoosier food traditions and the varied roles cafes fill in the lives of individuals and communities.

I have concentrated entirely on traditional cafes hiding in small towns off the beaten path. Sorting these out from today's colorful variety of other eateries called for a careful definition based on these criteria: (1) location in the town's original business district and typically on the main street, a requirement that frequently—but not always—eliminates old drive-ins and fast food franchises turned into family-type restaurants, as well as truck stops and cafes attached to gas stations and located alongside highways; (2) an established history in the community; and (3) a role as the year-round gathering place for local residents

Beyond this, traditional cafes are generally owner operated and have limited seating—usually a handful of booths and tables with one or more counters and stools. Seating generally averages about forty people; my upper limit is about eighty but sometimes as high as one hundred. The hours tend to be limited—for example, 5 A.M. to 2 P.M. Cafes typically do not serve beer, wine, or liquor. They feature daily, home-cooked specials based on traditional heartland "farm food": meat, mashed potatoes and gravy (affectionately known as MPG), vegetables, and desserts, especially pie. A good general rule is that cafe food is familiar and conservative, rarely trendy, with white bread and devil's food cake taking the place of croissants and chocolate mousse.

Bear in mind, however, that all of the above are guidelines rather than rules. They must be applied with a certain degree of flexibility. Some cafes are relatively new businesses; some are run by managers instead of owners;

some have liquor licenses; and some even specialize in desserts that were likely never served, let alone heard of, on the farm.

This balance between conservatism and change is what lures folklorists to their work. It is also what pulls pie riders out of bed before sunrise and sends them pedaling down county highways in search of good home cooking that is comfortable in its sameness, yet unique in its quality and innovation. Pie riders and other adventure eaters are much like folklorists in their search for things reminiscent of the past and symbolic of a way of life rather than merely a passage through—a way of life shaped by the hand, enriched by the heart, and impressed with community. So we search out cafes that recreate images of home with displays of family photos, dish up home-style cooking, encourage friendships through coffee groups, convey continuity in their architecture and decoration, and express commitment to community by virtue of their longevity. These cafes comfort us in their sameness, yet, in their uniqueness, incite us to adventure.

For three main reasons, I have limited my search for traditional cafes to small towns with populations of approximately ten thousand or less.

First, I wanted to explore Indiana back roads and discover humble, small town restaurants that still serve good home cooking.

Second, I wanted to understand how modest cafes—and small communities, too, for that matter—manage to survive in a world increasingly interpreted as distant, impersonal, mechanized, and fast paced.

Third—and most important for the adventure eater—in towns smaller than ten thousand, it's almost impossible to get lost. It's always easy to find cafes by their locations on the main business streets, by the soft drink sign hanging over the sidewalk, by the cars and pickups corralled on the street, and by the bank of newspaper vending boxes on the sidewalk out front.

To avoid dead-end meandering down every main street in the state and to make for less work on the road, I began by creating a master list of small town cafes. I first identified all small towns on the Indiana state road map. With the help of various Web sources, publications, restaurant guidebooks, newspaper articles, and the advice of people throughout the state, I created a master list of potential cafes based on names, addresses, descriptions, recommendations, and my previous experience and knowledge. Restaurants located on "Main Street" or on low-numbered streets were candidates, as were restaurants with names such as Coffee Cup or Cozy Kitchen, or any restaurant whose name included a personal name or initials, or the town in which it was located.

Even eliminating such obvious noncafes as Do-Drop Inns, franchises, and steakhouses, I still had a list of potential cafes that was far too lengthy. So, I phoned chambers of commerce, libraries, town halls, and post offices and asked for help in identifying community restaurants specializing in basic farm food and serving as local gathering places. I often called and conducted brief interviews with cafe owners, managers, or employees to determine whether or not a personal visit was warranted. I asked questions about the history of the restaurant, whether it was a popular hangout—especially with men's coffee groups—its seating capacity, and the type of food being prepared and served. The answers I received helped me to determine which restaurants I would visit.

Conducted between July 2004 and February 2007, my visits were spent chatting with owners and customers, taking notes, joining in story- and joke-telling sessions, taking tours through kitchens, studying old photographs displayed or dug out of storage by cafe owners, and inspecting building construction, outside facades, and inside decoration. I conscientiously attempted to visit every cafe on my list (which numbered nearly four hundred), but sometimes I came to a cafe after it was closed for the day or for the owners' two-week vacation. In such cases, I stopped back later for another try if I was in the vicinity; if a personal visit was not possible, I followed up with a telephone interview.

The sixty-four cafes featured in the following chapters have distinguished themselves by providing commendable food and/or atmosphere. My primary qualification for inclusion was good home cooking, which I judged on the basis of favorite "test foods": pie, baked goods, mashed potatoes, soups, hamburgers, tenderloins, and chicken or beef and noodles. While all of the featured cafes serve good home cooking, not all of them serve home-cooked everything. Some things have to be forgiven, so exceptional pie sometimes compensates for instant potato buds, homemade egg noodles for canned broth, and bakery hamburger buns for preformed frozen beef patties.

Next, I considered how open and receptive people were to me as a total stranger, especially whether owners were willing to take time out to talk, or whether customers welcomed me to take part in their pastimes.

If an owner refused to meet with me, if conversation came begrudgingly, or people were less than articulate, I found myself passing through a cafe particularly quickly.

A cafe's appearance was also important. I favored those that were comfortable, pleasant, clean, and homelike. It was thrilling to discover cafes that remain relatively unchanged despite the passage of years, cafes that still feature century-old pressed tin ceilings and walnut backbars or mid-twentieth-century soda fountains, polished chrome, and patterned Formica.

On the other hand, cafes whose histories had been obliterated in the pursuit of modernization left me empty and uninspired. With their impersonal, computer-printed checks, laminated print-shop menus, and identical, mass-produced waitress uniforms, they feel exactly like franchises, and I have not featured some that otherwise met my qualifications. Likewise, I was easily and frequently bored by cafes lacking personality, or those that seemed merely to be a hapless assemblage of plain-Jane tables and chairs set out between nearly bare walls.

Lastly, I invited cafe owners to participate in the creation of the book by providing input on the stories I had written. They were able to suggest corrections, clarifications, additions, and sometimes deletions. Some cafe owners chose not to be featured in the book for personal reasons, so if your favorite is missing, this is likely why. Unless specifically instructed otherwise, I listed these cafes as Next Best Bets.

The 181 cafes are mapped into Indiana's six tourism regions, each of which makes up a chapter. Within each region or chapter, featured cafes are listed alphabetically by the name of the town in which they are located. Listings include street addresses or locations, telephone numbers, hours of operation as of April 2007, and names of owners. This information is constantly changing, so I advise you to call ahead to avoid disappointment. If cigarette smoke is an issue with you, I further advise you to call and ask about air quality. Smoking is prevalent in Indiana cafes, especially in the southern part of the state.

Because I am repeatedly asked what cafes are the state's "best," I have designated those cafes I consider to be standouts with ☕ . These cafes excel at nearly every aspect of the business; more important, they are the only cafes I would not hesitate to drive one hundred miles out of my way for. "Next Best Bet" cafes, which deserve a visit because of notable menu specialties, decor, or people, are listed alphabetically by town at the end of each chapter. All cafes included herein are found in two alphabetical indexes at the back of the book, one organized by the name of the town in which they're located, the other by the name of the cafe itself.

The final chapter, an epilogue, summarizes the many roles that cafes play in small communities and in the lives of individuals and compares Indiana and Wisconsin cafe foods and culture. Normally, material of this kind appears as an introduction rather than a conclusion, instructing readers what to expect in the chapters to follow. But that is not how I learned about Indiana's small town cafes. I wasn't told what to see. My sight developed. I'd like you to come to understand cafes the way I did: gradually, through the words of owners and customers; through sights and sounds and tastes; through penetration of the past and perusal of the present.

This book can be used in several ways. It is both a reliable directory to Indiana's down-home cafes and an analysis of the varied roles cafes play in small towns. Like *Blue Highways*, it is a journey into the intimate lives of communities and individuals. Like *Adventures in Good Eating*, it is a reliable companion intended to delight and comfort travelers. Like "The Great American Pie Expedition," it is a celebration of the authentic and home-made and a rejection of the artificial. And like *Roadfood*, it is an exploration of regional food traditions that result in Hoosier food phenomena like pork tenderloins, biscuits and gravy, chicken (or beef) and noodles, sugar cream pie, fried brain sandwiches, fried biscuits and apple butter, and persimmon pudding.

And so, having found small town cafes serving simple dishes finely prepared, this hungry tourist shouts the glad news to all her friends.

Acknowledgments

With continued fondness I thank the original pie riders in Eau Claire, Wisconsin. They know who they are and what they mean to me.

Although I wrote the text that follows, the histories, anecdotes and many of the words themselves were given to me by cafe owners and their customers. It is their story I tell. I am particularly indebted to owners who generously engaged in hours of conversation, including Daniel Alemu, Daniel's Ligonier Cafe, Ligonier; Trini and Sherry Arias, Reme's Monon Family Restaurant, Monon; Tim Brown, Koffee Kup, Kouts; Ann Cain, Wolcott Theatre Cafe, Wolcott; Donna Friend, Gosport Diner, Gosport; Pieternella "Nel" Geurs, Nel's Cafe, Ossian; Tom and Gayle Gray, Brock's Family Restaurant, Brownstown; Tom Hackett, Town Square Restaurant, Howe; Marty Huffman, Marty's Bluebird Cafe, Laketon; Darrel and Betty Jenkins, Windell's Cafe, Dale; Susie Mahler, Cafe Max, Culver; Betty Melton, Sonny's, Hartford City; Beth Michaels, Flat Rock Cafe, Flat Rock; Debbie Montgomery, Velma's Diner, Shoals; Tony Shuman, Highway 341 Country Cafe, Wallace; Don Storie, Storie's Restaurant, Greensburg; Marsha Thomas, Corner Cafe, Nappanee; and Emma Lou Wilson, Emma Lou's Sandwich Shop, Princeton.

Lastly, I owe a heart full of thanks to my son, Pete, who spent the months I was away blissfully playing on the computer with no Mom yelling at him to get off; my husband, Mark, who lets me go and welcomes me home; Sandra Dolby, Joanne Flemming, Jon Kay, and Alice Morrison, who read the manuscript; Diana Cook and Adam Mehring at the University of Wisconsin Press, who read the manuscript again (and again); John E. Hurt Jr. and his late father, John E. Hurt Sr., who shared their lovely home on Lake Wawasee; and to Raphael Kadushin at the University of Wisconsin Press, who saw the project through from beginning to end.

North

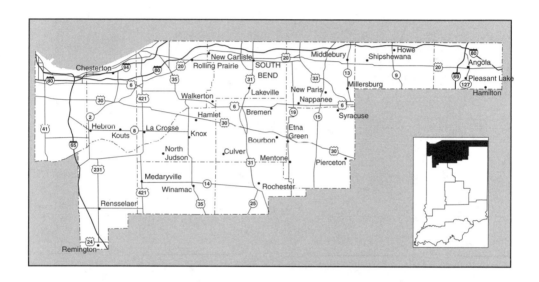

CULVER

Cafe Max ☒
113 South Main Street
(574) 842-2511
M–Su 6 A.M.–2 P.M.
Susie Mahler

I made my first trip to Culver on a bicycle several years ago, one of several hundred cyclists on the annual Touring Ride in Rural Indiana (TRIRI). We arrived early in the morning, but not so early as to escape dangerous rising temperatures and humidity. Through the silver-gray haze, the stunning brick buildings of the Culver Academies rose like apparitions warning us of the torturous day that lay ahead. It was nearly as hot when I returned to Culver, a jewel of a small town on the banks of beautiful Lake Maxinkuckee.

Due to the presence of the academies, whose students come from moneyed families, and Indianapolis millionaires who have erected pala- tial lakeside homes, Culver is a peculiar and enticing mixture of traditional small town culture and urban sophistication. The two-block commercial dis- trict, which in recent years has begun to enjoy a spirited renewal, perfectly represents the mix. Anchoring the south end of Main Street is Culver Pro Hardware, a workaday source of assorted necessities to keep both utilitar- ian houses and summer villas running without a hitch. It is flanked by a scattering of clever little shops selling gifts, fancy antiques and collectibles, and upscale clothing that survive on the pocketbooks of Culver's seasonal residents and visitors.

Culver native Susie Mahler's Cafe Max is a happy meeting ground for everyone who calls Culver home—both full time and part time—and for plenty of others who don't. Worn out by the heat and too many miles on the road, and with the discovery of a truly remarkable cafe long overdue, I step inside Cafe Max with considerable expectation. And though I have been told that the cafe doubles as a local museum featuring town, academy, and Lake Maxinkuckee history, I am not altogether prepared for the col- lection of wonderful stuff that I encounter! There are Culver High School marching band uniforms and tasseled hats (and a yellowed bass drum from the old junior high), framed historic photos, letter sweaters and yell sweaters, athletic trophies and discarded academy uniforms with insignia and badges and tassels and medals. But my hands-down, without-a-doubt favorite is a corduroy skirt with an impossibly small waist suspended from the ceiling above my table. It is the senior cords of Mimi Miller, a member of the Culver High School class of 1962. The cream-colored skirt is painted with color caricatures of a lanky basketball player (#3) and Mimi's chums, whose signatures testify to their undying friendship.

James and Rosalie Bonine, my neighbors at the next table, who have just retired from their Culver funeral home business, remember the tradition of senior cords very well. Explains Rosalie, "You'd hire an artist to paint scenes on them. I never had them myself because we couldn't afford that kind of thing." Jim, on the other hand, did have a pair of corduroy pants, but his looked more to the future than to the past four years he'd spent at Warsaw High School. "I knew I wanted to be a funeral home director when I was in school, so I had No Parking painted on the back of mine."

Having been regular customers of Culver's main street cafe for as long as they've lived in town—"We moved here forty-four years ago yesterday"—the Bonines have witnessed the transformation it has undergone in Susie's hands since she bought the former Nan-E-Lou Restaurant in 1985 at the young age of twenty-two. Because she'd grown up in the community, many of her customers expressed a parental interest in her welfare. They advised her to proceed cautiously with her new business—maybe wiggle a toe or two in the water before plunging in up to her neck. Touched as she was by their concern, Susie nevertheless began remodeling right away, mostly because she despised the "classic 1970s look" of the cafe, with its orange and gold casino-style carpet, plastic candelabras, and dropped ceiling.

"I had often gone to Chicago restaurants and was influenced by what I saw there," she explains, "but I didn't have a real plan when I began remodeling. I just uncovered, replaced, and restored as I went." She lifted the dropped ceiling panels and discovered a vintage pressed tin ceiling fourteen feet above the wood floor, exposed and polished after several layers of flooring had been laboriously peeled away. The original plaster walls were repaired and painted a cool sage green, and then spruced up with a wainscot of red brick veneer.

"My remodeling wasn't too well received at first," Susie remembers. "My customers were cost conscious for me. They warned me that the high ceiling would mean high heat bills. They were concerned that I was going backward."

Though they were fearful of falling into the past, it was the very same customers who suggested that history—in the form of memorabilia from Culver's own past—be used to decorate the emerging restaurant. Embracing the idea, Susie concentrated on three themes that have defined Culver through the years: town, academy, and lake. The unofficial museum got a considerable boost when the old town high school was replaced by a new consolidated building, and items that had been in storage since 1968 were transferred to Cafe Max. "The photos were taken down and the school colors changed from maroon and white to orange and black," Susie explains. "I guess they wanted to start fresh, so they put all of that old stuff in storage. We're fortunate that they saved it and we have it today."

As Susie's remodeling of the cafe moved from inside to outside, other property owners and merchants began to take notice. After she painted the building's tin cornice with different colors to highlight its design, it wasn't long before other cornices sported complementary new looks. The growing interest in making Culver more attractive and inviting led to a community-wide, collaborative planning process that formulated a vision for Culver's future. "The local merchants finally came on board with the idea that Culver is a tourism-driven community," explains Susie. "Out of that came ideas to enhance the downtown, like coordinating paint colors, awnings, and planters and window boxes."

With one foot set firmly in the past and the other in the present, Cafe Max boasts an urbane preservationist aesthetic in a genuine small town setting that many restaurants strive for but rarely achieve. The same comfortable commingling is evident in the menu.

I'm craving fresh vegetables after feasting on carb-laden Hoosier cafe food for days on end, and I am thrilled to discover inventive salads with a refined flair on the menu. The Mediterranean chicken salad, made with a variety of nutritious field greens including arugula, frisée and radicchio laced with mango chardonnay dressing, is delightfully unexpected. The bowl's flat rim is ringed with carefully placed mandarin orange slices, making the salad as beautiful as it is delicious.

I can't help but notice, however, that both James and Rosalie Bonine are lunching on the daily special: country-fried steak with mashed potatoes and gravy and a side serving of canned peas. If traditional Hoosier comfort food is what you're hungry for, you, too, will be happy at Cafe Max, where the

Bonines drop in daily for the noon meal and often for a morning start-up as well. "We're here every day," James tells me, "so people know they'll find us here. It's where we get our news. There was a bad accident last night, so this morning the talk was who was involved."

More likely than not, the Bonines find the daily special to their liking, but Rosalie confides, "We like their beef Manhattans quite a bit, too." Pausing during cleanup, my waitress stops alongside the Bonines' table and joins our conversation about the cafe's popular menu items. "Meat, potatoes, and vegetables are pretty much our bread and butter," she puns without seeming to notice. "Today's country-fried steak is always a good seller. Of course, there's always oven-fried steak, Salisbury steak, and swiss steak."

She laughs. "They're all pretty much the same thing."

All are gussied up, tenderized cuts of cheaper beef, such as round or cube steak. Country-fried steak (you might know it as chicken fried) is dipped in beaten eggs and coated with seasoned crumbs or flour, then pan or deep fried and served with milk gravy. Oven-fried steak is the same thing, only baked in an oven instead of fried in hot oil. Salisbury steak is the same thing again, although it is typically made from patties of ground beef. Last but not least—and my top choice of the four—is swiss steak, made by baking the same steak in tomatoes and green peppers until moist and tender.

Trendy radicchio and down-home, old-fashioned country-fried steak are fast friends at Cafe Max. Their best-selling buddies include homemade bread, soups, biscuits and gravy, yeast donuts straight out of the fryer, and cinnamon rolls swimming in butter. The same cinnamon rolls are sliced to make the sinful french toast, a hit with students from the academies, who loyally drop in every Saturday morning when school is in session. While the regulars return again and again for familiar favorites, out-of-town visitors and multimillionaire summer residents come in hopes of finding real home cooking that for them epitomizes the ideal small town. "They demand comfort food because they're living the 'simple life' in Culver," Susie notes, crooking her fingers to indicate quotation marks. Still others come as much for the food as for the journey. "I have cyclists who come from Valpo just to eat here. Then they turn around and go back."

HAMILTON
Baby Boomers II
7690 South Wayne Street
(260) 488-3244
M–Th 6 A.M.–2 P.M.; F–Sa 6 A.M.–8 P.M.; Su 7 A.M.–2 P.M.
Penny Hawkins

During the seven years that Penny Hawkins worked at Baby Boomers for previous owner Ed Sutton, her responsibilities gradually expanded from waiting tables to cutting meat, making side dishes, doing the payroll, and managing the staff. As an employee herself, she did not have to shoulder the worries of the business and could leave work behind her when she went home for the night. This all changed on Memorial Day weekend 2004 when Ed announced, "This is the last weekend you'll work."

"He called on Saturday at five o'clock and asked if I'd like to buy the business," Penny remembers. "On Monday I said yes."

The Hawkins family vacation out West that had been planned for months was canceled, and the month of June was spent getting the restaurant ready to reopen. "My husband and brother-in-law did a lot of repairs, replacement of equipment, and reorganizing. The biggest job was putting in new water and sewer lines in the bathroom. We always had problems in there. Now the toilet will flush your hat. That's what people say."

In 1991, Ed converted Hamilton's drugstore into the 1950s diner–themed Baby Boomers, tricked out with a black and white tile floor, the drugstore's 1943 stainless-steel soda fountain, funky reproduction chrome-legged tables, and matching chairs covered with sparkly pink and turquoise vinyl. Penny inherited it all when she took over, along with the restaurant's reputation for home cooking that customers in the tristate area have voted among their favorite.

Baby Boomers' burgers and milkshakes have earned multiple Honorable Mention "Best of the Best" awards by readers of three northeast Indiana newspapers. The cafe specializes in six- and ten-ounce burgers—real two-handers!—pattied by hand from fresh ground chuck. "When we put down a hamburger in front of you," Penny laughs, "you're going to know it!" My cheeseburger is nearly an inch thick in the middle, slightly tapering down to bulging edges that just fit inside the large buttered and grilled bun. Stuffed with lettuce, two slices of tomato, sliced onion, and mayo, the burger is stacked as high as a pillbox hat on a bouffant hairdo.

"A few days ago a guy ordered a double bacon cheeseburger," Penny says incredulously. "That's twenty ounces of meat! I asked the server if he looked surprised when she set it in front of him. She said no. That's twenty ounces of meat! Maybe he knew what he was getting."

While a burger this size scarcely leaves room for any extras, it begs for a Best of the Best ice cream accompaniment. The milkshakes shook up the newspaper voters, but I find Penny's old-fashioned ice cream soda to be the real cherry on top. The older crowd agrees, exclaiming with pleasure, "It's just like we used to get!" According to Penny, the most popular flavors are vanilla, strawberry, and chocolate. "But for those who actually break down and order the pineapple, wow! This is great!"

Of course, I order pineapple. At the soda fountain, Penny dips a scoop of vanilla ice cream from the lidded freezer, plops it into a large clear glass, and gives it one generous squirt of vanilla syrup. Adding soda water, she whips the contents by hand with a teaspoon until creamy. The staccato of the spoon hitting the glass sounds like popcorn popping in a microwave. Then come two more scoops of ice cream, more soda water, and ladles of crushed pineapple sauce that run in thick streams down the inside of the glass. Topped with whipped cream and a cherry, my pineapple soda is an unbeatable, unforgettable blast from the past.

Do not think that Baby Boomers is all about burgers and ice cream, however. There are so many splendors on the menu that you'd best come in famished—or better yet, in a famished party of at least four so everyone can order something different and share. Realizing that Ed's success was the ticket to her own, Penny determined right from the start that her "main goal was to continue what Ed had made." She follows his lead by buying only quality fresh ribeye, pork loin, and chicken from Harger's Meats in nearby Angola, which she trims and cuts herself. She pounds and breads her own tenderloins and even makes her own chicken strips. Other specialties include homemade soups, biscuits and gravy, breaded or grilled pork chops, barbecued chicken, and corned beef. Though Ed was not much for sweets other than ice cream, Penny has added a variety of desserts well represented by last night's selection of layered caramel cake and custard, raisin cream, and coconut cream pies. All were sold out but not yet erased from the daily specials board, as I discovered when I requested a piece of custard pie. My loss was my gain. I ordered the pineapple soda instead.

Straddling the Steuben–De Kalb county line, the town of Hamilton is located on the south bay of Hamilton Lake, which is ringed with both modest older dwellings and new homes valued in excess of a million dollars. Between Memorial Day and Labor Day, the year-round population of 650 swells with vacationers and summer residents who take over the lake and the town, forcing Penny's regular customers to adjust their daily schedules in order to get a parking spot out front and a place to sit inside. Surrounded by historic photographs of Hamilton displayed on the walls ("It's so important to show what Hamilton was," believes Penny), local residents mingle democratically with business executives from Chicago and Detroit, as well as bicyclists from Fort Wayne and fishermen and hunters from throughout the Midwest.

Baby Boomers also serves to bring together people who are part of the local community but whose difference in age would otherwise keep them apart. Wearing an Angola High School track team T-shirt with the words "If you believe, you will achieve" on the back, Penny's older daughter, Alysha, works as a waitress. Her younger daughter, Alicesun, spends Saturday afternoons drawing and coloring at a back table with Joe, a member of the men's coffee group and a meteorologist and artist. "He teaches me about weather, art, just about everything," Alicesun explains.

"Joe is a real teacher," adds Penny. "He has just so much uniqueness. He taught her how to carve a boat out of a bar of soap. Alicesun used to be afraid of the weather. Last week we were driving home and she said, 'Look, at those clouds, Mom. Those aren't tornado clouds.' She could identify the different types of clouds by name."

Using colored pencils, Joe sketches a monarch butterfly, a mayfly, and a brown trout on sheets of white paper and slides the completed drawings across the table to Alicesun. He teaches her not only their familiar names but also their scientific names, spelling out the genus and species of each in the lower right corners of the pages. When five men join them, Joe does not interrupt the lesson, and Alicesun does not leave the table. Gradually the conversation moves on to encompass other subjects, and still Alicesun stays, listening with her chin propped on the upturned heels of her hands.

"Joe's a good teacher," concludes Penny. "But he's an even better friend."

HOWE
Town Square Restaurant ౿
407 Third Street
(260) 562-3584
M 6 A.M.–2 P.M.; Tu–F 6 A.M.–7 P.M.; Sa 6 A.M.–2 P.M.; Su closed
Tom and Cindy Hackett
Just a few miles off the Indiana Toll Road, the Town Square Restaurant
specializes in home cooking so good that it makes "a hundred miles a rea-
sonable trip to go out to eat," confesses Mickey Strug of Crown Point. She
and Joe Jensen, a native southerner now living in Plainfield, Illinois, have a
passion for poking around urban nooks and along rural byways in search of
eateries serving not merely good but remarkable food. "We've been known
to drive 150 miles to go out to eat."

As experienced adventure eaters who recognize quality cooking, they
are finding it increasingly difficult to find food worth eating because, Joe
says, "people no longer know what good food is."

"Why do people settle for bad food?" Mickey wants to know.

Although they play a major role in the dumbing down of America's
taste buds, fast food franchises and frozen food companies don't deserve
to be singled out for indictment. A great number of small town cafes are
equally to blame. There are cafe owners who *really* cook, who regard the
preparation of food as a creative expression and a challenge to do one's
personal best. And then there are cafe owners who merely run restaurants, for whom cooking lacks emotion, an activity done to feed the body
and not the soul. It's the difference between soaking tenderized, fresh
pork loins in buttermilk, coating them with seasoned flour or crumbs,
and frying them to golden perfection, and tearing open a bag of frozen pork fritters, tossing them into the deep fryer, and calling them the
Friday special.

Mickey and Joe concede that adventure eating is a risky business
because you never know when you walk into a place whether the food
will be good or bad. Joe believes it's this take-a-chance uncertainty, this
fear of the unknown, that leads people to settle for less than quality food.
Mediocrity not only becomes an acceptable standard but desirable as well
because it is predictable, knowable, comfortable. Joe explains, "I think the
reason people like fast food is because you can get some really bad food

out there. It doesn't matter where you are. It's the same McDonald's, the same Burger King, the same thing everywhere."

Mediocre will never be used to describe the Town Square Restaurant. Cut that page out of your dictionary, crumple it up, and throw it away. No adjectives less than superlative sufficiently describe the genuine home cooking that has been carried out of the kitchen to waiting diners for over fifty years. Says owner Tom Hackett, "They all say, 'We have home-cooked food.' But we *really* do. Those cabbage rolls are made right back there by a seventy-year-old woman who has been here thirteen years."

This is Mickey and Joe's second visit to the Town Square—the second within four months—and already they are fast friends with Tom and his wife, Cindy. Tom puts his yeast rolls aside to rise and sits down for a visit, excusing himself now and then to check on the rolls' progress. The four met earlier in the summer at a toll road oasis. Mickey, Joe, and Mickey's sheltie, Zoe, were returning home from Maryland. "I met Cindy with her sheltie," explains Mickey. "We talked dogs. We talked food. And we came here."

As with all adventure eaters deserving the description, Mickey and Joe remember standout restaurants by the food they ate. "I had sloppy joes the first time, and were they ever good," enthuses Mickey.

Proving that a cafe's success lies in attention to details, Joe concurs. "The sloppy joe mix was delicious, but what I really like was the buttered, toasted bun. I don't want wet bread."

Joe and I both order the cabbage rolls, one of four daily specials along with beef tips with noodles, country-fried steak, and beef Manhattan—a hot beef sandwich with mashed potatoes and gravy. From an extensive list of side dishes, I choose cream of broccoli soup and a pleasant mayonnaise-based potato salad made with finely chopped boiled potatoes, celery, and hard-cooked eggs. Both sides were a teasing segue into the pair of cabbage rolls served in a ceramic ramekin. "Rolls" is not an accurate description. Much better is "logs"—as in hefty logs of seasoned ground beef and rice tightly wrapped in cabbage leaves and swimming in a light broth. They were so big that I could eat only one. The second was packed in a takeout box for tomorrow's lunch.

Scrutinizing the cabbage rolls as if they are a cultural artifact, Mickey and Joe conclude that the seventy-year-old cook must be of eastern European heritage. The tell-tale clue is the thin broth made from the stewing cabbage and beef that takes the place of a more common tomato-based sauce. Summing up their verdict, Mickey says, "I'm Croatian, and this is the kind of cabbage rolls I'm familiar with."

The size of the entrees at the Town Square requires hearty appetites or strategic eating—or both!—because you absolutely must save room for pie. The pie here is so good, Joe says, that "the waitresses don't ask you what kind you'd like to order. Instead, they order you to have pie!"

I discovered a scant handful of Hoosier cafes with truly outstanding pie, and the Town Square Restaurant may well be the blue-ribbon best. I wallowed in a slab of chocolate peanut butter pie (like the cabbage rolls that were logs, this was no mere "piece") layered bottom to top with peanut butter crumbs, peanut butter pudding, chocolate pudding, and real whipped cream dusted with cocoa.

Though stuffed to the gills with the Town Square's offerings, many customers think nothing of packing coolers with loaves of fresh wheat and white bread, whole pies, and pans of extra large cinnamon rolls to tide them over until their next visit. Tom and Cindy have even loaned their personal cooler to folks who didn't have the foresight to bring one of their own. They're that confident they'll be back.

"When we bought the restaurant in 1991," Tom says, "it already had a tradition of good food. We have made many changes and improvements so that we now have excellent food here. Once people find us, we have them forever."

KOUTS
Koffee Kup ☸
105 South Main Street
(219) 766-2414
M–Sa 5 A.M.–2 P.M.; Su closed (Central Time)
Tim and Donna Brown
From the window of the Koffee Kup cafe looking out over Main Street, and from inside the car he drives to and from his night job in a Gary steel mill, Tim Brown observes a landscape in transition. Sweeping farmland seasonally painted green and gold by soybeans and feed corn are being replaced by look-alike subdivisions. Inside the cookie-cutter homes live people Tim does not know and who, for the most part, do not patronize Kouts's little restaurant.

"People are moving here from the northwest—Valpo, Merrillville, even Chicago," Tim notes. "Younger people are moving here, and they don't know Kouts. They tend to shop and eat in Valpo, which is now just up the road. All the franchise stores and restaurants are helping to make Kouts a suburb or bedroom community. People sleep here and spend the rest of their lives somewhere else."

When the Browns bought the Koffee Kup in 1992, Kouts was "still this little town ten miles from Valpo." It supported lumber, hardware, and grocery stores, as well as several other businesses that made it fairly self-sufficient. Within a few short years, Tim noticed an onset of growth and change perhaps best represented by the introduction of Burger King, which, while welcomed by the kids, came to symbolize a fast, get in and get out mentality—a significant shift from small town life perceived as slower and more purposeful. Kouts boomed from a population of about eight hundred to two thousand in a decade, forcing its longtime residents to sit back and mourn the loss of its small town character. "It's slipping away," Tim says resignedly. "The old farmers are now retiring and selling land to developers. The farmer says, I'm done, I'm retired."

He continues. "I was raised in a small town. City people have different ideas. Not bad. Just different. People move away from city problems and come to the small town. Then there's nothing for the kids to do at night, and they demand services and things they enjoyed in the city. People want country living but still want the conveniences of the city."

With frustration hovering in the spaces between his words the way fog distorts an image in a mirror, Tim enumerates the large commercial businesses along Highway 49 that are slowly linking Kouts with Valparaiso to the north: Super Wal-Mart, Menards, Kohl's. The distance closed even more with the construction of Kouts's first strip mall immediately outside of town.

In the face of aggressive change that inspires both an ambivalent optimism and a sad resignation to loss, Kouts prides itself as a neighborly community rich in history. Two of the oldest institutions are the Kouts School—home of the Mustangs and Fillies from kindergarten through twelfth grade—and the Koffee Kup cafe, in business on Main Street since 1955. In fact, as Tim and I visit, a gathering of classmates celebrating the fiftieth anniversary of their high school graduation is enjoying lunch and laughter in the center of the cafe. A half-century after they received their diplomas, Kouts's graduating seniors selected the Koffee Kup's counter as the setting for their class photo. "They said, 'This has been here so long,'" Tim remembers. "I said to my wife, 'I hope the old building can hold up to all this weight in one place!'"

Back in the winter of 1992, Tim and Donna were heading to a basketball game at the school when they saw a For Sale sign in the Koffee Kup's window. Donna was between jobs at the time, and Tim quipped, "There's what you oughta do. Run that restaurant." A few days later, Donna said she'd do it.

"Donna had always been a good cook. A *real* cook. She tries to do everything homemade," Tim says proudly. "She doesn't go for fast food, Wal-Mart pick-it-up-and-zap-it-in-the-microwave stuff."

Real cooking at the Koffee Kup means homemade soups, comfortable daily specials, fresh burgers, real mashed potatoes, and homemade pies. If you're a breakfast lover, don't skip the omelets or biscuits and gravy, which Tim cites as some of the favorite items on the menu. The chicken and noodles is so popular that Donna has a list of people—including the girls at the clinic—that ask to be notified whenever it's served as a daily special. Spooned over mashed real potatoes, the chicken and noodles makes for a satisfying and filling meal.

"She still makes her own mashed potatoes," Tim points out. "People tease her and say, 'Donna, I found a lump in my potatoes,' and she tells them, 'I put it in there so you'd know they're real.'"

Tim and I have been talking for over an hour, so long that morning has moved into afternoon. Over his shoulder, I see a waitress erasing the biscuits and gravy breakfast special and replacing it with beef and noodles over *real* mashed potatoes, served with a dinner roll. Or you could choose tomato soup or chili with a side or two of applesauce, coleslaw, bean salad, cottage cheese, or tapioca pudding. Tapioca pudding is pretty darn close to dessert in my book, unless there's pie on the menu. Nothing is better than pie! Made with orange juice, my slice of orange cream was a fun, flirty choice that stood out from the other selections—oatmeal, cherry, french silk, custard, coconut, and pumpkin—on the board.

"Donna makes all the pies herself," Tim tells me. She uses fresh fruit for fillings, including apples and peaches gathered from the trees in the

Browns' own yard, rhubarb from their garden, and blueberries bought near Wheatfield and DeMotte.

Though the food at the Koffee Kup is mighty fine, Tim stresses that it is a working-class restaurant where farmers' shoes leave dirt under tables and booths. "We serve farmers who want a good meal at a good price." Even as the number of farmers dwindles along with the farmland, and as barns are swapped for strip malls, Kouts retains a strong agricultural identity. This is particularly evident at the Koffee Kup, where clusters of satiny ribbons hang over the kitchen window, providing nice testimony to the involvement of the Brown family in the county 4-H fair and Porkfest Parade. But they pale in comparison to Tim's impressive collection of miniature die-cast tractors, spreaders, combines, and other mechanical workhorses. There are hundreds of them tirelessly at work on top of the stainless-steel milk dispenser, on shelves and counters, and inside the glass display case beneath the register. I see orange Allis Chalmers tractors, yellow Case tractors, green John Deere tractors, orange Minneapolis-Moline tractors.

"I know Minneapolis-Moline because that's what my dad and grandpa had," my waitress confides as she helps me to identify the tractors by their colors. (Our efforts are helped out considerably by the color-coordinated metal street signs with names such as John Deere Road.) When we get stumped on the red tractors, she turns to one of the local farmers. "International Harvester," he says.

The two of us meet as we pay our bills at the counter. "They don't make 'em like that anymore. Those were the glory days when farmers could afford their own tractors. Now they can't hardly afford to farm."

LAKEVILLE

Hilltop Restaurant

303 South Michigan Street (Hwy. 31)

(574) 784-3474

M–F 6 A.M.–2 P.M.; Sa 6 A.M.–1 P.M.; Su 7 A.M.–1 P.M.

Vera Gouker and Karen Iovino

Lisa at the Lakeville Library told me about the Hilltop Restaurant when I asked where I could find a local hangout with good home cooking. "When people learn I'm from Lakeville," she said, "they say, 'Oh, that's where the Hilltop is.'" I knew Lisa had steered me correctly when I spotted cars lining the street out front of the restaurant for a block in either direction. Sure enough. On an ordinary Thursday morning in mid-September, the Hilltop is filled with people, voices, and a collection of old stuff so extensive that empty tables and empty space are both at a premium.

The Hilltop has been owned by Vera Gouker and Karen Iovino, who are mother and daughter, since 1979. Vera started the restaurant in 1977, was away for a year, and then returned. "Mom always collected antiques," says Karen, "and when she started the restaurant, she brought some of them in to decorate. The collection has kept growing ever since."

"Do you ever have enough?" I ask.

"There's always room for more," Karen smiles. "And this isn't even all of it. There's a lot more in the basement."

Study the contents of the Hilltop for thirty seconds, then close your eyes and try to recall what you have seen. I remember a pair of Raggedy Ann and Andy dolls, kerosene lamps, salt-glazed crocks, a wicker doll sleigh, an enamel wash pan and coffee pot, an old school slate, a crosscut saw, a whirl-igig that's a man cutting wood, historic photos of local buildings, framed needlework, and common school and high school diplomas. My pitiful inventory is an embarrassing attempt at my own game.

Inside the front door, a chalkboard advertises the daily breakfast specials, all attractive alternatives to typical Hoosier cafe fare found everywhere else. Anything out of the ordinary is bound to be good, so even before I sit down I decide on the french toast stuffed with pineapple cream cheese and served with orange syrup. Nevertheless, I pick up the menu to see what I may have missed. It is as artistic as the specials: hand-lettered and sprinkled with sketches, poetry, wise sayings, and tongue-in-cheek advice from the kitchen. "Everything is prepared with a sincere desire for excellence," I read. "Our staff are highly trained professionals that have studied at the Julia Wild School of Culinary Arts. We are proud of their work. Please be patient if, when we're crowded, it takes longer for your order than you'd like; and remember, we're cooking as fast as eggs can fly—this means it may take 15–40 minutes on weekends. God Bless."

"Weekends are crazy here," confirms Karen. "We get people from miles around: South Bend, Mishawaka, even Michigan. We hear all the time, 'The food is good, but it takes so long.' We are constantly trying to figure out how to get faster."

During the week, the locals have the Hilltop to themselves. At the rear of the dining room, they cluster at tables and along the counter left behind when Jacobs Drugstore moved out. The proximity of the kitchen puts them close to Karen and her staff, with whom they share talk and laughter. It is back here, too, that members of the Lakeville High School football team gather every Friday morning during the football season. They begin filling the tables about twenty after six, then move on to filling themselves with lineman-size breakfasts washed down with pitchers of Mountain Dew before heading off to the school just down the road. "We talk, shoot the bull, talk strategy, mostly socialize," a player tells me.

Wearing blue and white Lakeville home game jerseys, the football teammates anticipate tonight's game with Jimtown, whom they haven't beaten "in years." They seem resigned to the steady continuation of tradition, the same vague force that has brought them to the Hilltop for breakfast for the past five or six years. "My older brother used to come here with his team," I'm told, "so this must go back to at least 1999, I'd say."

Filling every available seat at the tables at the back of the cafe and overflowing into nearby booths, the teammates ignore the three men who drink coffee at the counter. The men also ignore them. This is not the Hollywood *Hoosiers* or *Titans* scenario, where adults manipulate players and meddle with the team behind the coach's back.

"No, that doesn't happen," says Shelly Vidmar, who has waited tables at the Hilltop for twenty-seven years. "And I'm not sure the kids are wanting that. This is just their thing. They're doing it on their own. They're keeping it going by getting the new kids to come."

The Lakeville Lancers bypass the frilly breakfast offerings that excite me, selecting instead farm-food standbys like boneless sirloin steaks, eggs, potatoes, omelets, biscuits and gravy, pancakes, and french toast accompanied not with coffee but pitchers of soda. After twenty-seven years, Karen knows she will never tear the locals away from their favorite food, like the Hilltop's homemade corned beef hash, but she continues to try "to make people eat more healthy. They're slowly coming around." One healthier alternative that has become a permanent fixture on the menu is the hi-octane oatmeal made with flax, sunflower seeds, and quinoa. Keep your engine revved up by ordering a bowl. But beware. The large bowl is really large, the small bowl is large, and the cup may be just right.

"We make as much as we can from scratch," Karen says. This commitment has earned the Hilltop rave reviews. "The man fixing our neon sign told me we're an icon. An icon! It was nice to hear that."

MIDDLEBURY
Village Inn ☙
107 South Main Street
(574) 825-2043
M–Th 5 A.M.–8 P.M.; F 5 A.M.–8:30 P.M.; Sa 5 A.M.–2 P.M.; Su closed
Kevin and Tonya Rhodes

I am the Queen of Turnaround. I'm never really lost, but I am frequently misplaced on the landscape, rarely knowing for sure whether I'm heading north or south, east or west. I have had success navigating by the position of the sun, but if it's cloudy or raining or if the sun is straight overhead, I inevitably find myself making U-turns. Such was the case when I left Bonneyville Mill with a plan: I'd drive County Road 8 along the tree-lined Little Elkhart River to Middlebury, a shorter and far more scenic route than the state highway. It wasn't five minutes before I found myself back in Bristol, which I had left an hour ago. It never fails. When faced with a fifty-fifty chance of selecting the correct arm of a T in the road, I inevitably pick the wrong one.

The state highway is always a sure bet.

The late August heat and humidity were oppressive, and the saturated air settled thick and heavy so that it was impossible to take a deep, cleansing breath. While most people cocooned themselves in air-conditioned cars or buildings with thermostats set at sixty-eight degrees (requiring me to throw on a sweater), the weather could not keep Amish bicyclists off the streets. Outside the Village Inn, four bikes were corralled in a rack on the public sidewalks, including a multispeed Diamondback hybrid with rear side baskets loaded with shopping goods, a thermos, and a lunch kit. I couldn't help but smile. Its owner hadn't eaten at the cafe today.

As its name implies, the Village Inn primarily serves the Middlebury community. A wall-mounted display inside the entrance containing brochures for furniture and quilt shops, restaurants, and other attractions indicates that it also caters to the tourist trade, but you are more likely to find area farmers and Amish families gathered around the table than folks with Chicago accents. Dressed in plain pastel dresses of polyester-cotton, the Amish girls waiting tables know who wants what without having to take orders. Only today they are fooled. It is so hot outside ("eighty-five degrees and 110 percent humidity," an older fellow announces) that the coffee group gathered in a booth near the counter rejects coffee for iced tea served with slices of cold cream pie.

Only a handful of tables are occupied at four o'clock in the afternoon. My waitress, a young Amish woman named Gynell wearing white Skechers, scurries about restocking little bowls with miniature plastic tubs of coffee creamer. She is very businesslike, pausing only briefly to take my order in accented English before returning to her end-of-the-afternoon chores. She uses English when dealing with the non-Amish (whom the Amish themselves call English) and slides effortlessly into German when chatting with a clean-shaven Amish man sitting alone at the end of the empty community table. He is an early arrival for the afternoon coffee session.

When I ask to see the owner, Gynell points to a man in a plaid shirt and denim shorts sitting at the counter. That's the owner? I was expecting an Amish woman perhaps, and if not her, at least a middle-aged woman with the thick waist of one who cooks well and eats better. I was definitely not expecting Kevin Rhodes, a man with a trim black mustache who's young enough to have a son playing peewee football. Kevin is a former wood-worker, a Mennonite, and a native of Middlebury whose family ate at this very restaurant when he was a kid. "It's been here over fifty years, I'd guess. Dad would always say, 'Let's go to Miller's for pizza.' We still sell a lot of pizza," Kevin says.

Kevin bought the restaurant from Marlin and Shirley Mast in 2004, after working alongside them for two years to learn the business. The Masts had been owners for ten years when retirement began to creep more and more frequently into discussions about their future. The Masts cast a line of inquiry and reeled it in. On the other end, hooked eagerly and securely, were their next-door neighbors, Kevin, and his wife, Tonya. The Masts couldn't have been happier. "They felt it was a hometown restaurant, and they wanted someone that the locals knew," explains Kevin.

Hometown and homelike, the Village Inn is as wholesome as the apple pies in the wallpaper border circling the room. The wall on one side of the restaurant is covered with a mirror, which makes you think that the dining room is twice as big as it really is. I studied the reflection in the mirror for several minutes before I saw myself looking back! The mirror also provides a great view of the cream pies—both whole pies and single pieces on white ceramic plates—in a Coca-Cola refrigerator against the opposite wall. A smaller glass case on the counter holds double-crust fruit pies at room temperature. There are so many pies and in so many varieties that it is obvious that the Village Inn is no mere cafe. It is a pie palace.

"I don't know what it is about pie," Kevin muses. "I think it is an Amish thing. I grew up Mennonite and dessert was always available. We always had cakes and pies, cobblers, cookies. People come up here and expect pie, so that's what we give them. We make any kind of pie you can imagine."

I seize his challenge.

"Ground cherry?"

"Yes."

"Gooseberry?"

"Yes. We also have grasshopper and German chocolate. We have so many kinds I don't know how many we have!"

Kevin is clearly proud of the Village Inn's immense pie repertoire, but no less so of its reputation for pie of competitive quality. Top sellers are rhubarb custard and red raspberry cream, selected as one of the top five pies in Elkhart County by Marshall King, restaurant reviewer for the *Elkhart Truth*. It lost to a lemon meringue pie from Goshen in King's grand champion round, Kevin explains with no remorse.

As chance would have it, Gynell brought my order of red raspberry cream pie before Kevin joined me. It consists of heavy vanilla pudding (with lumps that proved it was made from scratch) poured into a thick pastry crust, topped with a raspberry layer made from frozen berries and juice thickened with cornstarch, and on top of that, a spread of nondairy whipped topping sprinkled with red Jell-O granules. It is a pleasant piece of pie, but not particularly pretty; the layers fell apart when they were transferred from the pan to the plate.

Raspberry cream pie is always on the pie board, a blue plastic panel hanging over the counter. White snap-in letters spell out the other choices available according to the baker's whims, in enough varieties on any given day to make a second pie competition a very intimidating task. Imagine sampling your way through a lineup like today's: rhubarb custard, raspberry cream, pumpkin, cherry, dutch apple, french silk, peanut butter, pecan, peach, and fresh blueberry. I for one would be quite happy to be a judge!

Two other menu boards list the morning specials (there are so many that one board is not enough), testifying to the importance of breakfast at the Village Inn. There are the standard offerings available at any cafe in the Hoosier State but also some surprises that reflect the Pennsylvania Dutch heritage of the area's Amish and Mennonite. Adventure eaters who come in search of breakfast would not be qualified to carry membership cards if they left without sampling the cornmeal mush with tomato gravy, or the headcheese.

Mush is made by cooking cornmeal in boiling water, then packing it into a pan and cooling it until stiff. At the Village Inn, the mush is cut into slices, rolled in flour, and deep fried. It's served with tomato gravy made by thickening tomato juice with flour and milk, or with syrup. Kevin recommends trying it smothered in sausage gravy. I've seen cornmeal mush in plastic-wrapped chubs at Kroger (usually next to the eggs), a good indication that it is also a traditional southern breakfast food of interest to native Hoosiers.

The pairing of mush and headcheese, a transparent jellied loaf containing spices and bits of pork made by simmering a hog's head long and slow, is reminiscent of scrapple. Headcheese is eaten cold, sliced thick for breakfast or thin for sandwiches, as my German American grandparents preferred it. As a child, I always regarded the plate of headcheese on their lunch table with wary suspicion, but as an adult I developed a strange attraction to it as an edible capsule of my own family's heritage. You are what you eat.

At the Village Inn you can take the well-traveled route through the menu and stick to well-known traditional fare, or you can opt for secondary roads and take a chance on something a little more uncertain. It's the difference between the state highway and tree-lined county roads. You might end up just where you started. Or you might discover an adventure in good eating that will take you back to your beginnings.

NAPPANEE
Corner Cafe ⚇
161 South Main Street
(574) 773-2601
M–Sa 6 A.M.–2 P.M.; Su closed
Marsha and Robert Thomas

An ambulance is parked in front of the Corner Cafe when I arrive for breakfast about eight thirty. I joke to myself whether this is an inauspicious sign about the quality of food behind the door, but I open the door anyway and am reassured when I see over a dozen EMT personnel filling the tables in the front window. There is no emergency. It is merely Friday morning and the weekly breakfast meeting of the local emergency management team. All of the other tables are filled as well, so I take a seat at the counter, leaving a vacant spot between myself and the man drinking coffee at my left. Three seats down on my right is a young Amish girl eating chocolate chip pancakes.

With my back to the hometown crowd behind me, I am closed off from the talk and laughter that fill the cafe, a rather lonely stranger in a place full of friends. A man enters and takes a seat to my right, leaving one empty seat between us. This is an unwritten rule of counter sitting. Always leave a buffer between you and the next person. This way you will not be forced into unwanted conversation or accidentally bump elbows with a stranger.

Affecting confidence, I order a fried egg and toast without consulting the menu. "Would you like homemade bread?" asks my waitress. Is there any question? My spirits are buoyed to discover such a treasure, and I settle into the Windsor-back oak barstool with great satisfaction. From my perch, I spy two large cinnamon rolls in an aluminum foil pan behind the counter and weigh the possibility that they are homemade. Thinking the menu might provide the answer, I turn to the man at my right and ask to see the one he has just tucked behind the napkin dispenser. My question breaks the barrier of the vacant seat and invites further conversation. After the perfunctory, "Where you from?" he confides, "I figured you weren't a local because you asked to see the menu."

"You can *tell* we're not locals because we're sitting at the counter," I reply with a smile.

Marsha Thomas has had a front seat to the comings and goings of both the regulars and the out-of-town visitors since 1997, when she traded in a Hawaiian vacation for the cafe and a sixty- to seventy-hour workweek. "That's a funny story," she laughs. "I always loved to cook—I had five kids—and the previous owner asked me if I was interested in buying the restaurant. The time came for our twenty-fifth anniversary, and we were going to go to Hawaii. My husband thought it was the thing to do. But I'm afraid of water, airplanes, and boats. My husband said, 'You can go to Hawaii or buy a restaurant.' And I chose the restaurant."

"A vacation ends," I point out sagely. "This way you're still celebrating."

"That's a way to look at it," Marsha agrees.

Marsha has lived her entire life in Elkhart County, which combined with neighboring LaGrange County comprises the third-largest Amish and Mennonite community in the United States. Yet, she confesses, she is still trying to make sense of her neighbors' religious beliefs and cultural practices that keep them apart from non-Amish, or English, life, all the while situating them in the midst of it. Marsha employs Amish girls as waitresses and kitchen help until they are married and return to the family farm. "It is always hard to lose them because they are good workers and they become like part of the family," she says.

The Corner Cafe represents a cultural crossroads where Amish and English, local and nonlocal culture meet. Marsha shakes her head with amused amazement at visitors who regard the Amish less as living and breathing real people than charming tourist attractions. She emphasizes the tourists' ignorance by mimicking their mispronunciation of *Amish*, using a long *a* and not the correct schwa *a*. "They say, 'We came to find out about the Aymish.' They ask, 'Where can we go to look at the Aymish?' They want to see their farms. They want to know where they shop."

No search for the Amish is complete without dining on the home-style cooking that has come to be identified as "Amish cuisine." Marsha ticks off a list of homemade foods—mashed potatoes, noodles, gravy, dressing, bread ("That's one of their favorite things"), and pies—that tourists crave, demand, and fully expect during their brief dalliance in Amish country. In eating such food, tourists perceive their experience in Amish country to be both special and genuine. Yet, as Marsha aptly points out, Amish cooking is no different from the cooking at the Corner Cafe—and she is not Amish.

"Is there an Amish cuisine?" she asks. "I'm convinced that if you want to sell anything in Nappanee, just put the word *Amish* in front of it. What we cook here is the same food my mom fixed at home, the same food most of the people around here grew up on. What they know is what we fix, and what sells."

Among the favorite offerings at the Corner Cafe are the homemade bread, Tuesday's chicken stir-fry made with fresh vegetables ("Cutting them up is a lot of work"), rhubarb custard pie available every day during the summer months, and breakfast, breakfast, breakfast.

"Breakfast has become a bigger deal in the past few years," Marsha notes. "They'll pull the tables together and sit for hours. Every morning we have the same coffee guys at the front table. They're waiting every day at five 'til six before we even open." Unending talk and coffee are perfect sides to Marsha's biscuits and gravy, one of the breakfast best sellers. Other top choices include the haystack, a layering of hash browns, fried onions, scrambled eggs, gravy, and cheese; fried mush (try it with gravy or topped with butter and syrup or whipped cream); and baked oats. "I have people call me to find out if there's any baked oats," Marsha says. "If we're out, they won't come in until I've made a new pan."

NEW CARLISLE
Miller's Home Cafe
110 East Michigan Street
(574) 654-3431
M closed; T–F 8 A.M.–2 P.M.; Sa 8 A.M.–8:30 P.M.; Su 11 A.M.–6 P.M.
Bill and Diana Miller and George and Cindy Miller
If you're surrounded by people eating fried chicken at Miller's Home Cafe, it has to be Tuesday. That's the one day of the week that the popular poultry gets star billing on the buffet that makes up 95 percent of the cafe's business, according to Bill Miller. He and George Miller, his brother, are second-generation owners of the "family habit" that their father, William Miller, established in 1959. Nearing the half-century mark, Miller's Home Cafe is among the oldest family-owned cafes in the state.

Miller's is a fine example of a hybrid Hoosier restaurant combining several serving options under one roof. My waitress, Cindy, says, "It's three restaurants in one. It's a cafe for breakfast, a lunch buffet through the week, and a smorgasbord on Thursday, Friday, Saturday, and Sunday." Ordering off the menu is always an option, but those who do stick out like a sore thumb. I couldn't help but wonder why the gussied up folks at the next table insisted on burgers when they could have plumbed the depths of Miller's fine home cooking on the buffet. The only explanation that made sense to me—and that I made up to please myself—was that they had just come from a funeral and weren't in the mood for much more than perfunctory eating.

It would be such a shame to visit Miller's and not be prepared to really eat. By that I don't mean you should wear loose-fitting or even expandable clothing, although that is never inadequate preparation for a buffet the likes of Miller's. No, what I mean is that rewarding buffet dining requires an eager anticipation for everything you might encounter on the food bar, a spirit of adventure to try different things, and most important, the keen ability to zero in on only that which demands a second helping. There's no point in indiscriminately grazing on anything that comes out of a can, food service tub, plastic bag, or foil-lined paper packet. If the fruit is canned instead of fresh, skip it. If the mashed potatoes are instant, pass them by for bread dressing. If the corn is brownish-yellow, it's canned and not worth eating. (For better corn flavor, hold out for the bright yellow frozen variety.) If the dinner rolls are dusted with flour and too perfectly shaped, they came off a bread truck and not out of the oven.

Blessedly, words of warning and experience-based advice are of little concern at Miller's Home Cafe, where the buffet has achieved masterpiece status over the course of nearly a half century. Bill relates, "The original Home Cafe had a small buffet, and Dad expanded it when he bought the building next door in the early 1970s. It was a unique thing back then, but now it seems like there's one on every corner." Few are like Miller's, however. Rest assured that when you sidle up to the food bar with plate in hand, you will find real home cooking in such glorious plenty that memories of other buffets will melt away like real whipped cream on a hot July day.

Begin your sashay down the buffet with the salad bar, stocked with tossed lettuce and fresh vegetable toppings, plus a variety of homemade specialty salads including kidney bean, coleslaw, red skin potato with hard-boiled eggs, Italian pasta, sliced red beets, and confetti Jell-O salads with mixed fruit, minimarshmallows, and all sorts of other add-ins. The main entree or entrees vary by day, such wonders as fried chicken, barbecued ribs, fried fish, salmon patties, and shrimp and crab cakes. On weekends, baked pollock seasoned with lemon and dill or salsa is so popular that it is difficult to keep the buffet stocked. Side dishes appear in great variety—corn, carrots in brown sugar sauce, mashed potatoes (alas, they're instant)—along with familiar soups and those a little more exciting, such as the cabbage and sausage soup that I was lucky to discover. The buffet also comes with drinks and desserts like tapioca, pudding, bar cookies, apple crisp, and cake.

Miller's is a regional favorite, with people coming from as nearby as a few blocks and as far away as South Bend, Chicago, and the state of Michigan (not as far as it sounds since the state boundary is only two miles away). In 1997, Miller's Home Cafe was recognized as having the "Best Home Style Cooking" in the annual *Michiana Now* Reader's Poll. The framed award and accompanying news article, indeed the title itself, spotlights the shining star of the buffet: the chicken and noodles. Appearing daily, these humble golden glories (Bill calls them "buffet must-haves") are without a doubt the best chicken and noodles I found in all of Indiana. If all chicken and noodles were like Miller's, I could understand why Hoosiers are so enthralled by such a humble dish!

I have had plenty of chicken and noodles on my great Hoosier eating adventure, and most are memorable because they were so awful. I've been served wavy egg noodles from a cellophane sack, pinkish-orange chicken emptied out of a can, and gravy that started as a dry mix. I've eaten homemade noodles that could have sunk a ship, broth the consistency and flavor of school paste, and chicken so stringy it must have come from the oldest hen in the flock. Yet, regardless of the quality, chicken and noodles is time and again identified by cafe owners north of the Chicken and Noodle Line as being the most popular item on their menus.

The Chicken and Noodle Line is impossible to locate on a map, but it cuts Indiana into north and south with Indianapolis being the approximate dividing point. In order to keep things neat, let's somewhat arbitrarily assign the title to U.S. 40—the National Road. North of the Chicken and Noodle Line folks eat chicken and noodles. South of the Line, noodles become dumplings. You'll occasionally find noodles and dumplings in the other's territory, but you'll never find cafe owners claiming them to be best sellers on their menus.

The claim is well warranted at Miller's Home Cafe, where Bill estimates seventy-five to one hundred gallons of chicken and noodles are made and consumed every week. As they must be to be so good, the noodles are homemade and, until recently, were cut by hand. "When we all started getting carpal tunnel, we switched to cutting them by machine," he says. So cherished is Miller's chicken and noodles that customers quickly noticed the noodles had changed. They were now all the same width. Any complaints about altering an icon were silenced, however, when it became clear that the noodles tasted the same as always. They're still made with extra large eggs that make them dense and chewy. Simmered in broth thick with chicken picked off the bones, the noodles tint the rich gravy a beautiful lemon yellow. All gravy should aspire to be so lovely.

"How do you make it?" I ask Bill.

"Ah hah! That's the secret!" he laughs coyly. "Many have tried. Many have failed."

You must go to Miller's and attempt to decipher the secret yourself.

REMINGTON
The Lovely Cafe
12 South Ohio Street
(219) 261-2140
M–Th 6 A.M.–2 P.M.; F 6 A.M.–8 P.M.; Sa 6 A.M.–2 P.M.; Su 9 A.M.–2 P.M.
Thomas and Kathy Lovely, owner
Laurie Anderson, manager
A vowel-less, alphabet soup of railroads—the CSX, CR, KBS, NS, GTW—slice through northwestern Indiana at all angles, linking communities like beads on a string. Small towns with apt names like Wheatfield and Goodland jut up out of the prairie, breaking the horizon with behemoth grain elevators, two-story lodge halls, steepled Gothic churches, and commercial buildings that denote the past's prosperity and promise. Wide, optimistic streets are laid out in perfect grid patterns interspersed with houses ranging from Italianates and Queen Annes from the nineteenth century to workaday bungalows and even, in Remington at least, a pastel yellow, porcelain-enameled steel Lustron house from the twentieth. A town park with a veteran's memorial is commonplace, and, if it hasn't yet been torn down, so is a little depot with the town's name painted—once proudly, now faded—on the side.

Settled by New England and middle-colony farmers and tradesmen and Old World immigrants, northern Indiana has a different physical and cultural landscape than southern Indiana. It is marked largely by traditions that are European rather than Anglo-Appalachian, traditions that show up in buildings like Lutheran churches and in foods like the polish sausage sandwich accessorized with onion and relish served at The Lovely Cafe.

My first visit to Remington was in late 2005, shortly after Ron and the late Jerri Peppin brought the little main street cafe back from the brink of death. They were in their second go-around in the restaurant business, having run their own restaurant in Rensselaer for thirteen years before they ran out of steam, sold out, and found easier jobs. "We were retired for two and a half years," Jerri told me. "One day I had a bad day at work, and Ron had one, too. We went out to eat and Ron asked if I'd ever consider getting back into the restaurant business. I said I'd consider it under one condition: if the little cafe in Remington ever came up for sale. A week later it was on the market. Our kids thought we were crazy the first time, but they thought we were *really* crazy the second time."

The derelict Remington Cafe required extensive repair and redecorating, a lengthy project that Ron and Jerri took on themselves under the supervision of anxious customers who dropped in daily to check on their progress. The result is a perky and bright new cafe, with buttery yellow walls, forest green accents, and a wallpaper border decorated with folk-art buildings. Photocopies of historic photographs and postcards of Remington hang on the walls, and antique and reproduction food tins, kitchen utensils, crocks, and other vintage kitchen items are clustered on shelves. The yellow and green color scheme is attentively carried out in everything—right down to the Red Dot potato chip and Salerno cookies tins—reflecting the Peppins' work ethic and guiding principle that quality is in the details.

Made a widower with Jerri's sudden passing a few months after my visit, Ron put the restaurant up for sale. As beneficiary of the Peppins' legacy, Laurie Anderson knows she has been blessed. She acquired a building made new again, equipment that is efficient and clean, decorating that is fresh and charming, and customers like Larry and Carolyn Barkley, who have long been loyal to both the Peppins and herself. Laurie is well-known and much appreciated around these parts, having run first the little cafe in nearby Brook, and for the past several years the twenty-four-hour truck stop north of Remington. "Ron told my realtor that if he could have hand picked someone to sell it to, it would have been me," she says. "He knows I have the experience and will work hard to make it succeed."

"We were the Peppins' best customers in Rensselaer," Larry tells me between bites of his cheeseburger. "When they opened down here, we followed them. And when Laurie took over we followed her. I got a haircut in Goodland this morning, so of course we came here for lunch."

Looking up from her chicken fingers, Carolyn spies her sister and her brother-in-law, Janet and Dan Haskins, coming through the front door. Although the women enjoy going out to eat together—"It's an adventure," Carolyn says. "And sometimes it's a *real* adventure!"—their meeting is purely accidental. The Haskinses needed gas and figured they'd drive over from Wolcott to save a few cents at the pump. They have not yet tried the new Lovely Cafe, so why not stop for lunch?

The extensive makeover of Remington's longtime main street cafe restored both a building and a business and gave a boost to the local economy. Much has changed since Jane and Michael Stern featured the Remington Cafe in the first edition of *Roadfood* (1977), rating it a single star for its "mediocre food." Equally unflattering is their description of the cafe's clientele as "leathery-necked farmers and ample-armed corn-fed mamas in print dresses." Now, thirty years later, a return visit by the Sterns to the entirely new, entirely delicious Lovely Cafe is certainly warranted.

With years of restaurant experience under her belt, Laurie understands the "eating habits" of her customers. Daily specials are written in white chalk on a vintage train schedule board acquired at auction in nearby Monon. It's from the Monon Railroad, and it's not for sale. Don't even ask.

Laurie prepares the weekly menu every Monday, rotating among tried-and-true mainstays like chicken-fried steak, meatloaf, ham and scalloped potatoes, and chicken and noodles. Other main meal favorites are the popular soup and sandwich combos, tenderloins gilded with seasoned home-made breading, and burgers, especially the Cavalier burger, a fully dressed double cheeseburger served with mayonnaise and fries, named for the athletic teams at nearby Tri-County High School. For breakfast—served until eleven—there's a head-to-head rivalry between Laurie's from-scratch biscuits topped with homemade sausage swimming in creamy milk gravy and the "over-the-plate size" pancakes that come to the table with real butter and warm syrup.

Although The Lovely Cafe has been open for only a few months, word of Laurie's Friday night fish fry is spreading like salmon during spawning season. "I ran some ads in the paper the first Friday night, and we had about seventy-five people show up. People were standing around waiting for a table," Laurie remembers. The number has tapered off to a fairly steady fifty fish-lovers per night, all happy to celebrate the end of the work week with deep-fried or grilled perch, pollock, and catfish, plus shrimp, and one other non-fish entree. Every meal includes a foray through the salad bar loaded with lettuce and the typical toppings, plus six or seven tubs of homemade specialty salads—everything from Laurie's must-have pea salad to pasta and potato, pistachio and apple. "If I don't have something someone's looking for, I usually hear about it," she laughs.

As she gets acquainted with her new customers, Laurie has adjusted the cafe's hours to accommodate their requests. "When they said they wanted Sunday dinner, I told them it would be okay with me if I didn't have to work." While she attends church with her family and catches up on things at home, a friend and fellow cook comes in to prepare breakfast for the early arrivals, at the same time whipping up three different specials for the after-church crowd.

"I always tell people I have the best job in the world," Laurie says. "With a little help, I do what I want at my own pace and most days go home at two o'clock. I wouldn't want to be doing anything else."

RENSSELAER
Janet's Kitchen ☒
112 North Van Rensselaer Street
(219) 866-5804
M–F 5 A.M.–1 P.M.; Sa 5 A.M.–10 P.M.; Su closed (Central Time)
Janet and Ken Delaney
Four different recommendations led me to Rensselaer in search of Janet's Kitchen, a rosy-hued cafe that from the street looks like an out-of-place Swiss chalet. One was from Wendell Trogdon, author of *Main Street Diners*. Another came from Jim at the Rensselaer Chamber of Commerce, who told me, "It's a popular local hangout for everyone from the mayor on down."

The third came from Governor Mitch Daniels, whose campaign trail and victory tour brought him to Janet's to nosh on home cooking and schmooze with voters. The last, and by far the most persuasive, was a post on an Internet foodies' forum.

"This small place in this small town has THE best 'home-cooked' food," I read. "They have daily specials and fresh baked pies and desserts. Owner Janet Delaney is the best cook in the world! Very generous portions too. ☺ There is also a big table in the middle with a sign over it that says, 'This table reserved for farmers, fishermen, golfers and other liars.' They are all real nice people . . . it's family owned and operated. I live about 900 miles from there, but make a point to stop whenever I'm anywhere near."

If Janet's Kitchen inspires such passion from folks who don't even live in Indiana, I reasoned, it surely ranks a priority visit. I eagerly anticipated the day that my peripatetic cafe journey would land me in the Jasper County seat. I even made plans about what I would eat, starting with the daily special and finishing up with pie, of course. Chocolate? Apple? Maybe a hefty wedge of lemon meringue? In *Main Street Diners*, I read about Janet's homemade rolls and began to dream of hot, yeasty beauties smeared with real dairy butter. Visions of Janet's sugarplums danced in my head and tempted my taste buds.

You can understand, then, how absolutely crushed I was to have at last worked my way to Janet's Kitchen, only to discover a Closed sign in the window. Cupping my hands around my temples and pressing my nose against the glass, I saw a cafe suspended in daily use. Photos of the regulars were pinned to the wall behind the L-shaped counter, the sign hung from the ceiling over the Liars Table, and the daily menu board was still inscribed with the current day's specials. Not closed up, I sighed with relief. Just closed an hour earlier than I had anticipated.

Over chicken noodle soup and a ham salad sandwich the next day, I share the foodie's post with Janet and tell her how I came to be sitting at her counter.

"My niece, Lori, wrote that! She told me she'd put something on the Internet," she laughs with surprise. "She's a schoolteacher in Georgia."

Lori's comments inspired a post from "foodluvr," another foodie, who responded: "I did a search for this place on the net to find a site for it, but I guess it doesn't have one. What I did find interesting though is that there were several links to articles about the governor of Indiana making it a point to stop and eat there while out on the road. I think I'll have to make a point to try to get there soon as well."

Over Janet's shoulder, I see a photograph of Mitch Daniels during his April visit. The photograph is pinned to the bulletin board, along with a Rensselaer Bombers athletic schedule, a notice for an estate auction, business cards, and the photos of the regulars I saw through the window the day before. Daniels might be the governor, but at Janet's Kitchen he's just one of the guys. Our man, Mitch.

Janet has run the restaurant a block off the Jasper County courthouse square since 1988, first as a leaser and then, beginning in 1999, as its owner. During high school, she and her friends walked to the cafe, then the Sip and Bite, for french fries and Coke. "That was lunch," she recalls. "That's all we wanted. The owner peeled his own potatoes for fries and would say to us, 'Do you know just how many potatoes I have to peel?'"

With its jukebox, counter, and soda fountain, the Sip and Bite was the popular teenage hangout for lunch away from the school cafeteria, and again after school and before and after ball games. Today's teenagers have a lot more choices in where to eat, including several fast food franchises within Rensselaer city limits, yet many patronize the cafe. Several times a season, the entire football team comes in for lunch, and members of the junior and senior classes, who are allowed to go off campus for lunch, phone in their orders ahead of time. By choice, they bypass the premade in favor of Janet's homemade. And like Janet and her teenage friends from years ago, they pretty much stick with burgers, fries, and Cokes. Biscuits and gravy vie for second place.

Washed down with a bottomless cup of coffee, B&G is often the breakfast of choice for many of the men who begin gathering under the Liars Club sign as early as three thirty in the morning. Janet's husband, Ken, is one of them. He spends an hour here before heading off to his own job with the city street department. By the time the cafe officially opens at five o'clock, the table is packed and men overflow to the counter, trading talk back and forth across the room. Some days they are joined by a lone woman, but it is primarily a men's club that waxes and wanes with the passing hours. A few members remain all morning. "They just love sitting and talking," Janet says. "We've got one guy who sits at the end of the table for four hours. Others spend two and a half hours here in the morning, go home, and come back and spend another two hours here at lunch."

It's the food as much as the companionship that keeps the tables at Janet's Kitchen filled. "We make everything homemade," Janet says. For breakfast, try the skillet, a pileup of hash browns or American fries, ham or sausage, and eggs. Or go for the bratwurst, a German-inspired sausage served grilled for breakfast or sandwiched in a hoagie bun for lunch. Another specialty that's rarely encountered in the Hoosier State is corned beef hash. Other top o'-the-morning choices include Janet's biscuits and gravy, pancakes, and omelets. Later in the day, you'll find traditional meat and potatoes fare, including meatloaf, roast beef, and fried chicken, as well as soups and sandwich specials. My ham salad on whole wheat is actually Hoosier ham salad: minced bologna mixed with sweet pickle relish and mayonnaise. The chicken noodle soup is made with flavorful broth, diced carrots and celery, chicken picked from the bones, and curly egg noodles. A sprinkling of pasta stars makes me smile. I haven't seen those since I was a kid.

I surely would have indulged in Janet's homemade desserts if I had come a bit earlier, but I didn't want to keep Janet and her daughter-in-law, Kathy, from cleaning up and going home. "My mom used to do all the baking," Janet says, "but now I do it all. I make cake and cheesecake and pie: lemon, chocolate, all that stuff."

WINAMAC
Vicky's Restaurant ☷
124 North Market Street
(574) 946-4343
M–Sa 5 A.M.–2 P.M.; Su closed (Central Time)
Vicky and David Pingel

Vicky Pingel is a happy woman. She is in her second go-round at a job she loves, has countless friends who adore her (and whom she adores), and two years ago moved her namesake cafe around the corner into a building that was remodeled to satisfy her every need. The new cafe is a thing of beauty, with tongue-and-groove pine boards on the walls, sage tiles on the floor, and a variety of antiques to offset the newness. Everything is genuine, durable, and high quality. "That's what we were going for, because our food is the same way," she says.

Restaurants have been Vicky's home away from home for over half of her life, beginning when she was a seventeen-year-old part-time employee at Winamac's Miller's Restaurant, which she bought in 1992. She ran it for five years and then sold it when she was suddenly widowed. Happiness followed tragedy when she remarried and bought back the restaurant in 2001.

"It's just something I love to do," she enthuses. "My husband thinks I'm crazy. He says it's like being married to a dairy farmer because I'm here at three thirty every morning."

Vicky was only thirteen when she took on the role of preparing all the family meals and realized she had inadvertently discovered her life's passion. "Mom was an excellent cook, but she worked full time out of the house. My older sister went into the military, so cooking naturally fell to me," she explains. She began working at a local restaurant and soon came to the conclusion that "school was not teaching me what I needed to know to make it in the real world." At home and at the restaurant, she learned how to prepare shopping lists, budget expenses, pay bills, and manage employees. She also learned to cook and bake a variety of home-style foods that her customers clamor for. In the process, she acquired an entire town full of friends, and her restaurant acquired a blue-ribbon reputation.

"It's the kind of business that gets into your blood," Vicky says. "My customers are very loyal, and it's their appreciation of what we do that is my reward—*our* reward. I could never do this without the support of my husband and my crew."

Many of Vicky's customers deserve to be very appreciative indeed. She laughs when she describes the idiosyncrasies of some of her "babies"—older men who come in and order half a bacon and egg sandwich or a one-egg omelet. "They don't have any idea how hard it is to make an omelet out of a single egg."

"How about a two-egg omelet cut in half?" I ask.

"No, it's got to be made fresh," Vicky insists.

She continues. "We've got other guys who come in and order the same thing every day. We know when they're coming and put the order on the grill before they get here. That's the time they decide to have something else! Granny tells them—she's Granny because she mothers everyone—'This is ready today. You can have that tomorrow!'"

With four specials every day, plus a menu of day-in and day-out favorites, Vicky's babies are coddled with enough good home cooking to make them spoiled, fat, and sassy. "If they walk out of here hungry, that's their own fault," laughs Vicky. Everything possible is made from scratch, including soups, salads such as tuna and chicken, hand-shaped burgers and sausage patties, Saturday yeast rolls, roasts, breaded tenderloin, real mashed potatoes ("Just ask my girls in the back"), and pies. The lineup of daily specials is so extensive that it fills not just one but two dry erase boards: one for entrees, sides, and salads, the other for desserts. Prettied up with colored ink, lines, swooshes, and swirls, and organized just so in order to get the many selections to fit, the entree board is a tantalizing work of art:

```
Dinner        2-sides w/ Potato
*Lunch        1-side                              Salads   no sides
pork cutlet & dressing                                BLT salad
*taco or taco salad                                  mandarin orange
*beef & noodles                                       fruit plates
*Italian chicken                                  Cold Plates
chili cheese fries                                    stuffed tomato w/
pork cutlet sandwich                                    chicken, tuna or
Italian chicken sandwich                                crab salad
                                                  Soup
corn CB macaroni CB bean CB cinnamon CB Texas          beef stew
      salad       salad    pears      sheet            chili
                                        cake           chicken noodle
```

A reliable sign of a great cafe is the extensiveness of its specials board. If it looks like the one at Vicky's Restaurant, be prepared for a feast that you will long remember. I have been to countless cafes where the menu board showed only one hastily scrawled special, which I interpret as a pretty accurate reflection of the sparseness of the kitchen. It doesn't take a Betty Crocker to conclude that the best cafes are filled with food. The more food, the more variety. The more variety, the more likely it is that everything is made from scratch by someone who loves to cook. That's because there's a limit to what comes packaged, frozen, or otherwise prepared in advance at a distant location, and because good cooks like to stretch their wings a bit. The same goes for creativity in names. Texas sheet cake sounds like something made at home or discovered in a magazine rather than bought frozen from a food truck.

Better yet is when you find a menu board that prefaces variety with *homemade*, as does Vicky's pie board. A whole board just for pies! Oh, heaven! Yet what a dilemma it is to pick a piece from a list the likes of Vicky's: coconut, butterscotch, chocolate, cream cheese pecan, red raspberry, sugar-free apple, custard, and pumpkin.

By the way, when it comes to pie, do not confuse "home baked" or "fresh baked" with homemade. There are many tricky cafe owners out there who will try to pass off a frozen pie that has been baked in the oven for one made from scratch. If you're ever in doubt, don't ask, "Is the pie made here?" because many servers and cafe owners interpret "made" to mean "baked." Ask instead, "Is the piecrust rolled out here?" or "Is the filling made from scratch?" I've even asked whether the fruit in a fruit pie is fresh, frozen, or canned.

But I have no fears of trickery at Vicky's Restaurant, where home cooking is a sure thing and eating is a joy thanks to Vicky's own commitment and the eagle-eye supervision of her customers. "When I bought the restaurant the first time from the Millers," she says, "I was warned by the customers not to change anything." Vicky's great-uncle Russell Mays had it right when he hastily made up the following verse one morning as he sat with the coffee group: "We are a happy bunch at Vicky's Lunch; / there's no room for sorrow; / so eat your fill, pay your bill / and come again tomorrow." His ode is on the menu cover now.

• •

NEXT BEST BETS

ANGOLA
VILLAGE KITCHEN
109 North Superior Street
(260) 665-9053
A reliable sign of a good cafe is the number of newspaper boxes out front. Choose from six different dailies, then read the news behind the headlines while waiting for a table at Angola's most popular breakfast house.

BOURBON
RUTH'S DINER
102 North Main Street
(574) 342-0422
A For Sale sign in the front window didn't deter me from going in, and I'm glad I did. Made with crumbled sausage patties, the biscuits and gravy were so good I wiped the workaday ceramic plate clean down to its glaze.

BREMEN
DOWNTOWN'R
101 East Plymouth Street
(574) 546-5458
Saddle up next to the local men at the horseshoe counter and order one of the Downtown'r's fourteen varieties of omelets, including the one-of-a kind Philly Steak filled with sliced steak, swiss cheese, green peppers, and onions.

CHESTERTON
COUNTRY CAFE 🍴
213 Broadway Avenue
(219) 929-4567
A Polish American restaurant featuring fresh baked goods like bread, *paczki, kolaczki*, and *chrusciki*; entrees such as homemade sausage and *golumbki* (stuffed cabbage rolls); and side dishes ranging from sauerkraut to *pierogi* in fifteen varieties. As the Polish owners adapt to what their customers request, standard Hoosier fare like pancakes and pie is being added to the menu. An excellent cafe with many surprises, and definitely one to keep an eye on.

CHESTERTON
NORTHSIDE DINER
100 North Calumet Road
(219) 926-9040
Retro cool! Inside you'll find a Wurlitzer jukebox and yellow chrome-legged tables and chairs. Outside, a mural with celebrities from the fifties, everyone from Lucy and Desi to Lewis and Martin. And is that Jackie Gleason? The malted pancakes served piping hot with real butter are a dream.

CHESTERTON
PEGGY SUE'S DINER
117 South Calumet Road
(219) 926-8524
Yet another interpretation of a 1950s diner, with turquoise banquettes and vintage and vanity license plates (PSA CAKE) on the walls. A week after the Wizard of Oz Festival, the front window is painted with a picture of Dorothy, Tin Man, Lion, Scarecrow, and Toto in a pink convertible. The caption: "If I only had a brain, I'd eat at Peggy Sue's."

ETNA GREEN
ETNA GREEN CAFE
112 West State Street
(574) 858-9081
A sign behind the counter reads, "If you don't like my cooking, lower your standards." There are likely few complaints at this country-style cafe that pays tribute to NASCAR champ Tony Stewart.

HAMLET
HAMLET CAFE
403 Railroad Street
(574) 867-1855
Here is another fairly reliable rule: Good cafes can be found near grain elevators. The regulars at this tiny eatery near the mega Starke County Co-op arrive by any means: golf cart, motor scooter, cruiser bicycle, car, pickup truck, business van, and on foot.

HEBRON
COUNTRY KITCHEN
120 North Main Street
(219) 996-9221
A one-time cafe with big restaurant pretensions following an extensive makeover. Memorable blueberry pie—but I expect that in Indiana's blueberry country. I love the vintage sign trumpeting air-conditioning.

KNOX
FAMILY CAFE
14 South Main Street
(574) 772-7240
From-scratch fare in great variety, plus a Roundtable group of dreamers and doers who raise funds for hospice care, Habitat for Humanity, and other local not-for-profits. Big ideas brewed, blended, baked, and put to work.

LACROSSE
THE GRILL
13 South Washington Street
(219) 754-2266
The Grill is decades past its prime. But true adventure eaters will venture in and take the Dean Burger Challenge: eat two of these half-pound beef behemoths, get the third free, and be rewarded with your name printed on the wall. Since 1986, the wall has been repainted twice, with the old names transferred to a notebook for posterity.

MEDARYVILLE
NEW PRIDE OF 421
503 North U.S. 421
(219) 843-5031
Humble home cooking in comfy surroundings. Be sure to check out the bathroom.

MENTONE
TEEL'S FAMILY RESTAURANT
108 West Main Street
(574) 353-1091

Teel's Family Restaurant has expanded beyond the original cafe, still evident by the counter and blue-topped stools inside the front door. The lunch and evening all-you-can-eat buffets have people standing in line. The swiss steak is definitely worth having seconds. I did!

MILLERSBURG
CHECKERS CAFE
112 Jefferson Street
(574) 642-0029
A 1950s-themed diner done up in red, white, and black, Checkers is popular with the area's Amish and non-Amish farmers who appreciate meat-and-potatoes home cooking. A must-have is the fried fish breaded with the secret seasoned mix of Gropp's Famous Fish of Stroh.

NEW PARIS
FRIENDS CAFE
68453 North Main Street
(574) 831-5242
A friendly place—especially at breakfast when homemade coffee cake made with seasonal fresh fruit is a perfect accompaniment to coffee and chat.

NORTH JUDSON
KELLER AVENUE DINER
307 Keller Avenue
(574) 896-4021
Dine under the stars—cartoon stars that is! The dropped ceiling panels are airbrushed with all your favorites, including Elmer Fudd, Tweety, Betty Boop, a Disney Dalmatian, and Bam Bam from the Flintstones.

PIERCETON
PASTIME CAFE
129 North First Street
(574) 594-3292
Filled with Coca-Cola everything, this main street cafe provides the pause that refreshes during marathon antiquing in Indiana's "Antique Town."

PLEASANT LAKE
PLEASANT LAKE CAFE
1630 West Main Street
(260) 475-1920
I encountered a dead possum in the street outside the Pleasant Cafe and, inside, ads for the mythical Roadkill Cafe. The coincidence was twistedly funny. Over my lunch of chicken-fried steak (or is it?), I spotted these coffee rates posted near the front door:

ROCHESTER
EVERGREEN CAFE
530 Main Street
(574) 223-1809
Opened in 1945, this classic corner cafe retains its oh-so-cool half-round counter and a vintage LoBoy scale that still works. Mostly homemade food at modest prices.

ROLLING PRAIRIE
BLACKSMITH SHOPPE RESTAURANT
10 South Depot Street
(219) 778-2813
A perfect pie ride destination using the blue route of the Laporte County Bikeways system, this eatery was a blacksmith shop decades ago. It would be foolish to head back home without refueling on soup and coconut cream pie.

SHIPSHEWANA
COUNTRY CORRAL RESTAURANT
260-C East North Village Drive
(260) 768-4589
At Troyer's minimall just north of town, you'll find "cooking like Mom's." The lost-and-not-yet-found Amish woolen bonnets and children's overcoats on a hall table are proof that the Country Corral is a locals' hideaway from the tourists.

SYRACUSE
SYRACUSE CAFE
607 North Huntington Street
(574) 457-5293
Not a pretty place, this Hoosier house of omelets has the most inventive variety in the state, including cheeseburger, taco, grilled chicken, beef barbecue, and corned beef hash. A real belly buster is the "Dare You To" omelet made with four eggs, sausage, bacon, ham, green peppers, onions, tomatoes, and cheese, stuffed with American fries, and smothered with sausage gravy.

SYRACUSE
WAWASEE CAFE
615 South Huntington Street
(574) 457-3297
Preferred by Lake Wawasee's well-heeled and nattily dressed businessmen and lake
residents, this clean, fresh cafe serves food to match with a sense of humor. My
favorite among the signs decorating the walls is this one: "Don't make me get the
flying monkeys!—Wicked Witch."

WALKERTON
CROCK POT CAFE
70049 State Road 23
(574) 586-2005
Sold! Located about one mile north of town, the concrete block Crock Pot once
served bidders at the adjacent auction barn.

West

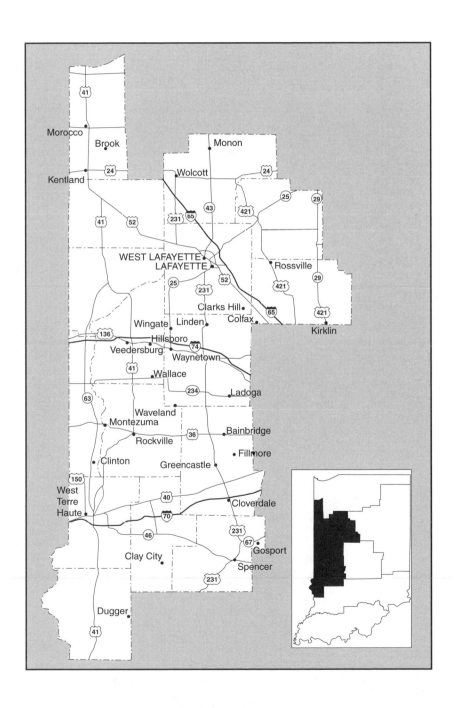

Morocco
Brook
Monon
Wolcott
Kentland
Morocco
41
24
24
25
29
41
52
231
65
43
421
WEST LAFAYETTE
LAFAYETTE
Rossville
25
52
29
231
421
Clarks Hill
421
Wingate
Linden
Colfax
65
Hillsboro
136
Kirklin
Veedersburg
74
Waynetown
41
Wallace
234
Ladoga
63
Waveland
Montezuma
36
Bainbridge
Rockville
Fillmore
Clinton
Greencastle
150
West
Terre
40
Haute
Cloverdale
70
231
46
67
Clay City
Gosport
Spencer
231
Dugger
41

CLAY CITY
Bob and Angie's Hometown Cafe
711 Main Street
(812) 939-3909
M closed; T–Sa 8 A.M.–8 P.M.; Su 8 A.M.–2 P.M.
Bob and Angie Freeman

By the time she was five years old, Erin Freeman had already acquired a lot of firsthand experience with the everyday operations of her parents' restaurant. As a baby, she supervised the kitchen work from her bouncy seat on the work counter, eventually graduating to a playpen in the corner. As a toddler, she tried out her legs in a walker barricaded by a ring of heavy pop tanks that kept her just where Angie and Bob wanted her. When at last the day came that she could walk on her own steady legs, she was allowed to explore the dining room.

"Erin is growing up here," Angie says. "She plays school with her baby dolls and takes them out to eat in the booth in the front window. I tell my customers, 'You all taught her this!'"

Not yet in kindergarten, Erin helps out in the cafe by doing child-size jobs such as restocking the tables and booths with sugar packets. "She peeled ninety-six hard-boiled eggs in one day for the salad bar," Angie notes proudly. Sitting in the booth next to Angie, Erin nods vigorously. "I like the restaurant, but I'd rather be at home," she admits.

"What's better about home?" I ask.

"It's where my bed is."

Erin goes home with Angie or Bob every afternoon for a few hours, and then returns to the cafe for the evening. In her time away from the cafe, she takes tumbling lessons at a local studio. "Would you like to see me do a cartwheel?" she asks, jumping from the booth she shares with me and her mom. She throws up her arms and plants one foot in front of the other.

"You're wearing a dress," Angie reminds her, "so you'd better be careful."

Erin pauses to think about the implications of doing a cartwheel in a dress. Her arms reach down for the floor and her bent legs fly up into the air before her smiling face remerges from the blur of body parts. Striking a ta-da pose, she asks, "How's that?" before zipping off to see what Bob is up to in the kitchen.

Angie laughs and shakes her head with amusement. "That's Erin."

After graduating from high school in 1989, Angie signed on as a cook at the former Firehouse Restaurant, which Bob had purchased four years earlier. Just twenty-one, he already had nine years of restaurant work under his belt. His bankers advised him against buying the restaurant because the building was in such bad shape, but he bought it anyway. It may have been the most fortuitous decision of his life. He and Angie got married ("I married into the restaurant," she says), sold the business on contract, and three years later got it back. "We really had missed it," Angie explains, "and when we got it back, we decided that this is what we were meant to do. We had another chance." Their grand reopening came after six weeks of cleaning, restocking, reorganizing, redecorating, and rechristening; the Firehouse Restaurant has since been known as Bob and Angie's Hometown Cafe.

From the first day, Bob and Angie settled comfortably into familiar roles, determined to "make as much as we can here." Their loyal customers drive from as far away as Vincennes, Brazil, even Plainfield, and bicyclists regularly show up on weekends from as far away as Terre Haute, a round trip of about eighty miles. "We've even gotten some from St. Louis," Angie exclaims with continuing surprise. "They come through Shakamak or Turkey Run State Park on their way to McCormick's Creek."

By car or by bike, from across the state or across town, customers can't get enough of Bob's coconut cream pie, Angie's well-stocked salad bar ("I've got people who drive here just for that—they tell me it's the best salad bar around"), and the all-you-can-eat buffets. Barbecued ribs are featured every Tuesday, with pizza on Thursday, fried or grilled Alaskan pollock on Friday, spaghetti on Saturday, and a full buffet with fried chicken and shrimp plus two other entrees available every Sunday. "Saturday morning breakfast is also really big," Angie says.

With the same food being prepared week after week, Angie admits to getting bored in the kitchen. Her customers squawk when she makes even the smallest change, however. "Once I put corn on the cob on the buffet, and got complaints. They said, 'Where's the regular corn?' I said, 'It's corn.' 'Yes, but we want the regular kind.'" Angie has learned not to be offended if some of the regulars stubbornly stick to items on the everyday menu instead of ordering her more adventurous offerings. "It's not that they don't like chicken cacciatore. It's that they won't try it." Fortunately, there is always a handful of customers receptive to her need to sometimes be a little more creative. "These are the people who go out to eat in Terre Haute," she explains.

Kneeling on the chair at a nearby table, Erin announces that she is making soup. She has carried a stainless steel bowl full of water from the kitchen and is busy tearing open packets of sweetener and tubs of nondairy creamer and emptying them into the bowl. Angie laughs. "She does this just about every day. Sometimes we have to remind her that some of her ingredients are expensive. One day I caught her in the kitchen opening the spice bottles and dumping them in."

I peer into Erin's bowl of watery cream of pepper soup, to which she wants to add hot cocoa mix.

"I think I'll stick with your mom and dad's soup," I tell her.

While Angie concentrates on the daily specials and buffet selections— and soup—Bob's gift lies in pie. "That's his baby," Angie admits.

Coconut cream, blackberry, peanut butter, and cherry were written on the board when I ordered lunch. Oh, madness! Which to order, which to order? I decided to ponder the question as I ate fried Alaskan pollock and potato salad, coleslaw, and fruit from Angie's well-stocked salad bar.

Now, I know better than to put off pie with a restaurant full of diners. I watch with increasing anxiety as Bob delivers pieces of coconut cream to the couple across the room. Pale yellow and hefty, it is exactly what I am hankering for. I begin to anticipate Bob's next visit to my table—"Is everything all right? Are you ready to order dessert?"—but he is so busy carrying plates of pie to other customers that he doesn't come my way.

Crisscrossing the dining room to deposit his treasure, Bob wonders aloud whether he should have made another coconut pie this morning. "Here it is noon, and it's just about gone." I feel a slight tremble of impending loss. Peanut butter pie wouldn't be a bad backup choice, I try to convince myself. And what about that cherry?

Bob disappears into the kitchen and emerges with a slice of coconut cream on a plate. Placing it on a table behind me, he announces, "That's the last piece." I quickly switch to peanut butter.

But the peanut butter is really banana cream. "The board is wrong," I overhear Bob tell another customer. So then, I'll have blackberry, I tell myself with unsteady conviction.

Turns out the blackberry pie is also in disguise. "I don't think it's black-berry," a man calls out to Bob. "It tastes like black raspberry to me." Better for me. I'm not a fan of blackberry seeds that get caught in my teeth.

I ask Angie to pack a piece for me to take home for dinner. Just fif-teen miles out of Clay City, the Great Berry Mystery begins to ferment like homemade wine. Do I have a slice of blackberry or black raspberry pie? I pull the car to the side of the road, put it in park, and lift the lid of the takeout box. Merely looking at the filling gets me nowhere. I poke my fin-ger into the dark purple jelly and lick it off. No answers there. I take a bite, evaluating the size of the seeds with my tongue. Definitely black raspberry. Satisfied, I return the piece to its box and head for home.

I'll be back next week for a piece of coconut cream and a piece of goose-berry made from berries picked by Bob himself. You can bet I'll be calling ahead to reserve a piece of coconut cream. Forlorn is forewarned.

GOSPORT
Gosport Diner
23 East Main Street
(812) 879-4992
M–F 7 A.M.–2 P.M.; Sa–Su closed
Floyd and Donna Friend

Growing up in nearby Bloomington, Donna Friend didn't know the town of Gosport existed. In 1995—after nearly thirty years away—she and Floyd were living in Florida when she began to dream of returning home. When they discovered the little restaurant in Gosport for sale, the couple came and took a look. "We thought, gee, this is perfect," Donna laughs. "We can sit out here and read the newspaper, flip a burger now and then."

Donna and Floyd ran the restaurant entirely by themselves for nine months before hiring a waitress. Their first customers were all men; they claimed the Bull Table the very day the Friends opened for business and have been there ever since. A month went by, and "then all of a sudden, the ladies started coming in," Donna remembers. "They were the white gloves, the ladies' clubs. They were the ones that saw that things got done around town. Once they got accustomed to us, it was party time in here at lunch. They had a ball. They served, set tables, had birthday parties. They ran this place like they owned it." The Gosport matriarchs have since passed away.

Today, Donna estimates that a majority of the diner's customers are in their fifties, with a fairly even split between men and women. This is consistent with most other cafes, yet the Gosport Diner is unique in attracting a relatively high number of customers who are kids. They come with parents and grandparents and also on their own, especially when school is out. One recent high school graduate, Tavis Rockwell, started coming in as a little boy with his grandparents. "He'd say to me, 'I want to work here. I want to cook,'" Donna remembers. Although Tavis never did get a job at the Gosport Diner, Donna is proud that his early enthusiasm for restaurant work inspired him to pursue a degree in culinary school.

Floyd and Donna received their chef's caps in other ways. Floyd earned his by working at Frisch's Big Boy. Donna earned hers on her own. "Mom hardly ever allowed me in the kitchen," she says. "When Floyd came back from Vietnam I'd cook for single GIs on holidays. I had a lot of requests for fried chicken and strawberry shortcake, and I just picked it up on my own."

At the Diner, Donna makes all of the daily specials, plus pies and biscuits. Floyd handles the grill and makes the gravy and meatloaf, butterflies and tenderizes the tenderloins, and prepares the roasts. "It's just us in the kitchen," Donna says. "We make everything we can ourselves."

Daily specials at the Gosport Diner include meatloaf on Monday, chicken or beef and noodles on Tuesday, ham and beans on Wednesday, spaghetti on Thursday, and hand-breaded, fried pollock on Friday. Served with two sides, the fish special is so popular, especially during the summer months, that people sometimes line the sidewalk down to the corner. Other consistent favorites are biscuits and gravy, Floyd's omelets, pan-fried chicken, salmon patties, liver and onions, and, of course, Donna's cream pies. She shies away from fruit pies, saying, "I cannot master a fruit pie. I never really know what that berry is going to do."

With a population of only about seven hundred, Gosport is as isolated and self-sufficient a small town as you're likely to find within an hour's drive of Indianapolis. "We have everything in town here that you could have but a vet," Donna says. People make daily visits to the post office to pick up their mail, often timing their trip into town around the Diner's hours. Other people schedule doctor and dentist appointments so they can make it in for breakfast or lunch, even selecting the day according to what's on the menu.

Even though she makes the same thing week after week ("I can make everything in my sleep"), Donna doesn't get weary of the routine. There are always opportunities to vary the menu, especially when special friends like Bob Carter, who played Sammy Terry, the vampire host of *Nightmare Theatre*, are expected. The first time Carter showed up at the Gosport Diner with a friend, Donna remembers, "It was a thrill for us all. Sammy gave out autographs and shared his ghoulish laugh with everyone." Now, when Donna knows Carter is coming, she prepares a special menu that includes Graveyard Leftovers and "ghoulash" and sets aside a whole coconut cream pie—his favorite—for him to take home. "The first time Sammy saw our menu, he was honored that we prepared it just for him."

The identity of another special guest eluded Floyd and Donna when he showed up unannounced on a summer day in 2004. "We had no idea who the man was," Donna admits about the day Mitch Daniels brought his gubernatorial campaign tour to the Gosport Diner. "He's a wiry little man and was running all over the place. I finally told my waitress, Annette, 'Tell him to sit down so we can work.' And he sat down and then was up and running again." Daniels lunched on chicken and dumplings, a dish that so impressed him that he named it the Hoosier State's best on his "Roadmap to a Comeback." Later, Daniels's secretary called and invited Donna and Floyd to a cook-off, but they had to decline because they couldn't leave the restaurant.

The visits of Sammy Terry and Mitch Daniels are highlights of Donna and Floyd's twelve years as owners of the Gosport Diner, but it's their everyday customers who are most appreciated. These are folks like Frank and Betty, who drive the twenty-mile round-trip from Spencer five days a week for lunch; the regulars who drive from as far away as Terre Haute and Indianapolis; and the local men at the Bull Table who enter the back door at six thirty, help themselves to coffee, and wait to order breakfast until the diner officially opens at seven. All day long at this table, theses are written, dissertations are defended, and honorary degrees are bestowed under the sign on the wall made and brought in by Jim Brock: "Gosport University. Learn it all here for free."

"Jim also made the library with the dictionary and *The Book of Totally Useless Information*," Donna laughs.

In fact, Donna and Floyd's customers have contributed nearly everything hanging on the green walls of the railroad-themed diner that once served as the town jail—the bathroom was the cell—and firehouse. There are framed enlargements of old postcards and photographs of Gosport, a painted mural depicting the town's Pennsylvania Railroad depot, and color prints of engines and trains. There's also a portion of Floyd's miniature and model train collection displayed on shelves. And surrounding the entrance up front are china plates that Donna has decoupaged with customers' anniversary announcements clipped from the local paper, old high school athletic team photographs, and other pictures.

With a little easy rubbernecking, you can see all the sights from your wood-grain Formica booth, but you'll need to get up and out of your seat to investigate the glass case of curiosities under the register. Go on. Go. You must not depart the Gosport Diner without taking in these treasures. There's a small Coke bottle with a wooden arrow through it and other intriguing puzzles made by clever hands, plus a variety of antique items from long closed Gosport businesses, but these do not utterly fascinate me like the money origami—the bill folds—made by the late Eddie Haulk. He took ordinary one dollar bills and folded them into a ring, bowtie, fan, a pair of lips, even a tiny dress with a Peter Pan collar and a placket front. "I stood and watched Eddie make a ring one day, and it was beyond me how he did it. I'm not that artistic," Donna says. Neither am I.

LADOGA
Patsy's Sun-Up Cafe
104 East Main Street
(765) 942-1015
M–F 6 A.M.–2 P.M.; Sa 6 A.M.–1 P.M.; Su closed
Patsy and Chuck Long
By her own admission, Patsy Long has "a pretty good set of pipes." She sings as she works in the kitchen of the Sun-Up Cafe and serenades her customers—especially the men—on their birthdays in the dining room up front. "I call myself the Singing Cook," she says. "I just love country music. Kenny Chesney, he's my man."

In the booth opposite me, Patsy draws my attention to her collection of Chesney posters and pictures on the paneled side wall. Suddenly and without warning, she springs from the booth like a Slinky stretched tight and then released.

"Jim, so help me, I'm gonna kill you!"

A single Kenny Chesney poster is left hanging on the wall.

Seated at the Bullshit Table with three of his late-morning cronies, Jim feigns injured innocence and denies the theft. "Me? I just come over here to enjoy the company!"

"You better give me them pictures back or you're gonna be wearin' that breakfast," Patsy threatens as she animatedly searches for the missing pictures. She finds them tucked under the tablecloth and carefully pins them alongside the poster. With her glossy, full color shrine to Kenny Chesney back in place, Patsy settles back into the booth with a sigh.

"Isn't he good looking?"

Patsy's Sun-Up Cafe just may have the longest Bullshit Table in the state of Indiana. Six white plastic utility tables stretch from the back of the cafe to the front, with room for a couple dozen Bullshitters. The first shift—mostly farmers and others who have to be up early—begin arriving about six thirty every morning. They help themselves to coffee while Patsy prepares breakfast. "We know what they like and can have it ready when they show up. They'll eat whatever we fix." The second shift—businesspeople on their way to work—show up an hour later. Beginning about eight o'clock, they're replaced by the "stragglers"—retired folks and others on their own schedules who often merge mornings into afternoons. "That guy that just left here? He's been here for the last two hours," Patsy tells me.

Patsy bought the Sun-Up Cafe in 1994 after years of working at local restaurants. The transition from employee to owner brought unexpected challenges, not the least of which was that the work turned out to be far harder than she anticipated. Patsy is up every morning at three thirty and at the restaurant by five. Most days she puts in ten hours before the last customer leaves at two o'clock, then another hour or two before she shuts off the lights and closes the door behind her. During the winter months, she has a staff of only three, including her daughter Jennifer, who is the sole waitress. On Fridays, Jennifer gets help from her sister, Kim. During the summer months when school is out and road crews and construction workers file in almost daily for lunch, Kim waits tables full time.

For Patsy, work often continues after hours with grocery shopping. She rarely plans the daily specials ahead of time; instead, they're conjured up based on what's on hand or what's on special at the stores. "I went shopping last night and found strawberries on sale, so today Jennifer made a strawberry pie," she says. "I try to keep changing things so people don't just sit down and order burgers, but sometimes it's a real challenge to come up with something. Sometimes I get in a rut and ask myself, 'What can I fix them today that they'll eat?' The people here are real meat and taters people. They want their roast beef, pork, and chicken and real mashed potatoes. We peel potatoes every day."

Two of the four Bullshitters huddled together at the end of the table closest to the kitchen—closest to Patsy's Kenny Chesney shrine—are forking into the day's roast pork special with tightly wrapped fists, leveraging dabs of mashed potatoes mixed with gravy to their mouths. The special comes with a choice of two sides: bright yellow corn or any one of Jennifer's homemade salads, such as coleslaw, macaroni, potato, pea, or a Waldorf-style apple salad. ("They'd have apple salad every day if they could," Patsy sighs.) The oldest man has opted for a tossed salad, whose vivid green color is a sure sign it is made from a crispy head of fresh iceberg lettuce. I rarely find such beautiful lettuce in a cafe salad.

Patsy's commitment to "food just like my grandma used to cook" translates into best-selling dishes, including biscuits and gravy, made fresh every morning, Monday's ham and beans, and Friday's skillet-fried chicken. "Breakfasts are unreal on Saturday morning," Patsy says. It is not unusual for her to go through fifteen or twenty pounds of pork sausage to keep pace with the demand for biscuits and gravy. Every Monday, more than three gallons of ham and beans are served with cornbread and fried potatoes with onions, the traditional "washday meal in a little country town." At the other end of the workweek, Patsy begins frying chicken in heavy cast-iron skillets at nine o'clock in the morning. Around eleven, the regulars start filing in, including a couple that makes the sixty-mile round-trip from Lebanon every single week.

"It's just a pleasure to stand back in the kitchen watching people enjoy what they eat," Patsy says. "There's not many restaurants like us that make everything homemade anymore."

Other constant favorites are chicken and noodles and Jennifer's peach cobbler and peach crisp. On Fridays, tilapia—a mild, sweet, flaky fish—shares top billing with fried chicken and replaces the find-it-everywhere-else fried cod that Patsy used to serve. She was supplied with tilapia by a local man who was raising it, but it quickly became so popular that he could not provide as much as she needed. He's since moved on to raising prawns.

Although Patsy has come a long way since the day in 1994 when she unlocked the door of the Sun-Up Cafe with her own key for the very first time, she admits that "some days even yet are overwhelming. I tell myself, 'Two o'clock will come no matter what.'" She's learned not to be overconfident because just when she thinks she's got the upper hand, a wrench inevitably is thrown into the gear works. It's never possible to predict customers' whims, the impact of the weather, the ripple effect of a special event in a neighboring community, and any number of other variables. "It took me at least three years to get into a groove," Patsy remembers. "I could have walked out a number of times, but I liked the work. I knew if I could stay with it, I'd make it. It's like that movie: 'If you build it, they will come.'"

And if you paint it yellow, it will be easier to see. Framed with cast-iron columns from the late nineteenth century, the front of Patsy's Sun-Up Cafe is as bright as the blazing sun, with rising suns on the large display windows and a perennially sunny smiley face on the front door. "I painted it yellow so people can find me," Patsy explains.

It works. Lined up party wall to party wall, the other commercial buildings in Ladoga's historic downtown blur into a muddled, mostly vacant mass. A few stores sell antiques, liquor, groceries and meats, and hardware—small town businesses that are stubbornly holding on. They get a boost from the Sun-Up's customers, who plan their daily trips to town according to Patsy's hours, the daily special, the gathering of friends at the Bullshit Table. Others from out of town, like the group of Lycra-clad bicyclists from Crawfordsville who join Patsy for breakfast every summer Saturday, are lured to Ladoga solely by the cafe. "People tell me that the town's dead when I'm not open," Patsy says. "I just feel good that they come in here and support me. I consider all of them my friends, and I enjoy spending my days with them."

LINDEN
R & S Cafe
115 North Main Street

(765) 339-4615

M–F 5:30 A.M.–7 P.M.; Sa 5:30 A.M.–2 P.M.; Su closed

Sue Hill

Contrary to the pair of initials on front of the building, the R & S Cafe is pretty much a one-woman operation. "I do everything," says Sue Hill about the cooking that goes on behind the kitchen wall. Twenty-odd years ago when she decided to take the plunge into restaurant ownership, her husband, Sam, advised her to "serve good food and keep it clean." Sam was a former truck driver with plenty of truck stops, diners, and cafes under his belt, so Sue figured he knew a thing or two about what it takes to make a successful restaurant. "I've been doing what he said ever since."

"Everything's made from scratch by me," she says. She tenderizes and flattens pork loins into twelve-inch tenderloins, boils and mashes real potatoes, makes her own noodles, slow-bakes her own pork and beef, mixes and rolls out her own pie dough, and makes her own fillings. Using a dry erase pen, she fills the daily specials board with traditional, home-cooked Hoosier farm food like ham and beans, meatloaf, and beef Manhattan that people like Bee Jones of Brownsburg drive out of their way for. "My husband's cousins lived in Linden and took us to R & S's," Bee enthused in "My Indiana," a Sunday feature article in the *Indianapolis Star*. "Sue without a doubt makes the best cream pies we've ever had. Of course she makes the crust from lard. . . . I just love these little cafes, which are a good reminder of days gone by. You get not only good food but also conversation and gossip in one place. You don't get that with fast food."

Sue remembers that article. "The day after it came out, I had four people drive here from Indianapolis. They had chicken and noodles and chocolate, coconut, and butterscotch pie. And they said, 'That article isn't wrong.' They wanted to buy four pies to go, but I couldn't do that."

Sue learned to make pie years ago by watching the baker at the old Romney cafe. When the time came for her to mix and roll out her own dough, she surprised herself by turning out "pies as good as what I make now. One of my customers said I was the best thing to hit Romney." She uses only lard because it makes a flakier, more flavorful crust, and mixes the dough with gloved hands. "You really don't want to mess with it too much," she advises, or the crust will get tough.

Praise for her cooking and the new customers it brings invigorate Sue and restore the joy that the long days periodically drain away. When Sue feels overwhelmed and depressed, she retreats to the kitchen and closes the curtains on the pass-through window so she can't see the customers packing the tables up front. "One morning a man came back and pulled my curtains open and said, 'Ma'am? Whatever you're doing, keep on doing it.' That about made my week."

By midafternoon, business at the R & S falls off to a lull, and Sue at last has the chance to pour a cup of coffee and sit down with friends gathered around the community coffee table. A wooden desk plaque with an engraved metal plate identifies the table as the Bull Shipping Department. ("We used to have a bull, but someone broke his ear off. Then we got a dancing diva, and then we got the plaque.") They chit, they chat, they pass the time. Talk ebbs and flows and circles around, topics invisibly linked by threads of association, memory, and shared experience. Although I am a complete stranger to the group, I'm immediately pulled in.

"Do you know about the Tunnelton tunnel?" Clint demands following the cursory introductions. I've just joined the group, so I have no contextual frame of reference to what has come before, and for a moment I am completely baffled. I rebound quickly. I happen to know a lot about the Big Tunnel in southeastern Lawrence County, built in 1856 by the Ohio and Mississippi Railway. I tell the Bull Shippers about my visits to the tunnel and about the legend that says it's haunted.

I'm feeling pretty happy—admittedly, even a bit smug—about my contributions to the Bull Shipping Department until Clint tells me, the self-appointed Big Tunnel expert, something I don't know. "My dad's first job during World War I was guarding both ends of the tunnel. It wouldn't've taken much to disable the railroad." Well into his seventies, and after years as a private pilot, Clint confides, "The tunnel is the last place I have a yearning to go."

Across the table from Clint, Bob reveals that for years he has been conducting his own great Hoosier food adventure, seeking out and eating at "local joints." We compare notes on the best and the worst of our discoveries—our worsts seem to be the most memorable!—and discuss the cleanliness or friendliness of this diner, that one's pie, or another's meatloaf. "My wife says I'll have on my tombstone, 'I ate at every greasy spoon between here and Lafayette,'" Bob says somewhat sheepishly.

Larry the preacher is opining on Sue's use of beans in the chili on his Coney dog ("I've never seen one with beans") when Shelly Wright and his wife claim the adjacent booth. Over coconut cream pie, Shelly shares news about his recent ninetieth birthday at his sister's house. It may be his birthday, but he's the one giving the gifts. He hands Sue three shiny stainless-steel pie pans and hints, "These are worth two big apple pies."

"You asked for two apple pies to take to your sister's house," Sue reminds him.

"Who told you that?"

"You did!"

"That's being ninety, I guess."

The laughter fades. Sue sips her coffee and leans back in her chair, the Bull Shippers framing the table around her. "How did I make it the last twenty years?" she asks, retrieving the question I'd asked forty-five minutes earlier. "I figure I have to work, so I might as well work here and make everyone happy—or miserable. I'd miss the people. I have so many good memories. That's probably why I don't quit."

MONON
Reme's Monon Family Restaurant
104 East Fourth Street
(219) 253-8550
M–Sa 5 A.M.–9 P.M.; Su 5 A.M.–8 P.M.
Trinidad "Trini" and Sherry Arias

Although it has begun in a perfectly ordinary way, Sherry Arias's day has swung into the slightly peculiar, thanks in part to the woman who has just left. I noticed her at the salad bar placing chunks of watermelon in her bare hand, but my enthusiasm in discovering Trini's rainbow of homemade salads pushed aside any contemplation of her odd behavior. Sherry is doing enough pondering for the both of us. "What a strange lady," she exclaims, shaking her head in bewilderment. "She complained four or five times about her pork chop, and then ate every bit of it. And what was she doing in the salad bar? Filching watermelon? Some days can be so strange!"

"My coming to write about you makes it that much stranger," I point out.

Sherry and Trini have been in the restaurant business long enough to have accumulated a large collection of unlikely events that make for great stories. At the top of the stack may well be the *Philadelphia Inquirer* column by Bob Neubauer, an amateur pilot, which featured a close-up view of their humble little restaurant. (That's Philadelphia as in Pennsylvania!) As he flies over the flatlands of the Midwest, Bob often wonders what life must be like in the specks of towns he spots from the sky. One day, on a drive from West Lafayette to Chicago, he took the opportunity to find out. Over breakfast of fried eggs and potatoes at the Monon Family Restaurant, he unobtrusively observed the locals and eavesdropped on their morning conversation. In the *Inquirer,* Bob wrote, "Every time I glance down from my plane at a cluster of buildings huddled at an inter-section, I'll see the tiny town of Monon in my mind, and think back on my breakfast in the Monon Family Restaurant and the collection of old farmers and their wives inside."

Now, imagine his surprise when the son of one of these very farm-ers, at home in Philadelphia, opened his morning paper and began to read about folks in his Hoosier hometown! It couldn't have been any less than the Ariases' own surprise when they read the column he quickly dispatched by first class mail. You can read the column yourself when you visit Reme's Monon Family Restaurant (named for Trini's mother). It's taped inside the glass counter under the cash register, next to newspaper clippings and pho-tos trumpeting the school accomplishments of Trini and Sherry's daugh-ters, Daniela and Felicia.

It's a shame that Bob Neubauer failed to mention Trini's food, for it just might make a trip from Philadelphia worth considering. "Everything is homemade," Sherry stresses. "Salads, sauces, soups, even the salsa. Trini's a real believer in fresh."

"Dad *insists* on fresh," Felicia chimes in. "He's real picky and can tell when food is real. He can tell if lettuce is from a bag or if it's fresh."

Trini spreads a salad bar so good it banishes my fear that I will never satisfy my craving for crunchy green vegetables. A truly fresh salad is nearly impossible to find in Indiana's small town cafes, where vegetables are pretty much limited to canned carrots, peas, corn, and mixed vegetables (a dowdy combination of the first two with perhaps a lima bean or two thrown in). Trini stocks his salad bowl with sturdy green romaine instead of the all-too common iceberg lettuce mix dumped out of a plastic bag. The packaged stuff is easy to recognize because the lettuce is cut into tidy little squares and tossed with sliced purple cabbage and julienne carrots that are usually dry—and too often brown—along the edges. Filling out Trini's salad bar are from-scratch potato and pasta salads, coleslaw, and specialty vegetable and fruit salads, as well as a variety of homemade dressings. As Sherry and Felicia attest, Trini is a stickler for real food.

He also has an impressive green thumb, validating one of my favorite theories: a sure sign of an excellent cafe is the health of its houseplants. (If they're tended by a loving hand, lush and hearty like Trini's, the food will likely be the same. If they're neglected or fake, you shouldn't expect more from the food.) The lavender walls of the Monon Family Restaurant—"We love purple," Sherry exclaims—are veined with a jungle of healthy pothos and philodendron vines the likes of which I have seen only in climate-controlled conservatories. Held in place by plastic push pins, vines amble up the walls from only five or six different pots. My own efforts with the same plants—said to be among the easiest houseplants to grow—never produce results like this! "They're Trini's babies," Sherry says. "He talks to them, spritzes them with water, and picks off their dead leaves."

A native of Mexico, Trini began his restaurant career as a busboy in a Greek-owned Chicago restaurant in the early 1980s. Over time, the owner persuaded him to learn to cook in preparation for the day he'd have his own restaurant. He'd regularly put in a full day out front, and then tackle another twelve hours in the kitchen. It was here that he learned to brew soups and prepare main dishes ranging from modest midwestern meatloaf to fancier fare like chicken cacciatore and prime rib.

It does not necessarily follow, however, that Trini's training prepared him for running a restaurant in a small town the likes of Monon. In 1989, he partnered with Sherry's mother, Sharon Fischer, and bought the Monon Family Restaurant. He stayed on at the Greek restaurant and drove back and forth on the weekends, but it soon became apparent that four kids, two jobs, and a long commute was too much. "That didn't work out," he recalls with a sigh, still wondering years later what madness made him think it would. In 1999, Sharon sold the restaurant to Trini and Sherry, who packed up their household, enrolled the kids in Monon area schools, and became full-time Hoosiers.

One of their early cross-cultural discoveries was the locals' madness for biscuits and gravy, a culinary quirk that Chicagoans had never demanded. "It was on the menu when we took over, so he had to learn to make it," Sherry explains. "The first thing Trini does every morning is turn on the grill and make biscuits and gravy. We go through three pots on Saturday and Sunday—and they're four- or five-gallon pots!" A bonus came in the discovery that sausage gravy is a basic building block in other dishes. "There's biscuits and gravy, gravy and scrambled eggs, gravy and potatoes, gravy over country-fried steak."

As a breakfast alternative, you might want to try the six-egg country omelet filled with sausage, green pepper, onions, tomatoes, and hash browns and topped with gravy. "It's the size of a football," gasps Sherry. "And people eat it!"

Later in the day, main meal favorites include Trini's Mexican dishes, especially the jumbo burrito, hand-breaded fried perch, fettuccine Alfredo, chicken à la king, and chicken or beef and noodles. The regulars are also plenty fond of Trini's Chicago-style pizza made in the standard varieties, plus a Mexican version topped with chorizo and jalapeños and an Alfredo interpretation made with chicken and broccoli. The owner of a Chicago pizzeria taught Trini the art of making exceptional pizza. The day a Chicago diner informed him that "you've got the best pie in the Midwest," Trini knew he'd aced the test.

Carnivores will be thrilled to learn that Trini cuts his own tenderloins, steaks, roasts, and other meats. He buys beef from the local 4-H fair and from local farmers, and relies on Monon Meat Packing down on the corner for processing. He insists on buying locally whenever possible because "we have to survive on the locals."

Sherry agrees. Area tourism—especially that centered on Lakes Shafer and Freeman and the town of Monticello—brings seasonal bursts of business, but "the locals are our bread and butter. We have to please the locals because we need them to return."

Among the reliable returnees are the daily groups of coffee drinkers that file in at informally established times for bottomless cups of coffee with friendly banter and the latest news stirred in. The Roundtable in the front window fills at five thirty each weekday morning with men needing a wake-up before heading off to work. They're replaced at nine with the first shift of retired men, whose places are taken by a second group an hour later. A coterie of women begins gathering at another table at nine, but by ten thirty or eleven they have departed for home. Most of the five thirty group returns at two for a midafternoon pick-me-up and a chance to catch up on news so recent that it hasn't yet had a chance to circulate. Laughs Sherry, "People are coming and going all day long."

SPENCER
Chambers Smorgasbord
72 West Market Street
(812) 829-3022
Breakfast: M–Sa 5:30 A.M.–1:30 P.M.
Breakfast bar: Sa 5:30 A.M.–10:30 A.M.; Su 7 A.M.–10:30 A.M.
Lunch smorgasbord: M–Su 11 A.M.–2:30 P.M.
Dinner smorgasbord: Th–Sa 4:30 P.M.–8 P.M.
Barbara Chambers

For seventeen years I have lived in Martinsville, and by reason of proximity that makes me a not-too-distant neighbor to the people of Spencer. I have noted the Chambers Smorgasbord billboards on State Road 67 for just about as long, yet I never ate there until I began work on this book. Just why I neglected to make the fifty-mile round-trip drive over the White River and through the hills of Owen County is impossible to say, but I now realize the error of my ways. I have missed out on years of fine eating courtesy of the Chambers family, and while I am not exactly making up for lost time, I find myself at their namesake smorgasbord more and more frequently.

On a Friday night in mid-October, I found myself approaching the end of a week-long stint of my Indiana food foray. I'd traveled hundreds of miles and visited nearly twenty-five cafes, and the unthinkable had happened. I was hungry. I studied my map and realized that suppertime would place me in Spencer. Chambers Smorgasbord, to be exact. As it turns out, my arrival intersected perfectly with that of a hungry bicyclist from Illinois who had ridden all day in the cold and rain to reach the start of the Hilly Hundred bike tour. He'd thrown up his tent at McCormick's Creek State Park, and then biked back into Spencer to find something to eat, bypassing the string of fast food huts along the highway in search of some-place truly local.

"I wanted to get inside where it was warm and dry," he confided as we huddled under Chambers's maroon awning. "I came downtown and saw the lights on and people eating inside and figured this looked like a pretty good place. I never would've dreamed I'd find such good food—and as much as I could eat. I'll be back tomorrow morning for breakfast." It had taken him one day and 110 miles to reach Chambers by bike from a neighboring state. It had taken me years and an 800-mile trip through southern Indiana to reach Chambers, a mere half hour from home.

Long-distance bicyclists demand starchy carbohydrates to fuel them for the road, but cafe hunters overdosed on country-fried Hoosier food, mashed potatoes, and pie crave nothing so much as crunchy fresh veg-etables. As I lined up at the smorgasbord, my knees quaked. Before me stretched a beautiful bonanza, the mother lode of salad bars. I rejected the skimpy glass salad bowls and reached for one of the large dinner plates on the hot food side of the smorgasbord. I plunged in with gleeful abandon, piling a little mound of crispy iceberg lettuce onto the center of the plate, then adding shredded carrots, sliced cucumber, rings of green pepper, bite-size pieces of cauliflower and broccoli florets, tomato wedges, sliced fresh mushrooms, and diced onion. Around the edge of the plate I spooned dol-lops of specialty salads: coleslaw, potato salad, ambrosia made with coconut and mandarin oranges, kidney bean salad, cauliflower, broccoli and carrot salad, pea salad, and Waldorf salad.

Did I say it was all homemade? No jars are opened and dumped into this salad bar, which I hereby anoint the Hoosier Queen.

I returned to the salad bar one more time for a refill before joining the folks in line for the entrees. The glories on this side of the smorgasbord were equally thrilling. There was freshly baked wheat and white bread and dinner rolls with pats of real butter, fried biscuits and apple butter, chicken and noodles, mashed potatoes and gravy, green beans flavored with bacon and onion, fried chicken, deep-fried catfish and shrimp, and rosy-hued slices of baked ham. I sampled a little bit of everything, went back for a second fried biscuit, and then headed off to the dessert bar where apple cobbler, no-bake cookies, brownies, and Tollhouse and seven-layer bars were lined up like contestants at a beauty pageant.

Oh, gluttony, thy name is Chambers. And I, for one, am willing to sin.

Established in 1972 by the late Bob Chambers (don't overlook the memorial bench carved from limestone inside the entrance), Chambers is a hybrid mix of traditional cafe, daily smorgasbord, and weekend breakfast buffet. Depending on your mood and the expandability of your waistband, come for the all-you-can-eat feasts or order off the menu. The restaurant format is reserved primarily for the mornings, when the locals and other regulars stream in for breakfast and rounds of coffee downed with talk. The Bullshippers, a group of local men, spend about three or four hours here each day around an Old Hickory table reserved by a handmade sign with the picture of a bull in a ship. The Bullshippers departed, taking their sign along with them, when the restaurant was declared a nonsmoking zone in January 2005, but they are gradually returning and falling back into their comfortable roles. "They talk about politics and everything else," says Barbara Chambers, Robert's widow. "They think all their talk is world changing."

In 1981, Robert expanded his original little diner located a block away and added the smorgasbord. Barbara recalls, "He was trying to increase business and added evening hours. He was also looking for a little more variety. We were traveling and went to a little place with a smorgasbord, and he came home wanting to try it. It was still a relatively new idea—that was long before Ryan's—and I was worried about the waste, but it worked."

Twenty years before Bob established his own business, his parents operated a restaurant near the entrance of McCormick's Creek State Park. The original Chambers Restaurant was known for Robert's mother's home cooking, and Robert himself "followed in her footsteps, making a commitment to home cooking from scratch," says Barbara. "What we make here is old-fashioned, just plain food. It's the kind of thing people grew up on and what they still want." That includes plenty of fried chicken, meatloaf, roast beef, chicken and noodles, ham, and swiss steak. "And fried biscuits and apple butter. We can never have enough of that."

Whatever day of the week, the smorgasbord always includes fried chicken and ham, with other entrees rotating on a set schedule. Wednesdays are reserved for bean soup and cornbread ("We've tried sometimes to switch, but they want to know they'll always get it on Wednesdays"), Thursdays feature meatloaf, Fridays catfish and seafood, and Sundays are always known for swiss steak. The regulars, including folks from as far away as Indianapolis and Terre Haute, know what they're hungry for before they leave home and don't hesitate to complain if their favorite items are sold out by the time they arrive. "When they say, 'I came all the way for swiss steak or home-baked cookies or peanut butter fudge,' and we don't have it," Barbara explains, "I feel just wilted. We tell people to call ahead so we can be sure to have what they want when they get here."

In 2002, Barbara was joined in the family business by her son, Jim, who started out working in the restaurant at age ten or eleven. "I was washing dishes, cooking, clearing tables, doing just about everything but baking," he remembers. After graduating from high school, he went to college and then worked four years in the tool-and-die trade. When Robert had a stroke, Jim returned to work in the restaurant. "Dad and I had sat down and talked about my getting back into the restaurant," he says. "I'd helped out in childhood and always said in high school that I wanted to take it over. Mom had kind of cultivated that interest in me, but then I veered away. Now that I'm back, it's kind of like home. It's what I grew up doing."

Chambers Smorgasbord moved to its current location in 1998 following an arson fire that destroyed the original restaurant's kitchen and rear dining room. Despite the devastating loss, going out of business was never considered. Instead, the Chamberses bought the vacant Mullenix building and tackled months of repair and remodeling under the supervision of customers who regularly dropped in to check on their progress and inquire just when they'd be ready to reopen. When the awaited day came, Robert and Barbara were overwhelmed by the number of people who came in to eat. For three months the hectic pace continued before slowly tapering off into a regular day-to-day routine. In recent years business has remained good but not increased. Since 9/11, observes Barbara, "It's just very erratic. We used to be able to count on regular business. Now we might have two hundred people on a Friday and be empty on Saturday."

Fluctuations in the economy, as well as aging buildings, changing demographics, customer demands, and the willingness of local residents to drive greater distances to shop and eat out, have contributed to a significant decline in Spencer's historic courthouse square. Despite the presence of the post office, courthouse, and library, all of which bring people downtown, businesses have abandoned the square for State Road 67. "A lot of the buildings on the square are empty, and that depresses me," Barbara says.

Chambers Smorgasbord, in fact, may well be the square's biggest draw, a destination business that attracts people from upwards of fifty miles away. It is also among the oldest businesses in Spencer today. In its second generation of family operation, Chambers is now serving "people who came in as kids who are now bringing in their kids," Jim notes. "We have a family who stays a week at McCormick's Creek every summer, and they come here every day for breakfast. The grandparents ate here in the 1970s, and they're now up to twenty-six or twenty-seven kids and grandchildren."

Breakfasts are both a big part of the day at Chambers and big all by themselves—especially with first-timers and tourists who haven't yet discovered just how big they really are. The "very large" pancakes are, at bare minimum, the size of a serving platter. But be forewarned: if the grill cook gets a little harried or slap-happy, they often end up hanging a few inches over the edge of the platter. A short stack consists of one "very large" oval cake. A full order of hotcakes consists of two "very large" oval cakes. It is so unusual for someone to polish off a full order of hotcakes that it becomes a momentous occasion when it actually happens. "We had someone just last Sunday eat a whole order," Jim says, "but that's pretty rare. Once people find out how big our pancakes are, they usually don't make the mistake of ordering two again."

Other memorable big breakfasts include the six-egg omelet made with eight or nine slices of cheese, a favorite of Tom Vedder, a local Jim describes as "just a normal-looking guy." Another fellow is identified with his regular full order of biscuits and gravy with a side of deep-fried diced potatoes (southern fries), followed by a second full order of biscuits and gravy and a side order of ham or bacon. Popular on-the-menu breakfasts include the Chambers Special, a layering of two eggs, bacon, sausage, or ham, hash browns, and cheese, and the Hash Brown Casserole, a "customer-created" jumble of hash browns, bacon, sausage, or ham, green peppers, onions, mushrooms, and swiss cheese. If these sound like a belly full, take a deep breath, loosen your belt a notch, and prepare for even more. They come served with toast or fried biscuits and apple butter.

WALLACE
Highway 341 Country Cafe ♻

3886 South State Road 341

(765) 397-3366

M–W 7 A.M.–8 P.M.; Th 7 A.M.–10 P.M.; F 7 A.M.–8 P.M.; Sa 7 A.M.–10 PM.;
Su 7 A.M.–2 P.M.

Tony and Linda Shuman

A farming community of about ninety residents, Wallace is the kind of place you're more likely to drive through than drive to. The downtown—the whole town actually—consists of a post office, lodge hall, fire station, Model T garage, a handful of houses, and the cafe that Tony and Linda Shuman purchased in 2003. Tony retired after forty years of installing commercial refrigerators, moved back home to Indiana from Alabama, and fulfilled a dream of running his own home cooking–style restaurant and making music on the side. The grand result is the Highway 341 Country Cafe and opry, as unlikely a little place as you're apt to find in a speck of a town like Wallace.

A Covington native, Tony inherited his mother's love for cooking and carried it into the restaurant. "We have all home cooking because I don't like that fast food stuff, and my mother was a really good cook. That's just what I was raised on," he says. He spent eight months perfecting his coconut cream pie and yeast rolls, which he makes at the cafe every Friday, Saturday, and Sunday. Other down-home offerings include pan-fried chicken, roast beef, Salisbury steak, and chicken and noodles.

Music is another gift that Tony hasn't squandered. He was a member of popular local bands during the 1960s and 1970s, and, as a member of Jade, recorded a version of "Chattanooga Shoe Shine Boy" that was a *Billboard* magazine country honorable mention in June 1984. The record played on seventy major radio stations in the United States, Canada, and Mexico. "Two years later I moved out of state, and the music stopped. Then I went to Alabama and met a couple of musicians and started jamming around a little bit. And the music came back," he says.

The Shumans bought the old Wallace general store and cafe in June 2003 and set about converting the old building into a music hall. Tony built a small bandstand and new restrooms, and used one hundred gallons of red and white paint to bring the whole place to new life. ("In the beginning, I did everything: remodeling, cooking, and music.") Once the paint had dried, the walls were literally filled with Tony's jaw-dropping collections of Wheaties boxes—there are ninety-one on display with another two hundred in storage—and coach Bob Knight collectibles. He has Indiana University and Texas Tech jackets, sweatshirts, and caps; a porcelain Bob Knight figure; an autographed basketball; photos and news stories, including a framed article about the February 2004 "salad bar incident" with Texas Tech Chancellor David Smith. There are hundreds of things, but my favorite is a cap referencing the notorious 1985 IU-Purdue game that reads "Bobby Knight Furniture Co. Buy a couch and he will throw in a chair."

Breakfast on a weekday is a fine time to peruse the decor, which also includes a Wallace historical display and "Memory Lane" plastered with photos of musicians and the regulars. With the exception of a table or two filled with farmers, retired gents, and deliverymen, you'll have the Highway 341 Cafe pretty much to yourself. Be sure to allow time for a leisurely, lingering visit because you won't want to miss a thing. You'll never, ever have the same opportunity on music nights, held every Thursday and Saturday beginning with dinner at four thirty.

First things first: Reservations are an absolute must. Do not expect to wander in off the street and find a place to sit, let alone stand. The Highway 341 Cafe really rocks, mostly with folks in their sixties and seventies who wouldn't consider missing a night unless there were was a death in the family. On a Thursday in early September, Tony had a place waiting for me right up front, at the end of a large community table I share with Montie and Betty Keller of Covington, Betty Davis, and her friend Tresley Noble. We get to know each other over massive amounts of chicken-fried steak and beef Manhattan with mashed potatoes and gravy, kidney bean salad, and Hoosier-style green beans flavored with bacon and diced potatoes. When Tony's daughter, Kathy, brings Montie a thick slab of raisin pie ("That's for breakfast," he tells me), I lay down my fork and push my plate aside.

"Bring me lemon meringue," I order.

Second things second: Be sure to put in your dibs for pie early or you will be disappointed. It will sell out. Betty guarantees that the pie "is the biggest and cheapest," and she's right. Half a piece is all I could comfortably manage.

Tresley is the first on the dance floor when the eight-member band opens the evening with "Folsom Prison Blues." Others soon join her, including Leslie "Sprout" Melvin, who wears striped denim overalls, a straw hat, and cowboy boots, and Lou McKinney, a septuagenarian with a dancer's elegant legs. She wears spunky red high heels, a denim dirndl skirt with a silk scarf tied around her waist, and a red and white striped T-shirt. Lou and her partner, Jerry Thompson, thrill me with their polished steps, dips, twirls, and spins. Lou tells me that she loves to dance and is at the Highway 341 Cafe without fail every Thursday and Saturday night.

Sprout is also in his seventies, a regular member of the audience, and the narrator in the band's rendition of "Roses for Mama." During "Elvira," he hooks his thumbs in his overall straps and jerks his pants up and down in rhythm with the music. Then he juts his elbows out, bends his knees, and struts about like a chicken. I am initially astonished by his complete lack of reserve, but quickly realize that he is so utterly at home here in the Highway 341 Cafe that he has no reason at all to be self-conscious.

In fact, it's the zany goofiness of the regulars that makes the Highway 341 Cafe an infectious delight. They do not put on airs. Instead, Jerry Griffith puts on a wig, a stuffed bra, and a T-shirt airbrushed with a bikini babe, and as Geraldine shimmies to "Hey, Good Lookin'." Sprout joins the fun by donning a set of clip-on devil's horns—with red bulbs that light up!—and dancing suggestively with Geraldine. "The devil made me do it," he tells the audience.

"Now that gives new meaning to the word ugly," Tony quips into the microphone when the song ends.

A half hour later, Geraldine reappears when the band breaks into Mickey Gilley's "Don't All the Girls Get Prettier at Closing Time." She is as surprised as we are when six women in wigs and bikini T-shirts (bought on eBay) join her on the dance floor. One wears the devil's horns, another a bunny tail. A third has glittery pasties glued to her painted breasts. The audience bursts out in peals of laughter. "You don't have to be crazy for coming here," singer John Covault says. "But it sure helps."

As the band takes a short break, I step outside and meet Allen Hayworth of Veedersburg, another one of the diehard regulars. We walk among the cars stretched along the highway two blocks in either direction, noting from their license plates just how far people have come. About half the cars are from Illinois, the other half represent five Indiana counties. With the light inside the cafe gleaming through the front windows and falling onto the pavement, the music fills the quiet night. "If Tony and Linda didn't come here, Wallace wouldn't be here," Allen says.

Allen and I drift back into the cafe as the band is winding down a three-hour set. When Tony asks for requests from the audience, Betty scribbles something on a napkin and passes it to him. Immediately a search is launched for Ross Houchens, a high school boy who works in the kitchen. When Ross appears, the band rips into "Wipe Out" by the Surfaris. With blond curls bouncing around his head, Ross begins a frenetic jiving, jiggering, jumping dance that's part break dancing, part rock-and-roll twist, and part Moondoggie surfing moves. On the song's final wipeout, Ross leaps high into the air with his legs outstretched like a hurdler and points to the band.

"You rock!"

WAVELAND
Brenda's Kitchen 🍴
205 North Cross Street (State Road 59)
(765) 435-3379
M–Sa 7 A.M.–8 P.M.; Su 7 A.M.–2 P.M.
Brenda Jones
It is four o'clock on a Wednesday in late September when I drop in at Brenda's Kitchen, located in the two-block stretch of Highway 59 that is Waveland's business district. Owner Brenda Jones is dunking Oreos sandwiched with jack-o-lantern orange filling into a glass of milk. I laugh at the irony of a cafe owner eating Oreos when her own homemade pies are temptingly displayed in a refrigerator just over her shoulder. Brenda smiles sheepishly, like a child caught with her hand in the cookie jar.

Brenda may be bored with pie, but I would sure like to eat a piece! Any piece. Banana cream heaped with toasted meringue would be just the ticket after dinner, and I promise Brenda I'll come back after pitching my tent at Shades State Park. But before I leave, as the sun slowly melts into the harvested fields, Brenda and I talk about life in Waveland during the past year that has brought a roller coaster of hope and despair.

Just about every morning, Lori Arts and Susie Calvert meet at Brenda's Kitchen to drink coffee and talk before heading off to work. One morning in August 2003, words and ideas fell like autumn leaves on the topic of Waveland's future. Like small towns all across Indiana faced with road-ways, sidewalks, and infrastructure crumbling from years of neglect due to shrinking tax revenues, residents of this southwest Montgomery County town worried that theirs was being drained of life.

"We talked about how to keep businesses in town, how to get the sidewalks and roads repaired, and how to help with the kids' ball field," remembers Brenda. Sadly, the pennies in the town's coffer didn't allow for much more than dreams about what needed to be done. When conversation shifted to a recent country music concert held in Greencastle, dim hope suddenly blazed into hundred-watt enlightenment. They'd put on a concert to raise funds for a wish list of municipal improvements that would help keep the town alive.

Dubbed Wavestock, the June 5, 2004, concert at nearby Lake Waveland Park featured country legend Kenny Rogers, Ricky Van Shelton, and Sara Evans. Organizers were optimistic that their gamble on the Gambler would attract twenty thousand fans willing to pay thirty to forty dollars per ticket that would raise an estimated $600,000 for the town. "We have no fears that this is going to work," Susie told AP reporter Ken Kusmer. "In my dreams I see new paved streets. I see sidewalks. I see storm sewers. This town has a lot of needs."

The novel and daring approach to generate revenue put Waveland on the map. "We went national," says Brenda. "In fact, we were even in Malaysia." The story was covered by Paul Harvey on the ABC Radio Network, Channel 7 News, an ABC affiliate in Washington, D.C., and featured on *As It Happens*, a program of Canadian public radio. It also appeared in regional newspapers, from the *St. Paul Pioneer Press* to the *Louisville Courier-Journal*. When *Country Weekly* magazine rejected the story idea, Susie says, "I e-mailed them that small towns are their most loyal customers. And they put us in. We just wouldn't say no."

To help pay the upfront costs of organizing and staging Wavestock, the community that was not ready to be a ghost town sponsored a spaghetti dinner, silent auction, golf scramble, and a number of raffles. The majority of funds came from five residents, who took out personal loans totaling $200,000, an investment in their community that was perhaps the most significant investment of their lives. "We wanted to see this town stay alive." Brenda says.

"People just don't know what they're losing," Susie believes. "The small town is a whole way of life. It's everyone knowing everyone else, when you take a shower. (That's both good and bad.) It's not like the big city. It's having the hardware store across the street that still smells like a hardware store."

Brenda nods. "The man from ABC was amazed! He'd never even driven a lawn mower before. He wanted to see around town, so we walked down the middle of the street. He kept looking over his shoulder, expecting to be hit by a car. It's not like that here. I told him people came here in their golf carts, and he thought I was fooling. He just loved our small town."

If, as Susie says, everyone in a small town knows who you are, then the corollary is also true: everyone knows who you aren't. As Susie, Brenda, and I talk, I am furtively watched by a couple finishing up the last remnants of burgers at the next table. Jim Perry and his wife, Marge, don't want to pull Brenda away from our conversation by paying their tab at the register, so Jim leaves a collection of bills and coins at her elbow. As the front door closes behind them, Brenda taps the table in front of me to emphasize her words.

"There's no such thing as a stranger in a small town cafe. Tomorrow they'll ask who you were and what you were about!"

Brenda opened her namesake restaurant in 1995, sold it in 1997, and a few years later bought it back. Since the first day, it has served as an informal town hall, a community center where schemes are concocted and implemented—and relived and rehashed afterward. When Wavestock fell far short of its goal—income failed even to cover the costs—it was at Brenda's Kitchen that residents gathered to shed tears, share heartache, and evaluate their next steps.

"It was a great concert although it didn't bring in the money we wanted it to," admits Brenda. "We're so far in the hole that the only thing we can do is have another one and climb a bit further out."

I am heavy with empathy and not just a little bit of worry for the folks of Waveland as I drive back roads through stubbly fields to Shades State Park. Many municipal needs and no money to pay for them is a familiar dilemma. My own town of Martinsville recently had water woes to the tune of some thirteen million dollars, and a courthouse closed due to unsolved health problems of its occupants—and empty pockets long ago turned inside out in search of pennies that might be hidden in the folds.

Only two sites are occupied by late season campers at Shades, and there is no park employee in the entrance booth. It is rather spooky being in a nearly empty park, and I set up my tent quickly before washing up and heading back to Brenda's Kitchen for dinner. It is comforting to know that I am expected, that people are waiting for me. I concentrate on memorizing each turn I make because I will be returning to my campsite in the inky blackness, where only the beady eyes of raccoons will greet me.

Not many regulars have turned out for Brenda's all-you-can-eat spaghetti dinner served with a well-stocked soup and salad bar and a side of simple garlic toast. It's a shame that all this excellent food is overlooked midweek by the folks who live around these parts. Perhaps it's the eat-'til-you-can't promise that scares them away. The amount of spaghetti noodles and meat sauce dished onto my plate is a gargantuan feast, easily satisfying all by itself the food pyramid's daily recommended servings of the bread group. I twirl spaghetti around my fork with considerable restraint. I haven't forgotten the banana cream pie waiting in the wings. It is lovely in pale yellow and a cap of meringue froth, and despite how much I've already eaten, I have no trouble at all polishing off the whole piece. It would be an unforgivable sin to send even a bite of pie this good to the dumpster out back.

Note: A second concert featuring Sawyer Brown held in July 2005 attracted about five thousand people but failed to generate enough funds to pay back the previous year's concert debts, let alone to pay for public improvements. Optimism that the town's difficulties could be overcome was shared with ABC News by Waveland's oldest resident, a ninety-two-year-old farmer: "Well, I had a bit of cancer back in 1967, and the doctors gave me five years. Now they're dead."

WINGATE
Spartan Inn 🍴
101 E. High Street
(765) 275-2649
M–Th 5 A.M.–7 P.M.; F–Sa 5 A.M.–8 P.M.; Su closed
Jo Ann and Luther Phillips
LeRoy Bunnell and Dallie Jones are holding huddle at center court, lining up plays for the rest of the afternoon. The farmers are here at the Spartan Inn, at the round table in the corner, nearly every day for lunch, not so much

watching over an investment as taking an active role in it. They are two of the six remaining founders of the Spartan Group that owns the building, a former implement dealership. "A sewer line was being put in, and the only cafe in town collapsed," LeRoy explains. "We had no restaurant for a year, and then we formed the Spartan Group and bought this building. The owner of the previous cafe opened the restaurant on July 10, 1991."

Named after the old Wingate High School athletic teams, the original Spartan Group had ten members, each with a share in the restaurant. As members pass away, shares are inherited by sons. This guarantees that the restaurant stays not only in the community but in the family, a legacy from one generation to the next.

But it's not quite that simple; there's far more than a restaurant at stake. The passing down of shares and the continuation of the restaurant means that the history of Wingate will not be lost, especially the magical years of 1913 and 1914 when the Spartans won back-to-back state basketball championships and established the state's first high school team dynasty.

As you enter town on State Road 25 from the north or south, you can't miss the billboards proclaiming Wingate's proud role in Hoosier basketball history. Not only did the Spartans claim two state titles and the first high school superstar in Homer Stonebraker, they went on in 1920 to seize the U.S. Interscholastic Tournament title from neighboring Crawfordsville. (Both teams were banned that year from the IHSAA tournament for infractions.) The billboards also commemorate two local men, Lee Haxon and Roy MeHarry, who made the first electric scoreboard in the nation.

That any of these achievements happened at all is amazing because the Wingate Spartans had no gymnasium of their own. The "Gymless Wonders" practiced at the school in neighboring New Richmond—the fictional Hickory in the movie *Hoosiers*—or relied on hoops nailed to posts. It wasn't until 1925 that the town purchased a livery stable turned implement dealership and converted it into a gymnasium. The Wingate gymnasium still stands at High and Main Cross Street, just a block west of the Spartan Inn.

Since 1991, the Spartan Inn has served double duty as a restaurant and museum, with an emphasis on the local schools—both Wingate, which closed in1954, and Coal Creek consolidated school, which was absorbed into North Montgomery in 1971. The walls of the side dining room are filled with old town photos and postcards, band and athletic plaques and trophies, vintage yearbooks, a letter sweater from 1941, newspaper articles celebrating the Spartans' one national and two state basketball championships, and athletic team photos spanning seventy years. Homer Stonebraker is the lanky boy shown straddling the basketball in the 1913 team photo.

Be careful not to miss the news story about Wingate's other famous son, Raymond "Gaumey" Neal, an Indiana Football Hall of Fame member. As DePauw football coach from 1929 to 1946, Neal coached the 1933 team to a remarkable undefeated, unscored-upon, and untied season. Team members donated the Raymond "Gaumey" Neal field house in the Lilly Center in his name in 1982.

Although she is not a Wingate native, Jo Ann Phillips is proud to be curator of the town's history. She'd worked for the Spartan Inn's previous owner for six years before she and her husband, Luther, bought the business in late 1999. "I didn't have much interest in taking over, but the guys [the Spartan Group] started bugging me about it, and my husband said, 'Why don't you give it a try?'" she says. She was joined by her three daughters, Patty Carter, Kathy Stephens, and Kimberly Clarke, and Luther, who cooks on weekends.

Together, the Phillips Group is a powerful force in the kitchen. From my perch on a stool at the end of an expansive stainless steel work table, I scribble notes as Jo Ann shares stories about life at the Spartan Inn. At eleven o'clock, the lunch orders are just beginning to come in from the dining room. Kim fries burgers on the grill and drops tenderloins into the deep fryer, then turns to the work table to dress the buns. She leans into the table like a sprinter in blocks tensed for the starting gun. Opening plastic tubs, she mounds homemade potato salad and Chinese slaw onto plates, adds the sandwiches, and pushes them aside for Kathy and Patty to deliver to the customers out front.

On any give day, more burgers and tenderloins will be sold at the Spartan Inn than daily specials, Jo Ann says. I think I understand why. Rote choice is much simpler than debating everything on the daily specials board! Are you hungry for pot roast or grilled cheese and chili? Green beans or corn? Butterscotch pie or pumpkin? Jo Ann tries to ease the dilemma by following a pattern established over twenty years. Monday is always set aside for ham and beans ("I tried pork loin, and they let me know what they thought of that!"). Tuesday is baked steak with brown gravy. Wednesday gets a bit tricky. Chicken and noodles alternate every other week with beef and noodles—but both are always served with green beans and real mashed potatoes.

"But aren't noodles and mashed potatoes pretty much the same thing?" I ask.

"They are," admits Jo Ann. "But the chicken or beef and noodles *has* to be on top of the mashed potatoes. That's just the way they want it."

Unique salads include the Chinese slaw made with shredded cabbage and broccoli, baby corn, water chestnuts, sunflower seeds, and Ramen noodles ("We go through a four-quart pail every day") and broccoli salad made with raisins and bacon bits. Even the ham, tuna, and chicken salads, served year round in sandwiches and cold plates, are homemade. For breakfast, nothing sells better than sausage gravy and homemade biscuits.

With everything possible made from scratch, Jo Ann is a stickler for quality. "It's a lot more work, but I don't serve anything I wouldn't eat myself." She confesses to being "a real critic" when it comes to pie, and is one of very few Indiana cafe owners who rolls out her own pie dough. At least seven or eight varieties of pie are available every day, two of which are always coconut and chocolate cream. Her rhubarb pie, sweetened with heaps of sugar and thickened with flour, reminded me of early summer back home in Minnesota.

Today's featured dessert is Holy Cow Cake, a Spartan Inn favorite recently requested by one of the regulars. It's a sinful, ooey gooey German chocolate cake soaked with sweetened condensed milk and topped with caramel ice cream topping, Cool Whip, and chopped Butterfinger candy bars. I've run into the same cake with several other names, including Better Than Sex Cake and Robert Redford Cake—a name that surely goes back a generation or two.

(Fifteen or so years ago at a Wisconsin cafe, the Better Than Sex Cake caused a sensation, with the local paper running letters complaining that a family cafe had no business serving a cake with such a name. The letters themselves proved more scurrilous than the cake and provided many laughs for the regulars gathered along the counter with the latest issue of the paper. The fun ended when the editor declared the whole issue a bunch of nonsense and refused to publish any more letters.)

"You've got to try the Holy Cow Cake," a hefty fellow at the Spartan Group round table tells me as he aligns his dessert plate for easy fork access. The two of us had received identical huge portions of meatloaf and mashed potatoes and gravy, and while he'd scraped his plate clean I was scarcely able to finish even half. There was definitely no room in me for cake.

Sizing up my dilemma, my partner in gluttony suggests, "You can take what you can't eat home with you."

And I did.

Update: In June 2006, the Spartan Inn was destroyed by fire. Lost in the blaze were all of the town memorabilia with the exception of a handful of photographs. The Spartan Group rallied to rebuild the cafe, which reopened in the summer of 2007.

WOLCOTT
Wolcott Theatre Cafe ☕
201 North Range Street
(219) 279-2233
M–Sa 6 A.M.–2 P.M.; Su 8 A.M.–2 P.M.
Ann Cain

As a longtime caterer and past president of the Wolcott area historical society, Ann Cain had two dreams: a professional kitchen that would allow her to expand her business and saving the town's historic movie theater. One became the solution for the other when her friend and partner, Walt Owens, bought the long vacant building "out of a fear that something would happen to it." A two-year rehabilitation project resulted in the conversion of the lobby into the classy Wolcott Theatre Cafe—what Ann calls "my midlife crisis."

Local nay-sayers didn't share Ann and Walt's vision and warned, "You're just gonna get farmers drinking coffee. You'll never make any money." Fortunately, they were proved wrong within months of the cafe's October 2004 grand opening. Their mistake was viewing the cafe solely as a place of business when, in fact, it quickly developed into an important social hub imbued with a sense of place and belonging. The cafe is a catalyst that tightens community bonds by bringing together lifelong residents with those who recently located in the area, retired folks with those who are still actively working, and high school kids with senior citizens. "We have one kid who comes in here every morning, and one of the locals—a sixty-year-old Vietnam vet—bought him breakfast for passing his ag-mechanics test," Ann says. "Where else are you going to see something like that?"

The cafe also provides Wolcott area residents with the opportunity to mingle with out-of-towners, especially travelers between Chicago and Lake Shafer who make up a valuable part of the cafe's business. According to Ann, they tend to be upper-class professionals seeking stereotypical small town experiences and genuine comfort food. Having stopped once out of curiosity ("They watched us working on the building and had to come in and check us out"), and ecstatic to have discovered exactly what they crave, they make return visits whenever they're in the area. One such Chicago couple—themselves restaurant owners—never return home without an omelet for their daughter and an order of sausage gravy for their dog waiting in the car.

Other out-of-towners convincingly sold on the Wolcott Theatre Cafe include bicycle clubs like the one from Lafayette that rode through town, spotted the red replica marquee over the sidewalk, and circled the block. "We saw them from the window, and pretty soon we heard the clickety-clack of their shoes on the floor," Ann says. "We've never seen so much Lycra and Spandex in Wolcott!" The novelty of their visit quickly warmed the locals, who welcomed them as part of the cafe community with questions about their bikes and their jobs. Curiosity became conversation. Conversation became camaraderie. Farewells became invitations to come back. That day, Ann says, "the locals sat a little straighter, a little prouder. One of the greatest aspects of the small town cafe is the locals' sense of ownership."

In 1946, local businessmen combined efforts and built the Wolcott movie theater, the first building in town to be "air cooled." Feature films, high school plays, graduations, and community events were held here until it closed in the 1960s. You can learn more about the Wolcott's glory days by perusing Russel Edmond's collection of photographs and theater memorabilia displayed on the wall. Or ask the old-timers circling the communal, self-serve coffee pot. (They drop a dollar in the cup and serve themselves.) They're the ones best able to put Ann and Walt's reincarnation of the abandoned theater into proper perspective.

Combining function with quality materials and a retro-aesthetic, the Wolcott Theatre Cafe is a real show stopper. Stark white walls contrast vividly with the black counters and chrome-legged stools, cherry red vinyl cloth–covered tables, and two large blackboards that announce the daily specials. (Behind the main counter, a third blackboard—a little Coca-Cola model—reports the score of a recent Tri-County High School football victory: JV Cavs 54, Trojans 0.) The epoxy composite floor is like a big checkerboard, alternating squares of black and white. And stretched out along the back wall is a gleaming stainless steel kitchen in full view of the customers.

"They can see everything we do," Ann says about her decision to put the kitchen "right up front." With customers watching her every move, Ann proves her commitment to homemade day after day. She had me at good morning. At eight o'clock, after a sleepless night in the campground next to the Interstate, I perched on a counter stool and watched with utter dejection as baker Brenda Bickett set a pan of huge cinnamon rolls aside to rise. It would be two hours before they were ready to eat. In front of me, a stainless steel bowl was heaped with thawing mixed fruit destined for pie. "The pies will be ready later in the day," Brenda explained. I immediately decided I had to come back. "We'll save a piece for you," Ann promised. "Brenda's pies are killer."

Ann hoped to experiment with a variety of foods at the cafe, but she quickly discovered that her menu had to be "customer driven." She wanted chicken cordon bleu. They wanted chicken-fried steak. "I hoped it would be a little more gourmet," she admits, "but that's maybe a little bit of a dream not realized." She sticks with tried and true comfort food like chicken and noodles, lasagna, biscuits and gravy, and Brenda's ultra-deep-dish pies and fruit cobblers, conceding to the fact that her regular customers "are pretty happy with the predictability." Even the drop-ins from Chicago, whom she regards as generally very "experienced eaters," demand "food like what Grandma made. So you gotta kind of bloom where you're planted. That means a lot of chicken-fried steak."

Ann orchestrates small victories over the routine by sneaking in new items, like her Italian marinated vegetable salad, that quickly become customer favorites. "How many times can I serve beans and corn? People eat the salad and don't even realize they're eating vegetables!" While it is Ann's own creation, other menu items are inspired by employees' suggestions and customers who bring in recipes. The Saturday Double Feature is one of these. Introduced by a waitress who remembered it from a restaurant in her Illinois hometown, it consists of a one-third-pound beef patty and grilled onion on a piece of grilled Texas toast, covered with french fries and smothered with cheese sauce. "People sauce it up with ketchup, mustard, hot sauce, Worcestershire. I kind of thought, well! But they love it," Ann says.

Breakfast is becoming an increasingly large part of the cafe's business, popular with everyone from high school kids eating together before school to retired men who while away an hour or two over eggs and coffee. A demographic group known as "echo boomers"—the children of baby boomers—today's kids have more disposable income than those of previous generations, and they spend it on themselves. "It's really interesting to watch the kids," Ann says. "They eat out all the time and are experienced eaters," yet they favor foods such as biscuits and gravy and sausage sandwiches that are considered old-fashioned and unhealthy. Omelets are another popular choice. Daredevils go for the three-egg Gypsy Omelet filled with four vegetables, three meats, and cheese and sided with hash browns—all smothered in sausage gravy.

With a cafe that seats only thirty-eight people at one time, Ann's success relies on a steady daily turnover. She sees many customers every day, with a handful showing up for both breakfast and lunch. The more frequently they come, the more of the cafe they appropriate as their own: a chair or place at the counter, a table for the coffee group, a menu item associated with a particular individual. "My daughter comes from Louisville to fill in, and Hank orders his usual. She doesn't know him or what he eats for breakfast everyday, so he tells her, 'Just write down "Hank's usual." They'll know what that is.' She gets a big kick out of that. The whole idea is that this is their place. There's this whole nonword dialogue going on in here."

Next Best Bets

BAINBRIDGE
Bon Ton Diner
110 West U.S. Highway 36
(765) 522-3221
My waitress tells me *bon ton* is French for "good times," but it is "good taste" she is after—*de bon ton*. I found plenty of that here, but the For Sale sign in the window foretells changes.

BROOK
Coachlight Cafe and Pizzeria
126 West Main Street
(219) 275-3484
A longtime cafe under new ownership, the Coachlight features a Saturday night buffet spread thick with salads and pizza that is all homemade, right down to the crust. You'll find charbroiled steaks, ribeye, and prime rib on Friday nights. Meatloaf is a favorite at midweek.

CLARKS HILL
Alexander's Sit-N-Bull Cafe
11437 U.S. Highway 52 South (intersection of Highways 52 and 28)
(765) 523-3304
One of eight authentic stainless steel diners in Indiana, this 1950s pink and chrome Mountain View beauty has had as many owners as names in the past thirty years. It's outside of town, but a true gem—with food to match—and definitely a local hangout.

CLAY CITY
Main Street Diner and Pizza
721 Main Street
(812) 939-2266
The daily lunch buffet draws plenty of hard workers and retired folks. Those with bottomless bellies cluster around the steam table midroom while widows and others share chitchat and companionship over burgers up front.

CLINTON
9th Street Cafe
121 North Ninth Street (State Road 163)
(765) 832-2138
A sign at the edge of the parking lot out front promises Home Cookin'—and it mostly is. Ninth Street has become Clinton's new main street, skirting the original commercial area and leading to the new: Wal-Mart and its typical sprawl entourage.

CLOVERDALE
Karen's Kafe
3 East Market Street
(765) 795-8067
Bypass the monotonous burger boxes and other fast food franchises at the I-70 interchange in favor of this side street cafe, where I was greeted with a direct stare and a slight nod of the head by the old-timer holding court at the community breakfast table.

COLFAX
Chatter Box Cafe
106 West Main Street
(765) 324-2199
A sign pinned to the bulletin board reads: The six phases of a project: (1) Enthusiasm (2) Disillusionment (3) Panic (4) Search for the Guilty (5) Punishment of the Innocent (6) Praise and Honors for the Non-Participants.

COLFAX
Colfax Grill
201 West Main Street
(765) 342-2993
How an Indiana prairie town of fewer than eight hundred people can support two cafes on one Main Street is somewhat of a mystery to me. Colfax presents a good example of how the locals sort themselves out by schedules, relationships, and what's on the daily specials board.

DUGGER
Dugger Diner
916 South Section Street
(812) 648-2142
Clean and fresh with food to match, the Diner is decorated with framed jigsaw puzzles and a bathroom door doing double duty as the community bulletin board.

FILLMORE
Bert and Betty's Kitchen
9 North First Street
(765) 246-6124
You'll find this diner next to Bert and Betty's house, and get this: in the middle of the only First Street in Indiana with two dead ends!

GREENCASTLE
Monon Restaurant
814 North Jackson Street
(765) 653-8012
Used to be the Monon engineers stopped the train and hopped the tracks for home cooking. The past is remembered in a nonstop collection of lanterns, Monon

photographs, and other railroad collectibles, including a mannequin conductor sitting on a bench up front. The Monon's so popular, he's been waiting for a table for years.

HILLSBORO
Chatterbox Cafe
115 East Main Street
(765) 798-3980
A basic cafe in the town that promotes itself as "Home to 600 Friendly People and a Few Ole Soreheads." The decorating scheme is part Elvis, a lot Billy Ray Cyrus.

KENTLAND
Kentland Truck Stop
409 South Seventh Street (U.S. Highway 41)
(219) 474-6473
This diner and truck stop serves as a local hangout while catering to long-haulers and pilots using the nearby Kentland airport. Real food is right at home with antique automobile and filling station memorabilia, including a Sinclair gas pump inside and a Phillips 66 sign outside.

KIRKLIN
Fredy's Restaurant
104 East Madison Street
(765) 279-5809
In tiny Kirklin (home to a surprising number of antique shops), at the corner of Madison and State Road 29, a hand-lettered sign attached to a wooden utility pole reads "Fredy's Home Cooked Meals 6–8." It hardly gets simpler, or more modest, than this.

MONTEZUMA
Janet's Family Restaurant
227 East Crawford Street (U.S. Highway 36)
(765) 245-2277
The blue ribbon goes to Janet's strawberry pie. The sweepstakes ribbon goes to the beef and noodles, made with genuine homemade egg noodles. But Best of Show goes without a doubt to this kindergarten essay written by Brianne McMullen on January 8, 1990:

Janit's Restront

Me and my daddy and Brogan go to Janits. And Anjee ushlee srvs as.

On sadrday thr is spgetee. Evree day tha have a noo speshl.

I like to go to Janits. It is fun. On Sunday we go sum times.

My mom gos sum times to.

THE END.

Morocco
Mel's Downtown
215 East State Street
(219) 285-0689
Pine boards on the walls lend a golden glow to this charming cafe, made even more so by the mix of vintage chrome dinettes and an earnest effort in the kitchen.

Rockville
Weber's Family Restaurant
105 South Jefferson Street
(765) 569-6153
Customer comment cards in the vestibule of this large restaurant tell a tempting tale. Writes David Wimm of Kenton, Ohio: "Very good food and staff. I've found my home away from home. Thanks."

Rossville
Hornets Nest Restaurant
356 West Main Street
(765) 379-2900
A few blocks out of town, but the hive of Rossville where burgers and tenderloins reign. Black and white photos of Hornets basketball teams decorate the walls, but the recent past is missing. Where are the photos of Jennifer Jacoby, the 1991 Indiana Miss Basketball, and the boys' team that claimed the 2002 Class A state championship?

Veedersburg
Bus Stop
201 North Main Street
(765) 294-2640
The too-frequent changes in name, owner, decor, phone number, and menu at this corner cafe keep the locals and adventure eaters on their toes. Worth a stop every now and again to see what's new.

Waynetown
Cracker Barrel Cafe
103 West Washington Street
(765) 234-2535
No rocking chairs, checker boards, or country store—just a small town diner with a chock-full daily specials board and an ode to cafe camaraderie by a local poet.

West Terre Haute
West T Diner
431 West National Avenue
(812) 533-2020
A funky 1940s-era box of green glazed brick and the requisite old-timers lined up at the counter like pearls of wisdom on the chords of memory. "Times were

tough in the mines in those days. A Rose-Hulman graduate signed on with a temp agency and was making five forty an hour. I was making fourteen. And he was a Rose-Hulman graduate. And I was making fourteen. He was a Rose-Hulman graduate!"

East

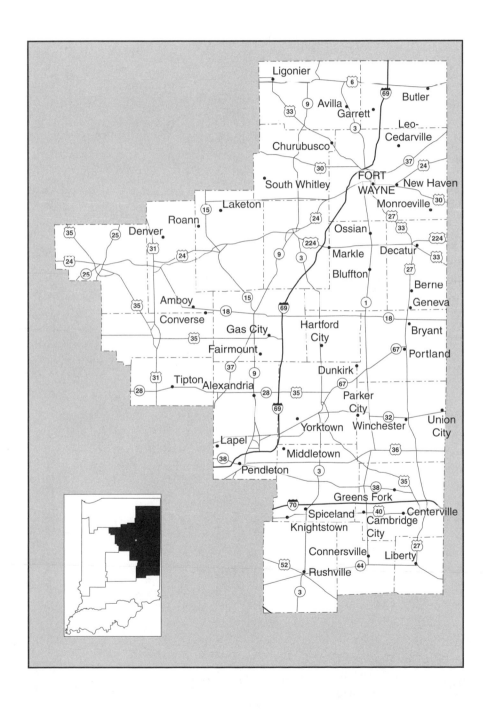

AMBOY

Stepler's Family Restaurant

116 South Main Street

(765) 395-7821

M–Th 6 A.M.–2 P.M.; F 6 A.M.–2 P.M. and 4:30 P.M.–7:30 P.M.; Sa 6 A.M.–2 P.M.; Su closed

Phyllis Stepler and Gary Stepler

A sign near the cash register of Stepler's Family Restaurant reads, "The way to a woman's heart is through the door of a good restaurant." This may also be the secret to a long marriage. Ask Richard and Rheba Weaver, who make the trek to Stepler's from Wabash as many as six times a week. They come for the consistently good home cooking, the company, and the high jinks. "It's just a spectacle for us. Even with the price of gas, it hasn't kept us from coming out," Richard explains.

While he enjoys a plate of mushroom steak, mashed potatoes and gravy, and lima beans, Rheba dines only on salad. She is on a very restricted diet and finds little on the menu that she may eat, yet she would never dream of staying home. Making the thirty-mile round-trip is a highlight of the day that holds a certain amount of suspense. "You never know what's going to be happening here," she smiles.

The cafe, owned by Phyllis Stepler and managed by Gary Stepler, her son, is a community theater with an ever-changing cast. On any given day, there might be a drama unfolding or a comedy spurred on by an innocent comment that strikes someone as hilariously funny. I am the only person in the restaurant before being joined by the Weavers about ten fifteen in the morning. By ten thirty, the place is nearly full, everyone having entered through the front and side doors within five minutes of each other—as if a townwide school bell had signaled the start of lunch period.

Four Public Service Indiana linemen were the first to arrive. They cluster at the register and order cheeseburgers in takeout boxes.

"I can't get these guys to eat anyplace else in town," one says.

Their waitress jokingly asks whose power they're going to cut off. The men don't miss a beat.

"We were up the road a bit talkin' to a lady, and she said she had a neighbor worked at the restaurant we could cut off."

I glance at the Weavers to see if they've overheard. Richard smiles and nods a conspiratorial "See what I mean."

The PSI workers liven up the restaurant with loud conversation, jokes, and laughter, drawing everyone inside into a spirited camaraderie. Even Gary, who has been confined to the kitchen making gravy, steps out to share in the fun. It's this adventure mixed with a deep feeling of belonging that the Weavers seek out each day. Community is at the heart of the small town cafe, and Stepler's is no different from others. Or rather, not so very much different.

In 1995, the restaurant burned to the ground. It was a disastrous loss to the Steplers and their customers. Like a tooth that has fallen out of a pretty smile, the fire left a gaping hole in the historic face of Main Street and a gaping emptiness in the town of fewer than four hundred residents. When government red tape hopelessly entangled the Steplers' efforts to rebound, Eric Turner, Indiana state representative, cleared the way for friends and neighbors to save the day. A donation drive by townspeople and area churches raised about one-third of the cost to rebuild. And rebuild they did. In 1996, they raised the new restaurant in a community building bee supervised by members of Amboy United Methodist Church and Amboy Friends Church that put the Steplers back on their feet and the folks of Amboy back at their dinner table.

This explains why the new one-story, vinyl-clad restaurant is out of step with its two-story brick neighbors built early in the last century. The building resembles a house, with a front porch overlooking the sidewalk and one large open room inside for dining. The restaurant's heart and the community's hearth is a gas fireplace flanked by a bookcase filled with children's storybooks and assorted toys. Nearby, two child-sized tables with chairs give little ones a place of their own to dine. A copy of the Ten Commandments on the mantel provides a model for Christian behavior, while the patriotic decorations—flags, Beanie Babies, wreaths, and flower arrangements—inspire civic responsibility. Without either, there would be no Amboy Restaurant. Thank the meritorious folks of Amboy when you visit.

And thank Phyllis and Gary for their commitment to home cooking that brings people like the Weavers coming back six days a week. You can go anywhere for food, Richard says, but there's no better place for eating. ("Tell me where there's other small town restaurants like this one, cuz we like to eat at them," he says when he learns of my search.) Each day begins with a breakfast special, such as today's sausage gravy over biscuits. Following, between ten thirty and two o'clock, is the daily plate special. Top-of-the-menu choices include chicken and noodles and Spanish hot dogs—"like a chili dog only meatier," explains Gary. Wednesdays always bring "Italian something," such as spaghetti, lasagna, or another pasta-based dish. On Fridays, batter-fried fish is rolled out at noon and again when the restaurant reopens at four thirty for the evening meal. Every day, two desserts are made from scratch, like today's sugar cream pie and butterscotch pudding.

As we meet at the register to pay our bills, Richard confides one key to the Steplers' success. "It's the meat," he tells me. "They get it at Amboy Market down the street. I'm going there now to buy some cubed steak so I can eat mushroom steak at home." While Rheba waits in the car, Richard heads to the market, with me following close behind. I am delayed slightly by a near-collision with a couple parking their bicycles on Stepler's sidewalk. "We live only a few blocks away, and it's a good place for lunch," they tell me after our mutual apologies.

Since opening the restaurant in 1986, Gary Stepler has been buying quality fresh meats from Amboy Market, a general purpose grocery store with one-on-one service that has anchored Main Street for over four decades. It's the kind of place where you can buy Band-Aids and basic school supplies, Pop-Tarts and duct tape while waiting for owner Chad Pond to wrap your meat order in waxed white paper. Chad specializes in fresh cuts of beef and pork, as well as chicken and sausage. "People come from all over," says Shirley Cunningham, the lone clerk. "For a small town, between the restaurant and here, we get a lot of business. There's a real loyal following, that's for sure."

BERNE
Palmer House

118 West Main Street
(260) 589-2306
M–Th 5:30 A.M.–7 P.M.; F 5:30 A.M.–7:30 P.M.; Sa 5 A.M.–2 P.M.; Su closed
Sharon and Roger LeFever and Saundra and Keith Minger
Polka music is playing over the town loudspeakers when I pull into Berne a week after the annual Swiss Days Festival has ended. At five thirty in the afternoon, the town looks deserted. The Palmer House is, too, with the

exception of owner Saundra Minger and her daughter and granddaughter, who are enjoying a quiet dinner.

"It's a good thing you didn't come last week," Saundra says. "I wouldn't have had a minute to sit down with you."

Saundra has lived in Adams County her entire life, so she has been both observer and participant in Berne's transformation from a fairly typical Hoosier farm community to Little Switzerland. Settled by Swiss Mennonites in 1852 and today a commercial hub of thriving Mennonite and orthodox Amish communities, Berne began celebrating and promoting its Swiss heritage in the early 1970s. Business owners were persuaded to remodel their buildings in a Swiss chalet style complete with folk art adornment and window boxes, and an annual festival was added to the calendar. "The festival started out as a town sidewalk sale," recalls Saundra. Over the years it has evolved into a popular three-day festival featuring Bavarian music, folk dancing, tours of a nearby Swiss-themed living history museum, a community musical performance titled *In Grand Old Switzerland,* street activities, and much more.

According to the town's official Web site, "Berne offers the discovery of historic nostalgia" with Old World hospitality, quaintness, friendly people, and "authentic Swiss architecture." Berne's traditions are not preserved and handed down from generation to generation, however. Rather, they are reinventions of traditions—of Swiss things rethought, reconfigured, and revived in a new time and place. They are not "historic nostalgia" but rather nostalgia that has been romantically historicized.

While Berne plays at being Swiss, real tradition and history merge in authentic and meaningful ways at the Palmer House, a landmark restaurant opened in 1939 by Ralph Liechty, a Swiss with the unlikely nickname of Ghandi. Liechty is remembered by the presence of two black and white photos on display in the Palmer House. One depicts the interior of Ghandi's Grill in the 1930s. The other freeze-frames the day Liechty locked up the restaurant and left a sign on the window announcing, "I'm gittin' hitched. Be back in 45 minutes."

Palmer Liechty followed Ghandi in the 1940s, renaming the restaurant Palmer House and redecorating it in midcentury fashion. This meant a good supply of natural birch cabinets with chrome handles, white Formica tabletops spattered with gold flecks, and a pair of horseshoe counters banded with wide blue stripes. This is the Palmer House today, where history *and* tradition remain hard at work.

Saundra and co-owner Sharon LeFever worked as waitresses for previous owners Gaylord and Agnes Stuckey. When the Stuckeys retired in 1986, they stepped in and took over. "We knew how much work it was, so we knew what we were getting into," explains Saundra. They also knew they were acquiring a successful business with a good reputation for quality, so they determined not to change a thing. Not the name. Not the looks. Not the menu. And most definitely not the legendary Friday night smorgasbord.

The every-day menu continues to include traditional Swiss-style foods that Saundra and Sharon grew up on, but Sharon notes that nothing is so unusual as to be exotic. "The Swiss just made good, common food: meat, potatoes, and vegetables." I recommend that you start your Swiss culinary journey with the *Schweizer* salad, a bowl of iceberg lettuce, sliced hard-boiled eggs, bacon chips, and hot bacon dressing. Then, move on to the best-selling swiss steak, which Saundra describes as "round steak, tenderized, floured, baked, and served with glop."

Saundra speaks the names of each dish in the Swiss dialect of German spoken by the Berne immigrants. I have a hard time deciphering, so she writes the names on the back of my check. I discover that I am familiar with other Palmer House specialties from my grandmother's preparation of special foods emblematic of my own German heritage. Saundra's *Himmelfrucht* is Grandma's fruit salad, *heisse Kartoffelsalat* is hot potato salad, and the mysterious *roesti* nothing other than potato pancakes.

You'll find all these and much, much more on the Friday night smorgasbord served from four to seven thirty. While tending to the regular daily business, Saundra, Sharon, and their staff somehow manage to prepare a bountiful end-of-the-workweek feast that has become legendary in this part of the Hoosier State. This kind of food, and in this quantity, is guaranteed to make gluttons of us all. Be sure to wear pants with an elastic waistband or a belt with holes to spare.

Multiple trips are needed to move through this heroic lineup of homemade salads, hot entrees, and desserts. Start with the salad bar, which is wisely stocked with both plates and small and large bowls. In the spirit of objective science, I decide to try a little of everything and fill my plate with green bean salad, potato salad, fruited Jell-O, tuna salad—all found under the hooded bar. On the table to my right I find a divided tray of assorted cold relishes and homemade ranch dip. I pass over the bowl of pickled whole beets and hard-boiled eggs dyed a bright fuchsia; I do not like beets. Continuing on, I sample jellied cranberry salad, strawberry-pineapple salad, and Waldorf salad. I conclude my foray with a few slices of cheese, a bit of cheese ball, and a few crackers. Believe it or not, I fit all of this onto a single plate, which I take back to my table and polish off in remarkable time.

Clean plate in hand, I study the hot food bar with considerably more restraint. With a side helping of sweetened sauerkraut, the sausage made at Manley Meats in nearby Monroe is hands-down my favorite entree, but I also like the slow-cooked pot roast richly flavored with thickened broth. Several members of the Wally Byam Caravan Club camped out at Bear Creek Farm rave about the boneless pork ribs, while others can't seem to get enough of the chicken and noodles. Other hot items include homemade bread dressing, green beans, fish sticks, and breaded and deep-fried cauliflower.

Senior citizens all, the Caravan Club has been led to the smorgasbord by an advance scout who questioned Keith several times about the Palmer House's ability to seat and serve the large group. Twice he asked for confirmation about the price per person, which at less than ten dollars is an unbelievable bargain. The price includes a dessert bar to die for.

Only shame at my gluttony, so cruelly exposed to the entire Caravan Club (who, to my astonishment, emptied the bowl of pickled beets and eggs in wicked time), kept me from taking some of everything. Stretched out before me is a dreamlike candyland, a veritable feast of sweets: thick butterscotch pudding, a layered spice cake with vanilla icing, fudge brownies, and pie, pie, pie! A three-tiered, stair-stepped shelf holds tempting triangles laid out on ceramic plates like gems in a jeweler's case. Apricot, lattice-topped raspberry, old-fashioned cream, peach cream, rhubarb custard, chocolate, dutch apple. Mercy! How can I possibly choose?

Keith directs me toward the peach cream (the top seller of twenty-five varieties of Palmer House pie) and the baked coconut, his mother's favorite. Just one bite of each substantiates a fundamental principle of adventure eating: anything out of the ordinary is bound to be good.

With a kind of deflating sadness and not just a little discomfort, I say good-bye to Keith and Saundra and the Palmer House. Before I am out of Berne, I am already planning my next visit. I can't wait.

BLUFFTON
Snug Cafe ☷
126 West Market Street
(260) 824-0718
M–Sa 6 A.M.–2 P.M.; Su 7 A.M.–1 P.M.
Walt Mitchell

The laminated placemats at the Snug Cafe that double as menus are generously sprinkled with the adjective *homemade*. In red capital letters, the word leaps out at you like a flashing semaphore. Homemade muffins, homemade biscuits, homemade mush, homemade pie, homemade large cookies, homemade cinnamon rolls. The food at the Snug is so good that months after your visit, you will be scheming ways of returning for more. I woke up this morning from just such a dream, with a great scenario sketched out for my next trip. My husband and I will return with the tandem bicycle, set up camp at Quabache State Park, and spend a few days pedaling to the areas best cafes.

I don't know why it is that Wells, Adams, and Allen counties have the greatest density of blue-ribbon cafes in Indiana, but I am not overly concerned with coming up with an answer. I'd much rather eat. And in my way of thinking, a bike provides an ideal way to move from cafe to cafe while burning enough calories to warrant the progressive feast. From Quabache, it's a quick ride to the Snug Cafe for breakfast, then on to an early dinner at Rich's Cafe in New Haven. We could begin the next day with breakfast at the West End Restaurant in Decatur, then swing north into Amish country before circling back to Bluffton for an end-of-ride feast at the Snug. The third and last day would have to be a Friday because we wouldn't—absolutely couldn't—miss the Friday night smorgasbord at the Palmer House in Berne. Surely, this would be the pie ride to end all pie rides!

It is the German pumpkin pie that makes the Snug Cafe creep into my sleeping and waking dreams. As I sat with owner Walt Mitchell early one morning in August, he drinking coffee out of a Three Stooges mug and I with a plate of fried eggs and buttery hash browns, we talked pie. Upon learning that whole pies are available with a day's advance notice, I mused, "Maybe I should take one home."

"How would you like a German pumpkin pie?" Walt asked. "It's our best seller."

Before I could respond, he wrote the order on a paper napkin and carried it back to the kitchen to find out if pie maker Anna Liby could have it ready by eight o'clock Saturday morning. Two days later, the pie was on its way to Martinsville where it was dissected by four discriminating pie eaters. From the flaky golden crust perfectly fluted by experienced fingers to the creamy pumpkin pudding topped with pecan-coconut streusel, the pie was sweepstakes quality. "The word's out in Bluffton," Walt says. "We'll sell over sixty pies at Thanksgiving, and half are German pumpkin."

Anna's German pumpkin pie is a fairly recent addition to the Snug's menu, which has remained pretty much unchanged for years. The regulars insist on it. They fight for continuation and constancy, letting Walt know when his efforts to update or make changes run contrary to Snug tradition. "I tried to change the name of the Big Bob Burger," he laughs. "It's huge. A real two-hander. I was going to call it the Big Bluffton Burger. You'da thunk World War III had broken out. I got snuffed on that one from everyone!" Another change that threatened the timeless security of the Snug occurred a few years back when the Ossian Packing Company was closed for a month and Walt couldn't get its award-winning thick-cut bacon. The customers complained about their misfortune and moaned almost daily about when-oh-when their rapturous rasher would return.

Blessedly, there's a scarcity of worries at the Snug, where things have generally remained modest and true since the doors first opened in 1927. Imagine the conversations that have been carried out at its tables and booths over the past eighty years. On the menu-placemats you'll find a partial list of topics: Lindbergh's flight over the Atlantic, the Great Depression, four major wars, Neil Armstrong's landing on the moon. The Snug has endured through it all, as has the attention to quality home cooking. "The Snug's a landmark known for breakfast and lunch specials," says Walt. "When people hear the name Snug Cafe, they think homemade pies and soups."

Folks come far and wide for longstanding favorites, such as Thursday's pan-fried chicken served with homemade dressing, mashed potatoes and gravy (the potatoes are instant "oomphed up" with sour cream), one side dish, and a roll and butter. On Fridays, the best seller is hand-breaded fried fish; on Tuesday it's beef Manhattan. Other Snug specialties include chicken fried rice and soup and sandwich selections that vary day by day. Try the Ham Dinger made with ham, summer sausage, and swiss cheese on a hoagie bun.

"I've got six people who come in and order them every time," Walt says. "It's probably not cost effective to keep it on the menu, but no way could I face the six of them." Your order could help save the Ham Dinger! Much more popular are hamburgers and pork tenderloins. For breakfast, served until eleven o'clock, you can't go wrong with the skillets—jumbles of fried potatoes, eggs, meats, cheese, and vegetables—served in a ceramic skillet.

Walt must carefully balance the Snug's longtime popularity and success with the need to keep the restaurant up-to-date with changing fashions and customer demands. "The Snug's a landmark," he explains. "It has a real nostalgic feeling that made me want to be connected to the place. And that hasn't changed in the seven years I've owned it." Anticipating retirement after a twenty-five-year career as food service director for Indiana Tech in Fort Wayne, Walt began casting about for a restaurant to buy. He consulted a broker, who kept him informed of each new possibility. "I was taking my time because I hadn't yet retired," Walt says, "and I didn't look at this one for quite a while because it was twenty miles from home. One Sunday I drove down. It was closed, so I peered in the window. 'This is the place,' I thought. 'This is exactly what I've been looking for.' I don't want to be overly dramatic, but I could hardly wait to tell my wife. I flew home to Fort Wayne as fast as I could without getting a ticket."

What immediately charmed Walt will charm you. "It was the appearance of the place, its genuineness," Walt remembers. The Snug has all the elements of a classic and vintage small town diner: a front window with a great view of the street from within (and, as Walt's story indicates, a great view of the cafe's interior from the sidewalk), green vinyl banquettes still hanging around from the 1950s, and a long central counter lined with "coffee stool sitters."

Walt laughs. "I see them sitting there everyday and am reminded of a Garrison Keillor monologue about the Chatterbox Cafe. 'A cup of coffee is $0.85. Coffee all morning long is $1.25. Coffee all day $1.75. Ask about our weekly rates.'

"Really, though, it's not a situation where they're taking up room and keeping people from sitting down. The regular coffee drinkers are on a very tight schedule."

CONVERSE

Herschberger Essen Haus ᕽ
223 North Jefferson Street
(765) 395-5905
M–F 6 A.M.–8 P.M.; Sa 6 A.M.–2 P.M.; Su closed
Freeman and Ruth Herschberger

It took me far too long to get to Converse and the Herschberger Essen Haus, especially considering the great number of times I'd heard about the all-you-can-eat Tuesday fried chicken and Friday fish dinners, the homemade bread, and Ruth's honest-to-goodness pies. You know what they say: if I had a dime for every time . . .

At three o'clock on a Tuesday, I hope to catch Ruth Herschberger in a lull, with time for a chat before the onslaught of fried chicken lovers arrives for their weekly fix. But she is not here. Writing down the Herschbergers' home phone number on an unused guest check, my waitress, Bre, suggests I call Ruth at home. "They have eleven grandchildren and two more on the way, and Ruth likes to spend as much time with them as she can." I let the home phone ring six times before hanging up.

Ruth's postnoon meal—is it lunch or is it dinner?—getaway is the only break she has in a sixteen-hour day. She and Freeman are up every morning at four o'clock. At five thirty, they're at the restaurant. By seven thirty, Ruth has fruit pies in the oven and cream pies cooling on the counter, and Freeman has settled in for a two-hour stint at the community roundtable. Their day ends about nine o'clock, when they turn the key in the Essen Haus door and head for home. It's been the same way for the past thirteen years.

"The restaurant takes about 150 percent of my time," Ruth confides when we finally connect. "It takes a lot of dedication, patience, and perseverance. You just have to keep pushing on."

A practicing Mennonite who wears traditional plain dresses and a white mesh head covering, Ruth had been making pies and side dishes at a local restaurant for two years when the opportunity came to move out on her own. "I thought I had enough experience after two years to run my own restaurant! There were times the first three months that it was a real battle to keep going. I asked my husband how long we were going to do this, and he said, 'Let's try five years.' We got to five, and then the next year and the next year, and we're still going. We have been very blessed."

Nevertheless, one of the most trying difficulties is finding experienced help. The Herschbergers hire a lot of high school kids that have grown up on prepackaged and fast food and "don't know home cooking. They have no training like we have. Mennonites are raised to know how to work and how to cook." All too often, Ruth has to show them basic skills, like how to peel potatoes and work the grill, which leads her to ponder the future of from-scratch cooking. "If people aren't brought up with cooking, I don't see how it will last."

Her concern was shared by Duncan Hines, the obscure real man behind the red and white logo on dry-mix boxes of cake and other baked products. He was not always so unknown. Fifty years ago and more, Hines was both a household name and trusted travel companion. As a salesman with a penchant for eating, Hines authored *Adventures in Good Eating*, a series of red-covered guidebooks to "harbors of refreshment" along American highways and in cities coast to coast. By directing Americans to restaurants that he approved, Hines hoped to upgrade America's palate and reform its back country eating habits.

If such a cultural transformation could be achieved on the road, why not also in the home? In the early 1950s, Hines was persuaded to endorse a variety of packaged food products that made the home cook's daily success not so much easier as more assured. Ironically, the very products he endorsed have contributed to the virtual disappearance of the authentic, from-scratch cooking he championed in print. The result is, as Ruth observes, a generational succession of kitchen incompetents.

As the original Adventure Eater, Duncan Hines would surely have endorsed the Essen Haus, where the Herschbergers' commitment to home-made is evident morning, noon, and night, beginning with fried cornmeal mush, light-as-air biscuits, and creamy sausage-studded milk gravy. Prefer it hot, as I do? Shakers of cayenne pepper on the tables allow you to season it to taste. Other surprises include noodles mixed, rolled, and cut by Freeman's aunt; white and wheat bread—order it for toast and sandwiches; and cinnamon-spiked apple butter served in clear plastic dispenser bottles. If your table is missing a bottle, ask your neighbors to share. Don't be shy. Apple butter is public property at the Essen Haus.

With an hour to kill before the start of the Tuesday night all-you-can-eat chicken dinner, I head down to Converse's 1918 Carnegie library and browse the local newspaper until closing time. Then I take to the streets, ambling along the length of Jefferson Street, from the three-story IOOF lodge to the old Pennsylvania Railroad depot.

Converse has a stock of historic buildings that are sadly neglected and empty. Faded signs for a discount grocery and resale shop reflect recent failed business attempts and hint at the community's general economic decline. The Converse Economic Development Corporation is optimistic that a turnaround is possible, thanks in part to businesses like Herschberger Essen Haus that attract visitors seeking an authentic small town experience. "On any given night a simple check of the abundance of out-of-town license plates reveals the popularity of Converse eateries," the EDC boasts.

When I return to the restaurant at five thirty, the dining room is nearly filled. My table along the wall has only recently been vacated and has not yet been wiped clean, a sure sign that diners come as quickly as they go. A group of local citizens concluding a two-hour roundtable meeting are preparing to leave, while families including kids and grandparents, retired couples, and miscellaneous parties of two, three, and four are polishing off dinners of fried chicken, tenderloins, burgers, and swiss steak. On every table I see pieces of uneaten pie or stacks of square white takeout boxes.

I know what that means. Order pie first or risk going without. A white dry-erase board labeled Ruth's Homemade Pies is a real conundrum. What's for dessert? Cherry, rhubarb, dutch apple, or peach fruit pie? Coconut, chocolate, banana, butterscotch, peanut butter, or chocolate peanut butter pudding pie? How about sugar cream, pecan, or custard? Or sugar-free custard and strawberry rhubarb?

I hungrily eye my neighbor's wedge of rosy rhubarb and decide: a piece of rhubarb to eat here and pieces of cherry, pecan, and coconut cream to take home for later. Easy as pie.

"I'm sorry, we're out of rhubarb," my waitress Teresa, Ruth's sister-in-law, tells me. Pointing to my neighbor, she says, "That guy got the last piece."

Sigh. Banana cream here. Cherry, pecan, and coconut to take home.

The Tuesday all-you-can-eat chicken dinner starts out with four beautiful pieces of plump, golden fried chicken—a breast, wing, thigh, and leg—sided with bread and apple butter, two choices from a lengthy list of sides, and baked or mashed potatoes. I find it unbelievable that anyone can plow through that amount of chicken and ask for more, but Teresa assures me there are plenty who do.

I'm generally not too keen on fried chicken because it is far too easy to make badly. Too long in the deep fryer or on the steam table means one tough and dry bird. Consequently, I approach my Essen Haus fried chicken with some doubt. I scratch off a flaky piece of breading from the knobby end of the wing and slide it onto my tongue. Mmm, light and well seasoned. I pull off the white flesh with my fingers and eat it. Mmm, moist and sweet. I giggle wryly when I realize I'm nibbling at the wing's puny tip as if it were the only morsel of chicken on my plate.

I turn my attention to the plump breast, stabbing into the center and twisting my fork until the meat pulls free of the ribs. Hot juice runs out where the breast breaks in two. Despite the abuse I inflict, the seasoned-flour breading remains fused to the skin, adding flavor and crunch to each and every bite. This is excellent fried chicken: hot, tender, moist, and flavorful.

The mashed potatoes, too, are an adventure in good eating. Because real mashed potatoes have lumps that preclude a slick appearance, I'm always suspicious of spuds when they're mounded on my plate in a perfectly shaped globe, sides as smooth as a scoop of vanilla ice cream. But the beauty of Essen Haus mashed potatoes is not deceptive. Here, musky russet potatoes are peeled and boiled before undergoing some serious mashing by strong-armed cooks. Topped with silky white gravy made from rich milk and flour, they're as good—no, better!—than Grandma used to make. Duncan Hines would have been well pleased.

DECATUR
West End Restaurant
702 West Monroe Street
(260) 724-2938
M–Tu 5:30 A.M.–8 P.M.; W–F 5:30 A.M.–9 P.M.; Sa 6 A.M.–9 P.M.; Su closed
Phil Wolpert and Jared Lengerich
Located seven blocks from downtown Decatur and adjacent to the old Penn Central railroad tracks, the West End Restaurant has been serving area residents for 120 years. That's a record for Indiana cafes, making the West End the granddaddy of them all. It has a Quaker Oats–Wilford Brimley, old-fashionedness that never goes out of style yet successfully adapts to the

changing times. This challenge has been successfully met by the Wolpert family for over sixty years!

Paul Wolpert worked in the little restaurant in 1945 after returning from World War II. When age made the work a little too much for even a seasoned veteran, his brother, Louie, resigned as manager of the Elks Club and joined him. The restaurant became a two-generation affair with the addition of Louie's son, Phil, who worked his way through high school washing dishes. Never intending to stay on, Phil got married and moved to Wabash. But one day Phil received a call from his father that would alter the course of his young life. Uncle Paul was sick. Could Phil come back and help out for a year or two?

Two years became three, then ten, then twenty, explains Phil. "I didn't want to run a restaurant per se, but I was attracted to owning my own business. Among the first things I realized was that it was what they did that made it a success. It was a very seductive business."

What the Wolpert brothers did was to stick with the same real food that had been slow cooked in the side kitchen since the restaurant's beginning, resisting the efforts of food salesmen to get them to try something new, something cheaper, something quicker to make. They made a habit of working alongside their employees, visiting with their customers, and taking a hands-on approach to all aspects of the business. They also cared for the old building, updating and remodeling as necessary to keep things fresh and current.

Phil has heard stories of the old days before Paul and Louie, back when the restaurant was still owned by Andy and Bessie Appleman. "Andy's customers served themselves," he tells me. "He never had a register, so they paid their bills by leaving money in a bowl." The stories are a legacy of the past that keep the reigns of ownership untangled and tight and grasped securely in the hands of each successive proprietor. Phil also tells stories of his uncle's and father's ownership and his as well. The days and nights might seem endlessly repetitive to outsiders looking in, but Phil shakes his head. "Every day here is different. Like the time a lady drove her car through the front door." The accident inspired a remodeling that eventually included the replacement of the rear dining room. "You wouldn't believe the number of people who were sad to see that old lean-to removed," says Phil, shaking his head. "One couple shared memories about how they met back there, had their wedding reception there. But it had to go."

With its bright, smoke-free spaciousness, the new dining area reflects the sanitized tastes of the present day. If you're hungry for a vintage diner experience, grab a booth up front. Better yet, lasso a spot at the counter. Straddle one of the candy apple red stools on sturdy tapered steel posts and lean your elbows on the gold-flecked Formica countertop. This is where I want to be, front and at center, absorbing the West End's unique 120-year history.

Not everyone shares my sentiments or my sentimentality.

"I'll be standing there drying dishes and see people come in, and I hear them say, 'And this is it?' Meaning, 'What's so great about this place?' Let me tell you, that really brings you down to earth," Phil says.

Down to earth aptly describes the eating at the West End. You'll be starry-eyed over noon and evening specials in enough quantity and sterling quality to warrant twice-a-day visits, as many of the regulars are known to make. The week begins inauspiciously with sure-to-please offerings such as grilled ham and meatloaf, loping along until Wednesday when southern-style pan-fried chicken bursts on the scene. If you're like most folks fooled into thinking fried chicken is cooked in a vat of hot oil, your taste buds are in for a full-throttle thrill.

The cooks are in the kitchen at six every Wednesday morning, dredging fresh chicken pieces in a seasoned flour mixture before dropping them into hot, oiled, cast-iron fry pans. When the pieces are golden brown and cooked through, they're transferred to a warm oven to wait until the first orders come rolling in about ten thirty. The chicken sells until it's gone. "It's nothing for us to serve 150 to 175 dinners every Wednesday," says Phil.

The folks around these parts love chicken, and that includes chicken gizzards and livers. "I just love them," confides a nattily dressed fellow in a fine three-piece suit sitting alone at the table next to me. He is Chris Harvey, the Adams County prosecutor, who has escaped the office for a quick lunch. "But I only eat them twice a year because they're so bad for your cholesterol."

If, like Chris, you periodically throw caution to the wind by feeding your addictions, you must splurge on the West End's crispy, hand-dipped onion rings. The secret recipe batter was developed and perfected by the Applemans more than seven long decades ago. It also appears on a number of other items, including fish and chicken innards. My Friday french-fried cod loins were as close to perfection as you can expect outside of Wisconsin, the fish fry capital of the world. Featherweight and crunchy, the batter enhances the fish instead of overpowering it.

Other home-cooked menu winners include meatloaf, swiss and Salisbury steak, and pork tenderloins made from tenderized fresh butterflied loins dipped in the Applemans' magic batter and deep fried. These are no pulverized fritters of pork on an undersized bun. These are tenderloins worth eating! Served with mashed potatoes and gravy, two unbunned tenderloins make a dinner in demand. Side dishes include vegetables and a variety of salads such as coleslaw, macaroni, kidney bean, and pickled beets and eggs. Favorite soups are cream of potato, chicken and rice, and beef and barley.

The West End is also well known for pie, but Phil unashamedly admits that it is the frozen variety. "The kitchen is just not set up to make pie," he explains. The peach pie in particular is considered so good that customers have refused to believe it isn't homemade. "I've threatened to show them the box," Phil laughs, "but they still don't believe me."

DENVER
Denver Cafe
90 South Payson Street
(765) 985-2040
M–W 5:30 A.M.–2 P.M.; Th–Sa 5:30 A.M.–2 P.M. and 5 P.M.–9 P.M.; Su closed
Emerson and Carlene Wood
A sense of déjà vu swept over me when I pulled into Denver and began to poke around. I'd been here several years before during The Ride in Rural Indiana (TRIRI), a week-long bicycle adventure. It was darned hot and Hoosier humid, and my family and friends found refuge under a huge shade tree opposite the wood-floored grocery store, where we purchased supplies for a picnic lunch. We didn't know about the Denver Cafe just a few blocks away. As it turns out, owners Emerson and Carlene Wood were equally unaware of the hundreds of cyclists invading their town like locusts in search of anything at all to eat.

Oddly enough, it happens that Denver is located on the northern route of the TransAmerica Bike Trail, which spans the country from Anacortes, Washington, to Bar Harbor, Maine, a distance of more than four thousand miles. This means that cyclists are not strangers to the little Miami County town, which often plays the role of overnight host, though it may not always know it. The TransAm maps advise cyclists that tents can be pitched on the ball field at the southeast edge of town, just catty-corner from the Denver Cafe. This makes the cafe the perfect spot for two-wheeled trekkers to grab a quick dinner after setting up camp or breakfast before rolling out of town.

The Woods realized something unusual was occurring when, shortly after they purchased the Denver Cafe in 1979, one or two cyclists a summer began stopping by. "One Sunday, a gang came through," Emerson recalls. "They sent out a van ahead of them to look for a place. They were due on a Sunday, the day we're closed, but we opened up and fed them and got them on the road."

The Woods began keeping a logbook for the cyclists to sign. Most leave brief messages about their journey, but others pen witty and insightful commentaries like these, my favorites:

From Bobbi and Vin McCabe of North Andover, Massachusetts, July 17, 1999: "North Andover Mass to Seattle Wash—Almost died on the hills in N. Y., breezed around Lake Erie, lots of corn in Ohio and met wonderful friendly people in Indiana.—Please plant corn *on both sides* of the road so it will block the wind for us bikers heading east to west. Indianans are the friendliest people in the U.S.A. Hope you get rain!"

From Matt and Julie Ritzman, July 7, 2000: "Riding from Syracuse, NY, to Oakland, CA. If you're reading this you already know how cool the people are and how great this place is, so we'll just agree with you!"

And the best of all: From Big Baltimore Bill: "Did RAGBRAI [Register's Annual Great Bicycle Ride Across Iowa] this year, decided to bike back to Baltimore solo. I walked in here, dark coming from the early morning sunshine. All eyes on me—'What the f—?' is what I think they're thinking. Then the waitress gives me this book. Bella! Happy Trails. P.S. Raye is an angel."

The Denver Cafe is located in a brick building one block south of State Road 16 with a misspelled sign out front that reads Denver Tavern Cafe & Dinning. The tavern is up front; the cafe is in back. As Big Baltimore Bill discovered, the cafe is rather dimly lit, nearly dark when coming in from the bright sunlight outside, and it takes a minute or two for my temporary blindness to pass.

Despite the tables and chairs and a salad bar along a side wall, the cafe could be mistaken for a history museum. On the lime green pebbled walls are line drawings of Denver's landmark buildings and a faded map depicting the town the way it used to be. Norma Imhoff, a former cook, drew them all from memory and research. Over there is a display of chaps, spurs, photos, and newspaper articles remembering Peru-born Walt Kinsey, a cowboy, Hollywood extra during the 1940s, and expert saddle maker. And in back, on the walls surrounding the elevated rear dining area, Emerson has arranged a variety of antique farm implements and other antiques culled from the Porter County general store operated by his grandfather B. C. Wood.

Of all the things displayed on the walls, it was a little blackboard advertising the Thursday night special I found most attractive. Deviled pork steak, it read, with a choice of potato, salad bar, and dessert. Alas! It was only Tuesday. I'd be in the area for a few more days, however, so I decided to return for deviled pork steak and the opening night of the annual Denver Lions Festival.

A girls' softball tournament was underway at the ball field, and men and boys were tinkering with their souped-up garden tractors in preparation for the six thirty start of the tractor pull when I arrived back in Denver. The kickoff festivities had enticed so many people into town that I had to park several blocks from the festival grounds. With ominous skies overhead, I picked up my umbrella and began to walk, hoping I'd be able to find an empty seat at the cafe. Carlene gave me a hasty greeting as she headed to the festival tent to watch Riley, her granddaughter, participate in the Sweetie Contest. I ordered the deviled pork steak dinner, loaded up at the salad bar, and then sat back to observe the goings-on in the cafe.

Throughout the year, but especially during festival time, folks come to meet their neighbors and eat a good meal. "The old-timers come in and tell war stories, personal experiences, just what's going on," says Emerson. "Everyone mixes: the retired banker, the butcher, the local farmers. In here there's no differences." It's this spirit of commingling that drew David Letterman's sidekick, Biff Henderson, to Denver in early 2002. He spent three days in town filming footage for a five-minute segment that aired on the *Late Show* that May.

It's a shame the deviled pork steak didn't make the cut because there's nothing like it in any other cafe in the Hoosier State. The recipe was handed down from the previous owner and remains a tightly guarded secret. "Carlene's the only one who makes it," my waitress tells me. "She won't even let us know what's in it. I've tried to look over her shoulder, and pretty soon she's turning her back so I can't see what she's doing." Someone more skilled than I could no doubt decipher the blended taste of herbs, spices, and sauces that Carlene rubs on these steaks long before they're cooked on the charbroiler and brought out to your table. I found my steak intriguingly delicious and reminiscent of Chinese barbecue. The thinly sliced russets fried on the grill with rings of sliced onions were an ideal accompaniment.

Although I had to wait about forty minutes for my pork steak, I wasn't prevented from seeing three-year-old Riley crowned Festival Princess. I caught the first few rounds of the garden tractor pull as well.

GARRETT
Dinky Diner
202 West Keyser Street
(260) 357-0041
M closed; Tu–Th 7 A.M.–4 P.M.; F–Sa 7 A.M.–6 P.M.; Su closed
Ozia Clancy and Steve Frappier
Combination vintage and fanciful recreation of the past, the Dinky Diner is a porcelain-coated steel diner, a prebuilt, modular type of restaurant hauled into Garrett in 1938 and christened the Superior Diner. Steve Frappier, co-owner with Ozia Clancy since 2004, leads me outside and points out how the old porcelain has been covered with layers and layers of paint, but not quite so much as to completely hide the words HAMBURGS ICE CREAM FROSTED MALTEDS painted in capital letters across the diner's front. "I want to repaint them someday," he says. The advertising pretty much sums up the old Superior Diner, a neighborhood hangout that featured classic diner food served inside by waitresses and outside by car hops.

A chef by training, Ozia had long dreamed of running her own restaurant. When she and Steve were laid off from a Fort Wayne steel factory, the two headed south in search of a stainless steel diner in which to set up shop. There was none to be found. Disappointed and dejected, they headed home to work out an alternative plan. When they discovered the Dinky Diner for sale in Garrett, they drove up to take a look. "Ozia sat in the car and didn't even want to go in and look at it," Steve remembers. "But when we did, it began to grow on her. We drove hundreds of miles looking for a diner and found one in our own backyard."

Times have changed since 1938, and the Superior has changed, too. After forty years as a neighborhood hangout serving up burgers, fries, and ice cream fountain treats, it was converted into a beauty salon. Over-the-counter talk became under-the-hair-dryer gossip. By 2003, the salon itself had become obsolete. In stepped Deb Osborne, who was looking for a restaurant with which to expand her mobile hot dog vending business. Thinking the best way to move forward was by moving backward, Osborne converted the salon back into a diner.

Retaining its dining car–like proportions, the new Dinky is a zippy twenty-first-century interpretation of a 1950s diner with a red, white, and black Coca-Cola theme creatively carried out on a limited budget. Since all of its original furnishings were removed long ago, the requisite pieces had to be refashioned. A diner just isn't a diner without a counter. A new one was made out of two-by-fours and plywood topped with shiny black and white ceramic tile. Though the traditional behind-the-counter grill has been moved to a galley-type side kitchen, a quilted aluminum backsplash is recreated with sheets of silver foil glued to the wall. Along the front wall and facing the counter, round tables and chrome chairs double as Coca-Cola advertisements.

The diner is so narrow that Ozia and Steve are in constant interaction with their customers. Talk and banter, jokes and friendly bickering are freely tossed back and forth, so that the diner is as much a restaurant as a theater specializing in improvisational comedy.

While Ozia works her magic in the kitchen, Steve works the audience from his "up-front" position behind the counter, carrying on a steady dialogue with customers while filling orders for shakes and malts. He digs three scoops of vanilla ice cream out of the container and drops them into a stainless steel cup, then adds whole milk, a squirt or two of vanilla syrup, and Hershey's chocolate syrup. The concoction is whirred in a mixer for a few seconds, stirred with a long-handled spoon, and then whirred again. Steve pours the shake into a large Coca-Cola glass and tops it with a swirl of aerosol whipped cream. The crowning touch is a long-stemmed maraschino cherry fished out of a large jar. "Here you go, young lad," he says as he passes the shake to a little boy patiently watching from the counter.

"I do a lot of shakes," he confides as he hands me a glass filled with the remaining contents of the mixer cup. As if on cue, a neighborhood girl walks through the door, announcing to everyone inside that she has seven loose teeth. We all express surprise while Steve utters a one word response— "Chocolate?"—and heads back to the mixer. She is a regular customer for Steve's hand-dipped shakes. When she comes up eighty-nine cents short on her bill, he makes up the difference. "We're just your friendly neighborhood diner," he explains.

The Dinky Diner is busier than most small town cafes on a Saturday afternoon in mid-August because Saturdays are barbecue day. Wearing a black cap with orange and yellow flames on the front, Ron Mayes, Ozia's brother-in-law, tends a smoking barbecue parked at curbside. A restored 1930s Model A is parked nearby. Of the contents of the grill, only the half chickens are not yet spoken for. I express dismay that there is nothing for smaller appetites. "Girl, this is barbecue day!" admonishes Ron. "Why don't you take some home?"

Inside the Dinky, I disregard the barbecue specials and order the Dinky's spinach salad topped with feta cheese, bacon, mandarin oranges, and other delights. I am craving fresh greens after more than a week on the road and am thrilled to find such an out-of-the-ordinary salad. As Ron did outside, Ozia scolds me for my choice. "Salad? This is barbecue day!" Her sister, Robbie, wearing a junior police badge ("I was deputized by the town marshal"), tsk-tsks me from behind the counter. She, too, lends a helping hand every Saturday.

Don't think that the Dinky's barbecue is a hard sell. In fact, it's so popular that Ozia has a hard time believing people would actually prefer something else. "We usually sell out on the barbecue grill before one o'clock," Steve confirms. "They place their orders at breakfast on Friday, and by noon I usually have six or seven racks of ribs sold for the next day. Chicken, ribs, sausage—we pretty much permeate the air in and around Garrett."

Saturdays are special at the Dinky, but Ozia's cooking is memorable every day of the week. She makes all the usual standbys in high style, but adds daily specials, sandwiches, and soups in enough variety that dining at the Dinky never becomes mundane. Unlike many other cafes that serve soup only in winter, soup is available year-round. "This town will eat soup any day, even chili," says Steve. "I don't care if it's a hundred degrees. They'll want soup."

Other favorites are cheeseburgers ("They just about cheeseburger us to death") and the salads—the spinach version that enthralled me, along with cobb and chicken—and Steve's own Coney dogs. Nicknamed the King of Coney Dogs, Steve makes his own secret recipe sauce with eight different spices. "We use a nice sized hot dog, grilled, then add chili, onions, and cheese. That's a dog 'with tail a waggin.' A dog without anything is a dog 'with tail a draggin.'"

Breakfast favorites include biscuits and gravy, omelets, oatmeal, and Ozia's baked goods so tempting they rock the stability of Dinky society. "The Breakfast Club meets every day at seven o'clock," Steve says. "They'll drink coffee for a while, then they'll start lookin' at those cinnamon rolls or apple fritters. One morning, a lady came in and bought them all. It was a Kodak moment, I tell you! They made up a rule right then and there: No women before eight o'clock!"

If the Breakfast Club misses out on the sweet rolls, there's always Ozia's desserts, available in three or four varieties every day. My spinach salad left me feeling smugly health conscious, so I splurged on a piece of black walnut cake made by the mayor's wife for a fundraiser. Neatly stacked in four layers sandwiched with a light cream cheese frosting, it was as delicious as it was beautiful.

As I polish off my last forkful, my empty salad bowl cast aside, Ron comes in from tending the grill. Feigning hurt, he scowls at me and growls, "I thought you were going to order something off the barbecue!"

GAS CITY
Jackie's Family Restaurant
105 North Harrisburg Avenue
(765) 674-7509
M–W 5 A.M.–2 P.M.; Th–F 5 A.M.–8 P.M.; Sa 5 A.M.–2 P.M.; Su closed
Jackie and Merle Ingle
Before crossing the Mississinewa River to Gas City, I paused to investigate the Cardinal Greenway Trail, an asphalt-covered recreational trail stretching from Richmond to Marion. It was a rainy late afternoon, so I left my headlights on and the engine running while I sat at the side of the road. Within thirty seconds, a Jonesboro police car pulled up behind me. I couldn't imagine what I'd done wrong, with the possible exception of the U-turn I'd

made in the middle of the road when I realized I'd missed the entrance to the trailhead parking lot. With rising anxiety, I peered in the rear view mirror and watched a blond officer get out of the cruiser and walk toward my car. It was Dennis Conrad, Jonesboro's chief of police, just checking to be sure everything was all right. "If you're heading into Gas City," he advised when I told him what I was up to, "you'd better go to Jackie's. They have the best food around. Just cross the river and go three blocks, then turn north. You can't miss it."

An hour later, after a dinner of pot roast, boiled potatoes and carrots, and corn bread, I am convinced that Chief Conrad has not steered me wrong. Owner Jackie Ingle smiles when I relate Conrad's stellar recommendation. "He comes in a couple of times a week," she says.

Jackie's Family Restaurant is identified by a large plastic sign with snap-in black letters topped by a row of white light bulbs. Three of the five light bulbs are lit, casting elongated white reflections on the glossy black pavement of the parking lot. With its rustic board covering and chunky boxed entrance, the building is more utilitarian than pretty—the kind of restaurant you would drive past without paying much notice. Inside, the walls are covered with wood-grain paneling and unpainted wafer board. Decorations are limited to a collection of golf clubs, framed prints, and a Tiger Woods Wheaties box that reflects Merle Ingle's passion for the game, and a smattering of Elvis photos hanging on the walls.

But look more closely. There are one, two, three, four, five, six calendars to help diners keep track of the months and days. Jackie is unfamiliar with William Least Heat-Moon's wall calendar method of rating cafes in *Blue Highways,* his best-selling American travelogue. At the don't-bother-eating-here end of the scale are one-calendar cafes serving "preprocessed food assembled in New Jersey." At the other end are seven-calendar cafes—golden dreams of the past talked about fondly by old-time travelers and businessmen. She laughs when she realizes just one more calendar will elevate her restaurant to legendary status. "I guess we'd better find another one."

The folks around Gas City—and the truckers passing through—don't need calendars to confirm what they have known for the past twenty years. Every day, Jackie and her staff prepare enough good food in enough variety to satisfy just about everyone who drops in. This includes Chief Conrad, local farmers, retirees, widows and widowers, adventure eaters like me, even the

Mississinewa High School cheerleaders who come for breakfast on Thursday mornings during the school year. ("They order cheeseburgers, hot ham and cheese sandwiches, that sort of thing," Jackie says.) Jackie cites as favorite menu offerings the half-pound burgers of hand-pattied ground chuck, fried potatoes and gravy, fried bologna, breakfast burritos, Friday pot roast, and the homemade desserts, including fruit-filled and cream pies and cakes. Served with boiled potatoes and carrots, the pot roast was slow cooked until it fell into moist, melt-in-my mouth shreds. Topped off with a piece of chocolate cream pie spread with nondairy whipped topping and a sprinkling of miniature chocolate chips, dinner was a six-calendar celebration of Hoosier home cooking that transported me back to Sunday dinners at Grandma's house.

HARTFORD CITY
Karen's Cafe
120 West Main Street
(765) 348-0458
M–Sa 7 A.M.-8 P.M.
Karen Stafford

The streets and sidewalks around the Blackford County courthouse square are blocked by barricades set up by the construction crew working on the downtown revitalization project. I circle the block, maneuvering the closed streets so I can pull directly into a vacant spot in front of the restaurant. As I pull open the door, my eyes light on the posters taped to the front window advertising everything from Hartford City's annual Civil War Days to Cowboy Church at Trinity United Methodist Church. Cowboy Church? I study the poster. That's church with "gospel music country style."

The downtown revitalization project has brought an anticipated slump in business, one that owner Karen Stafford hopes will rebound once the last of the construction crews have departed. A native of Hartford City, Karen remembers the days when the downtown bustled with people shopping, conducting business, and socializing. As businesses relocated to the outskirts of town or were forced out of business by the large box stores, and as the historic buildings fell into a state of long-term neglect, the courthouse square hit hard times. Today the high number of vacant buildings and the lack of diversity among the businesses that remain have Karen worried about the future of her cafe.

"We're doing this downtown beautification, but how is anyone going to see it if they never come downtown?" she asks. "The solution to my problem could be the solution to the downtown's problem. I tell my seventeen-year-old niece that instead of cruising, she and her friends should park on the square. This might be a way to get back to what it was like years ago when people would drive downtown for the afternoon."

The cafe provides a front-row view of Main Street, which, at least while it is under reconstruction, allows Karen to shape an alternative vision of it based on her memories of the past. The success of her business is tied directly to the success of the downtown, and she ponders ways to bring people back to the community's historic center. Her two strongest suits are her conviction that she is doing precisely what she was destined to do, and that she is doing it as authentically as possible.

For several years Karen worked as the dietary manager of an assisted living facility in Muncie. She had begun contemplating running her own restaurant but was diverted from this dream when her mother passed away. "I went out to Mom's grave and asked for a sign of what I should do. That was on a Monday. That night, my cousin called and asked if I'd be interested in taking over her tea room. The next day I was fired. I was absolutely devastated. But they really did me a favor, because here I am."

Karen worked alongside her cousin for a month before making a solo leap from the tea room to a full cafe. She expanded the menu and hours and added daily specials more consistent with the appetites of her middle-aged and senior customers. No deep fryer means no french fries or tenderloins, but no one seems to miss them. They are entirely content with Karen's homemade specials like chicken and noodles. "I'm getting known for that," she says. "I had to add beef and noodles because the beef people got mad. I used to have it one day a month, but now I have it every Monday because they could never remember when."

"My noodles are homemade," she continues. "That's something I got from my mother. I like to cook like her. And every time I make them, I think of her."

Other specialties at Karen's Cafe include cappuccino muffins with cream cheese spread that are popular with the courthouse workers, thick, yeasty cinnamon twirl rolls, and butterscotch pie. "I think desserts are what cafes are known for," Karen explains. "You can't go to McDonald's or fancy restaurants and get pie or cake. But I'm not a pie maker. I'm a cake baker. I don't make pie often enough to have recipes in my head. I feel a lot more comfortable with the recipe in front of me." In addition to baking treats for the cafe, Karen also bakes and decorates specialty cakes and caters birthdays, reunions, receptions, and other parties.

Comfortable also describes the cafe's homey decorating, which is not so extensive as to erase all clues that it was Dorothy's Dress Shop in a former life. (Look closely: a fireplace mantel fills the nook where a clothing rack was removed.) The walls are covered with wainscot, plaid wallpaper, and a birdhouse border, and window sashes filled with mirrored panels are framed with shutters. A white picket fence and potted silk flowers line the front window. Everywhere—on shelves, hanging from the ceiling, on top of cupboards—are birdhouses that belonged to Karen's mother, who loved birds of all kinds.

"The old guys like the birdhouses," Karen laughs. "One day they were pointing out which ones feed which birds. The one over there feeds the bluebirds. The one hanging over their table feeds the crows. And I said, 'Well, I guess I've got that one hanging in the right place, don't I? Above a bunch of old crows!'"

HARTFORD CITY
Sonny's
200 East Washington Street
(765) 348-9965
M–Sat 5 A.M.–2 P.M.
Sonny and Betty Melton
In the after-hours semidark of their knotty pine–paneled restaurant, Sonny and Betty Melton relax after their first day back from a Las Vegas vacation. Sonny played in a poker tournament with a thousand other people, and though he doesn't play much poker at all, "he lasted longer than most," Betty tells me. Thanks to their trustworthy, competent staff, the brief getaways they are able to make allow them to sample what life will be like without the restaurant they have operated since 1986. After twenty years in the business, they are looking to retire. "I think about retiring all the time," admits Betty. "My body is feeling it."

The youngest of thirteen children, Betty grew up in Hartford City. Her father was an avid gardener, growing vegetables on four lots to feed his large family. Sonny was a Kentucky boy brought to the area by his share-cropper father. "We were both raised on plenty of fresh vegetables," Betty says, "and we always looked for restaurants with fruits and vegetables." Unable to find any to their liking, they opened their own.

The restaurant is a second career for both. Sonny worked at a factory in Muncie for forty years while Betty did bookkeeping. Their first entry into the food service business was a tavern up the street known as the Glorious, short for Glorious East Washington Street Bar. The tavern didn't have the kind of hours suitable for experimenting with food, however, so when the opportunity came to buy a restaurant, they did. "We were always looking for a place to serve breakfast," Betty says, "and this served that purpose."

Betty is the public relations member of the team. While she chats with me, Sonny is busy making plans for tomorrow's menu. Each day after the restaurant closes, he scribbles tomorrow's specials into a stenographer's notebook, and then makes up a grocery list before heading off to the local stores for the best buys. If he gets in a rut, Betty points out, "he'll leaf back through the notebooks until something catches his eye." Sonny insists on shopping at the local stores because he believes they provide the best prices and products. It also allows him to buy in "usable quantities."

"Most of our menu is from our moms," Betty explains. "The food we cook here is the same we had growing up. When my oldest brother married an Italian woman, the family started eating spaghetti, lasagna, and pizza. We don't use her recipes, but it's certainly her influence."

Family is a dominant theme in Betty's narrative about the life she and Sonny share both inside and outside the restaurant. Joining her at the table is one of her brothers, wearing a hat that reads "If you can read this, you're fishing too close." Also present is Betty and Sonny's son Bill, who helps out at the restaurant in his spare time. Other people who are not physically present are strongly felt. These include Betty's father, who tended the large garden; Betty's mother, who cooked and canned the vegetables he raised; a son who died of Hodgkin's disease at fourteen; Betty's Italian sister-in-law; a son-in-law in the navy who gave them the picture of the Blue Angels flight team hanging on the wall; and Sonny's mother, who worked in restaurants for many years. Sonny says, "She'd be surprised I'm running a restaurant, but she'd probably be up here helping, telling me how to do things."

The concept of family expands to include Betty and Sonny's customers, as well as members of their staff who call Sonny Dad. "Everyone in town knows Sonny," Betty says matter-of-factly. "We'll be walking down the street or working in the yard and people will drive by, honk and wave, 'Hi, Sonny!'"

Sonny's daily afternoon shopping trips also help to make him a familiar figure around town. After his swing through the local grocery stores, he packs the food back to his namesake restaurant and readies it for the next day. The menu includes one fixed daily special plus three others drawn from the repertoire recorded in his notebooks. In this way, the regulars can count on their favorites while not getting bored with the same thing week after week. On Mondays they'll always find ham and beans, Tuesdays meatloaf, Thursdays beef and noodles, and so on through the week. Daily specials are typically served with potatoes, vegetables, a trip to the salad bar, and bread or a corn muffin.

"Mondays is ham and beans because it was traditionally washday," explains Betty. "When we were growing up, Monday was washday. Mother would put on five or six pounds of beans and cook them all day. She'd make fried potatoes and corn bread, and that would be dinner. She didn't have an electric washer or dryer. She'd hang lines in the utility shed and take them down at the end of the day."

Most everything that Sonny and his staff cook up is a winner, but he points to breakfast as being the most popular meal of the day. A sign on the wall written with a fat felt-tip pen advertises the start-of-the-day best sellers, among them Sonny's Big Boy Breakfast: three eggs, three strips of bacon, two sausage patties, and toast. Breakfast begins when the cafe officially opens at five o'clock, a half hour after the first coffee drinkers begin their bleary-eyed wait for the doors to open. "We've got a loyal bunch," Betty says proudly.

LAKETON
Marty's Bluebird Cafe ☃
15 North Main Street
(260) 982-7147
M closed; Tu–Sat 6 A.M.–2 P.M.; Su closed
Martha "Marty" and Bart Huffman

At the corner of State Road 114 and the Laketon turnoff, I encounter a billboard-type sign modestly promoting Laketon as "Just a nice little town." The sign is plastered with ads for various Laketon businesses, including Earl's Restaurant, which became Marty's Bluebird Cafe more than eight years ago. This sign may be out-of-date, but the one with the pert little bluebird on the side of the cafe in the heart of this out-of-the-way Wabash County village certainly isn't. "Hungry?" it reads. "Good eats here."

Owner Martha "Marty" Huffman and her husband, Bart, are passionate about two things: cooking and collecting. They are avid fans of cooking shows and like to eat out at upscale restaurants and try a variety of food, often experimenting with recreating favorite dishes or inventing new ones in their kitchen at home. Restaurant road trips provide the opportunity to comb antique shops, flea markets, auctions, and yard sales for pieces to add to their collections. Over the years, Bart has accumulated a dazzling array of pie pans, many of which are found in the Bluebird Cafe. "This is just a small portion of his collection," Marty says as she points out a few prize pans. "He's got probably two or three hundred more at home. Amazingly, only about six are duplicates." Marty has recently begun collecting ceramic whistle cups—blow into their handles and they whistle—but they are still so few in number that it is somewhat difficult to pick them out from the huge flock of bluebirds filling the cafe.

I had an inkling that any Bluebird Cafe worth its name would have a bird or two here and there—maybe a bluebird wallpaper border or a few birds on the menu—but never, ever did I expect to find so impressive a collection of bluebirds as Marty and Bart's! "Anything with a bluebird theme, we collect," Marty says, as if it wasn't obvious. "We came across a Bluebird Cafe in southern Indiana, and I thought if I ever had a cafe of my own, that's what I'd do."

Do it she did. I am delighted to discover a Bluebird bicycle ("I paid $8.95 for it on eBay and it cost $20.00 to have it shipped," Marty says wryly), bluebird figurines, ceramic pie vents, lusterware, dinner plates, old advertising pieces and calendars, paper labels for crates of Bluebird Pears, Idaho license plates, pictures and posters, framed needlework—even vintage sheet music for popular tunes such as "Bluebird Waltz," "A Bluebird Singing in My Heart," and, last in this list but by no means last at the cafe, "Bluebird of Happiness," the 1948 hit by Art Mooney and His Orchestra. "We always associate the bluebird of happiness with the cafe," Marty says.

In regard to both happiness and bluebirds, Marty believes "there's always room for more!" Her regular customers happen to agree. They bring in bluebird items or mail them to the cafe while on vacation, and then scour the cafe for their gifts when they come in to eat. "They'll look and look for their bluebirds. It gets to be a real game. I move them around to keep them guessing, and they think everything's new."

After eight years, Marty continues to get pleasure from running the Bluebird Cafe, a regular Saturday morning destination for people who drive in from as far away as Fort Wayne. Others have been known to arrive by bicycle. Being a cyclist myself and knowing that they ride to eat, I'll pass on this tip: a reliable sign of a good cafe is the number of bicycles leaning against the front window. Still others arrive by canoe, putting out on the banks of the Eel River and hoofing it the two blocks to the cafe. "They just kind of filter in from all over. We had a couple here from Florida who heard about us from some of the locals who winter down there. And we had a gentleman from Australia. His wife was from Wabash. She brought him home to meet the folks, and they brought them here for breakfast."

As was the biblical hometown prophet, the Bluebird Cafe is, oddly enough, perhaps not so much rejected as it is overlooked by the finicky people of Laketon. Marty estimates that only about 5 percent of the town's five hundred residents are regular customers, with most of these being fifty years old or older. Being perhaps the last generation to have grown up on "old-fashioned farm cooking," Marty's regulars stick like glue to the tried and true. "This is a meat and potatoes place," she says. "People here like their meatloaf. Anything out of the ordinary—well! Oh, my gosh!" Not surprisingly, from sunrise opening to early afternoon close, Marty concentrates on traditional Hoosier home cooking like real mashed potatoes ("I always leave lumps in them so you know"), beef and noodles, tenderloins, biscuits and gravy, fried cornmeal mush, and desserts ranging from summertime ice cream treats to "occasionally a cake." Other favorite menu items include the

Bird's Nest, made by topping hash browns, onions, green pepper, mushrooms, and cheese with two eggs and two pieces of bacon; the "Mickey Special," another name for a bacon cheeseburger and fries; and oatmeal made with dried apricots, raisins, cranberries, and walnuts.

Fancy-schmancy, Marty has found, just doesn't sell. "I get bored and kind of aggravated because they want only that old-home cooking. We'd love to get away from all of the noodles and grease—not that the food's greasy!—but they're just not receptive to that. If it's not burgers and noodles, they don't want it." She does find ways to flex her creative muscle and slip in more exciting fare, however. For the past five years, she and Bart have prepared a Valentine's Day gourmet candlelight dinner. One year they served rabbit. Another year they prepared grilled pork ribs rubbed with herbs and spices. Though the dinners have never been in great demand, Marty hopes that the locals' gentle introduction to alternative dining may pave the way to nightly experiences with "finer, more experimental foods" once Bart retires. "We think about opening at night to share our passion about food," she says. "Until then, I've kind of learned from trying not to zing things up with spices. It's a real struggle sometimes. But you put a Coney dog in front of them, and they'll fight you to the bone."

LAPEL
Bulldog Corner
701 Main Street
(765) 534-3746
M–F 5:30 A.M.–3 P.M.; Sa 5:30 A.M.–11 A.M.; Su closed
Julie Terry

Approaching Lapel on State Road 13, I began looking for Main Street. I passed a pizza place, the Lapel High School, a minimall boasting a Subway and General Dollar. I crossed State Road 32 about the time I realized I had missed downtown Lapel, so I pulled into the parking lot of the Fisherburg Wesleyan Church and began to turn around. It was then that I caught sight of the message on the sign that asked, "Are you feasting or snacking on God's Word?" I was dumbfounded! What an ironic question for someone eating her way across Indiana one small town cafe at a time!

By the time I arrive at Bulldog Corner, plenty of feasters and snackers have already come and gone. Though the restaurant doesn't officially open until five thirty, men are waiting at the door when owner Julie Terry arrives at four forty-five. They circle the Roundtable in the dark, starting the coffee pots while Julie turns on the grill and begins preparing the daily special. When the lights go on and the Closed sign is flipped to Open, they begin ordering breakfast. By the time the sun is up, they are off to work, leaving the Roundtable for the groups that follow like clockwork throughout the remainder of the morning.

At nine o'clock, those on hand to witness my arrival have a laugh at my expense as I stumble over the raised threshold. "Watch your step," I'm advised by a gentleman with a Santa Claus beard, one of six people eating breakfast at the Roundtable. A few minutes later, on my way back in from retrieving something from my car, I jump playfully over the threshold. The six laugh again. "You sure do learn quick," says the bearded man.

His name is John. His nickname is not Santa but Grandfather Time. ("I lost the reindeer," he explains.) Although it is still early, it is already John's second visit to the Bulldog today. He would not miss the preopening coffee klatch, but neither would he miss the opportunity to have breakfast with his ten-year-old granddaughter, Whitney. Together they are here nearly every morning. Whitney not only joins in the conversation at the Roundtable, she is sometimes at the center of it, as she is today when back-to-school shopping is being discussed.

I eye Whitney's bowl of fresh strawberries hungrily and enviously. Why didn't I order some, I ask myself, especially when fresh fruit is so rarely found at small town cafes? Whitney has bypassed her standard breakfast fare for french toast, while I have opted for a quarter order of biscuits and gravy. I learned long ago that a full order is much too much for me, but at the Bulldog, even the quarter order fills a dinner plate. Here, biscuits and gravy is among the most popular items on the menu.

"When I bought the place in 2004, people were concerned that I would change things," remembers Julie. "I was told in all seriousness, 'Don't ever change the biscuit and gravy recipe.' People are very serious about their biscuits and gravy! I have one gentleman who comes in once a week with all his kids, ages four through eleven, and they all order biscuits and gravy."

Most people eat Hoosier favorite B&G just as it comes from the kitchen, while others accessorize in creative ways. "Some order biscuits and gravy and then want eggs over easy on top," Julie says. "Sometimes they'll add hash browns or fries. And sometimes they'll add both!" The sausage-studded milk gravy is itself very versatile, used on everything from break-fast fare to pork tenderloins, chicken-fried steak, mashed potatoes, even crumbled bread.

Concerns about potential changes to the Bulldog's chicken and curly egg noodles, served every Wednesday, were also brought to Julie's atten-tion, especially by Whitney, who is positively addicted. During the summer, she has lunch at the Roundtable every Wednesday. During the school year, she gets picked up at school and brought to the Bulldog for her weekly fix. "Chicken and noodles are my favorite," she explains. "I just love them because they are so chicken-y and noodle-y and gravy-y."

Bulldog Corner has a strong attachment to the Lapel school, one of sev-eral small community schools in Madison County to have successfully resisted consolidation. Its name is a tribute to the black and gold high school mascot, and its walls are filled with decades of photos of Lapel sports teams. Basketball players wearing belted wool shorts and singlets peer out from 1920s black and white photographs mounted on the front wall. On a side wall is a photograph of the Lady Bulldogs basketball team, each player sporting the big hair styles of the 1980s. But without a doubt, the real prize of the collection is the over-sized portrait of the 1940 Bulldog basketball team that reached the Final Four of the state tournament before bowing out to Hammond Tech. The glory of that celebrated long-ago season has not been forgotten. And owing to today's multiclass tournament, neither has it been upstaged by the 2005 team that took the Class A title from Loogootee.

In a small town like Lapel, the high school athletes are not only the hope but the ambassadors of their community, and the cafe and the gym are its most important community centers. The football players meet at the Bulldog Corner for breakfast every Friday morning during the school year. In recent years they have been joined by other teams—both boys and girls—and cheerleaders. The Bulldog Corner and Bulldog athletics are so intertwined that Julie is considering the town policeman's suggestion that she reopen on Friday nights so people can gather and listen to piped-in radio coverage of the away games. "Either that or open later so people can talk about the game," she says. "There's a lot of people who can't get out to the games. Sports are important to everyone, and we want to let our teams know we support them."

LAPEL
Woody's Family Dining Room
737 Main Street
(765) 534-3878
M–Th 6 A.M.–9 P.M.; F–Sa 6 A.M.–10 P.M.; Su 6 A.M.–9 P.M.
Terri Wiles

Woody's diner is tradition in transition. While retaining its beer and spirits roots, owner Terri Wiles has expanded Lapel's hometown tavern in a new direction. "I like a competition thing with myself," she explains. "If I can do this that much better, I'm happy." Terri converted a long unused storage room into an inviting eatery decked out with secondhand booths and tables, mismatched china plates, and sturdy knives, forks, and spoons picked up at yard sales and flea markets. She tweaked the basic bar food menu to attract an after-church crowd, adding inspirational breakfasts and home-cooked daily specials. The rest of the transformation was completed by her contented customers who, having discovered Woody's, come back again and again.

The foundation of the diner half of Woody's (the tavern is still located next door) is the same bar food that originated with Remley's Tavern more than fifty years ago. Photos of both Remley's and Woody's hang on the wall, freezing in black and white imagery the life of a small town tavern across the decades. The photo of Remley's depicts a Christmas party in progress. A sign over the bar reads "Step this way for holiday cheer." It is 8:20 P.M. on December 16, 1953. Men in plaid work shirts, caps, and rubber galoshes hoist bottles of beer to the photographer, while bartenders in semiformal short-sleeved white shirts stand at the ready behind the bar. Fast-forward some twenty years to Woody's. It's Christmas again, but acknowledgment of the holiday is reduced to a strand of tinsel garland pinned to the ceiling. Woody himself stands behind the bar.

Step this way for everyday cheer. The Woody's of today has changed significantly, but you will still recognize it in the old photos. Note the golden knotty pine, the growing collection of wood-sided miniature cars and trucks known as woodies, the room filled with happy regulars—locals and out-of-towners alike. Chances are they've come for Terri's oversize tenderloins. Cubed pork loins are pressed by hand to a quarter-inch thickness and then soaked in buttermilk. They receive a coating of cracker crumbs before they're dunked into the deep fryer and served golden brown between two halves of a substantial bun.

"Our tenderloins are so big that people can share," Terri says. This often leads to friendly arguments about how best to eat them. "Some people deck them out with all the accessory toppings: lettuce, tomatoes, pickles. Some people insist on mayonnaise, others on mustard. But some people eat them plain. Some people cut them into strips and dip them in our homemade ranch dressing. There's one guy who trims away the edges and just eats the middle part filling the bun. He throws away the edges every time!"

Personal tastes and quirks aside, the tenderloins are perfect sided with Woody's hand-dipped, deep-fried onion rings, mushrooms, hefty pepper-jack and mozzarella cheese logs (these are no mere sticks!), and breaded dill pickle spears. Sound a bit strange? Do not leave Woody's without trying these treats that are an addicting combination of salty, sour, hot, and crunchy.

Other can't-miss menu items include the dinner specials served with fried biscuits and apple butter; beef Manhattans made from fresh roasted and shredded beef; Friday's hand-dipped Icelandic cod; and the Oink Burger—a nine-ounce beef patty topped with barbecue sauce, grilled onion, American and swiss cheese, and a slice of ham. You'd think the regulars would need to reserve belly room for a burger this size, but they're often the same ones filling up on Woody's popular breakfasts featuring hash browns made from boiled and shredded real potatoes.

In steering Woody's in its new direction, Terri has succeeded in losing "the small town tavern feel and bringing in the after-church crowd by staying pretty much within Woody's tradition. You can't change tradition, or your customers will let you know it," she explains.

"I want Woody's to be that little hole-in-the-wall place where people say, 'Have you been to Lapel? Have you eaten at Woody's?' One of those small town secrets that leak out and grow, you know? I want Woody's to be just like that."

LIGONIER
Daniel's Ligonier Cafe
319 South Cavin Street (State Highway 5)
(260) 894-4901
M 5 A.M.–2 P.M.; T–Th 5 A.M.–2 P.M. and 4 P.M.–7 P.M.; F 5 A.M.–2 P.M.
and 4 P.M.–8 P.M.; Sa 5 A.M.–noon; Su closed
Daniel Alemu

Sarah at the Noble County Visitors Bureau tipped me off to Daniel's Ligonier Cafe. "It's a great place, and they have Ethiopian or some kind of ethnic food once a week."

Huh? A cafe in Indiana's former marshmallow capital serving Ethiopian food? Either Sarah had made a mistake or I didn't hear her correctly over the phone. Some weeks later, on a rainy night in late August, I happened to be passing through Ligonier after every downtown door was locked. I was so curious about Daniel's that I pulled to the curb and got out. With my hands cupped around my face, I peered into the darkened cafe.

"Are you looking for Daniel?" a voice called out from across the street.

I turned to see a man silhouetted in a lit doorway. "No," I replied evasively. How could I, a stranger in town, explain why I was peering into a closed cafe on a rainy night? Feeling a bit like a kid with her hand in the cookie jar, I began to stammer something about Ethiopian food.

"Oh, yeah, that's right," the silhouette tells me. "Every Friday night. You've got to come between five and eight. Daniel's Ethiopian."

Of course, I thought to myself. Daniel's Ethiopian. That explains the ethnic fare. But how on earth did an Ethiopian end up running a cafe in small town Ligonier? A mystery like that screams to be solved. This is why on the following Friday my friend John and I found ourselves at Daniel Alemu's dinner table, hearing his story and experimenting not only with Ethiopian food but also with the Ethiopian manner of eating it.

Born and raised in Ethiopia, Daniel came to America in 1982. He lived in New York before moving on to Clarion University in Clarion, Pennsylvania, where he received an undergraduate degree in computers. He returned home to New York confident he'd soon be hired for the perfect full-time position, but freelance work was the only thing that came his way. Family members in Fort Wayne encouraged him to try the Hoosier State, and when his computer degree again failed to produce a job, he began to consider other options. "I'd always liked to cook," he says, "so I began looking for a restaurant and found this one." After spending about six months working with the previous owners, he welcomed his first customers in July 1994.

"My first day was terrifying," he remembers. "I couldn't sleep all night. I finally fell asleep at four o'clock and woke up late. The previous owners are amazed I'm still here! A *lot* of people are amazed I'm still here."

Daniel's years in the United States, especially a job as a busboy in a New York restaurant, exposed him to mainstream American food and eating habits. That is not to say, however, that he understood exactly what Hoosiers expected. "It's nothing like New York. I had trouble in the beginning with homemade soup because they were used to canned. I remember I tried lentil soup and no one ordered it. But I learned if I put sausage or something like that in it, they'll eat it. I made coleslaw with vinegar like they eat in New York, and I noticed my customers putting sugar on it. Once I got to know the people, I'd ask how they like this, how they like that. Everything's easy now."

Daniel describes his menu as "mostly Hoosier food made from scratch." Every day he prepares four or five daily specials like meatloaf, hamburger steak, burgers, and soup and sandwich combinations to feed his friends in Ligonier, including members of the steadily increasing number of Mexican immigrants who prefer breakfast over other meals. (Breakfast is Daniel's favorite meal as well. "I can eat breakfast at any time of day and be happy," he says.) There's enough variety and exchange of ideas to keep everyone content, including Daniel himself.

"I don't get bored because cooking is not boring," he asserts. "If you take it as a talent, it's never boring. If you open a can and dump it in a pan, then sure, it's boring." A challenge greater than creative satisfaction is figuring out what his customers will like on any given day. Daniel laughs at how many times his thinking runs contrary to theirs. "It's a hot day. I think it's a good day for chicken chef salad, and they'll all order a Texas cheeseburger—a burger topped with chili."

Friday evenings may be the one sure time during the week that Daniel and his customers are in sync. The locals who are not culturally curious either come in early for standard Hoosier fare or do not come in at all. "The regulars go out to eat on the weekends," Daniel notes. "People who live in a small city think they'll get more in a big city, and vice versa." Ninety-nine percent of the people on hand for Ethiopian fare come from out of town, with the Goshen College "contingent" being Daniel's best customers. Many of the students—including the thirteen gathered in the cafe the night of our visit—get their first taste of native food at Daniel's before heading to Ethiopia for overseas study or Mennonite mission work.

John and I watch the students intently for tips on how best to approach the platters of unusual food that Daniel carries out to us. He is used to coaching new recruits and spends a few minutes putting us through our warmups before letting us master the plays.

"We don't use knives and forks in Ethiopia," Daniel explains. He shows us how to pinch a piece of *injera,* a fermented flatbread made from teff, between our thumb and fingers and use it to carry food from our plates to our lips. Cooked in a dry skillet on top of the stove, the crepelike injera is brownish-gray in color and laced with tiny popped bubbles. It reminds me of the underside of a mushroom cap, with a flavor somewhat reminiscent of hazelnuts or buckwheat. A calcium and iron-rich staple in Ethiopia, teff is relatively unknown in other parts of the world. Needless to say, this makes it difficult to come by for someone living someplace the likes of Ligonier. Daniel purchases teff from Idaho, where it's being raised to satisfy a growing popularity in the health food and vegetarian food market.

In the absence of American table utensils, injera is a culturally consistent (and at first a bit awkward) way of enjoying Daniel's traditional Ethiopian dinner selections. John and I didn't want to miss out on anything, so we ordered the combination platter that included a spicy beef dish known as *wot,* a chicken leg paired with a hard-boiled egg ("chicken and egg go together traditionally in Ethiopia"), pink lentils, and a vegetable stew made with potatoes, carrots, green beans, and snap peas. The meal includes hot injera and cottage cheese, used to clear off the lingering burn of onions, red peppers, and other spices used in both the wot and lentils. The degree of heat from the spices was tame compared with the same dishes prepared for native Ethiopians, but it was plenty hot for us. Daniel had to bring an extra supply of paper napkins to mop up the beads of sweat sprouting on John's forehead and to catch the steady stream running from my nose.

"Ethiopia is the only country in the world making food like this," Daniel says. "No one else uses teff. When I came to America in 1982, there was one old woman operating an Ethiopian restaurant in Washington, D.C. She used to make injera by substituting flour for the teff and using lemon juice to give it the sour taste.... Chinese food, Mexican food, you can find it everywhere. It's become Americanized, I think. Ethiopian food is unique."

MARKLE
Davis Family Restaurant
165 North Clark Street
(260) 758-2263
M–F 5:30 A.M.–9 P.M.; Sa 5:30 A.M.–2 P.M.; Su 7 A.M.–2 P.M.
Robin Phillips
It was because Diane Enyart took her cocker spaniel to the vet in Ossian and decided to meet her son, Walter Klefeker, for breakfast at Nel's Cafe that I found myself eating lunch at Davis Family Restaurant. Diane and Walter regularly make treks to three of their favorite cafes in the area, confident that they'll be eating genuine food in friendly surroundings. "You'll like Markle," Walter assures me. "It's like a museum. And be sure to have black raspberry pie."

Owner Robin Phillips has heard the word *museum* applied to her cafe many times before. "People say, 'You've got too many things,' but I say, 'No, I like it like this.'" The walls of her restaurant, which retains the name of the longtime previous owner, are virtually nonstop with historic photos of local people, places, events, and scenes on loan from the Markle historical society. In the absence of a local museum, Davis Family Restaurant successfully plays the role. "I regularly trade in photos for new ones so people always have something new to look at," Robin explains. "People say, 'Oh, that's my grandpa,' or 'That's my sister's graduating class.'" In this way they close gaps in their genealogies and flesh out stories they've heard about Markle in days long gone, often asking Robin to make them a copy of photographs depicting, say, a bird's-eye view of Markle from the top of the quarry stone crusher, the 1909 Fourth of July parade, or the covered bridge just east of town.

It thrills Robin when customers get out of their seats to study the photos on the walls. That's when she knows that her museum is successful: when it brings together people who have remained strangers despite having lived in the same town their whole lives. But she didn't set out with such a goal in mind. Referring to her impressive collection of photos, treasures from yard sales and auction box lots (many of which are tagged for sale), and family mementos brought in by customers to display, Robin laughs and says, "It just kind of happened."

Robin laughs easily and often because she's having fun running Davis Family Restaurant. She spent sixteen years managing a franchise restaurant before going into business for herself in 1997. "People ask, 'Are you glad you bought the restaurant?' This is the best job I could have. I do what I want, and I'm not working any harder for myself than when I was working for others. I get great satisfaction in knowing we have just plain ordinary food that is inexpensive."

Having been featured in several other Indiana restaurant guides, Robin has come to realize that Davis Family Restaurant is a dining destination for many Hoosiers, yet she notes that there are "some people in Markle who don't know the restaurant is here." This perplexes her, especially since she is committed to supporting the town as a local business owner. In past years, she has sponsored both a float and booth during the annual Wildcat Festival, donated coupons for fundraisers, and filled plastic eggs for the Markle Easter egg hunt. As a resident of Zanesville, Robin also provides eggs for the Zanesville Easter egg scramble and supports the Zanesville Lions Club by serving food at the club's dinner meetings. "I'm always the food person, of course," she says.

While some long-term Markle residents are oblivious to the home cooking treasure right under their noses, others of temporary duration have quickly seen the light. Every day for the past few weeks, Robin has fed workers on the Buckeye gas pipeline running "west from Pennsylvania to I don't know where. They tell me they're glad to have home cooking, and I'm glad they're here."

Like cafes throughout the Hoosier State, Davis Family Restaurant "serves all the basics: fish, chicken, and hamburgers." Specialties include ham and beans and all-you-can-eat chicken on Mondays, beef and noodles on Wednesdays, and all-you-can-eat fish on Fridays. You'll find it a challenge to select from the four specials offered every day, especially if you plan to save room for an apple dumpling or any of the ten kinds of pie made fresh every morning. Because it is Wednesday and I'm determined to get to the bottom of native Hoosiers' passion for noodle dishes, I opt for the beef and noodles.

Carrying a 1980s plate decorated with a goose with a blue bow around its neck, I head off to the salad bar. Perched on its hood is a Royal Copley rooster proprietarily guarding the tubs of fixings, along with a Franciscan pitcher, decanters, and an assortment of other ceramic pieces all tagged for sale. I carefully spoon onto my plate a little of each offering, starting with chopped iceberg lettuce and fresh vegetable toppings and moving on to potato salad, kidney bean salad, and hard-boiled eggs pickled in beet juice.

As it turns out, I prefer the salad bar selection over the main dish. How do I begin to convey my inability to appreciate a beloved Hoosier dish? I have no warm memories of beef and noodles as a family dinner, no associations with grandparents or holidays or home remedies for childhood discomforts. Back home in Minnesota, Mom would occasionally serve egg noodles with melted butter and pepper, but they were more likely to be a side dish—sort of an afterthought to the main meal.

My waitress sweeps past and asks, "How do you like them?"

"I don't," I mumble.

She looks at me blankly, failing to comprehend.

"I just don't see the attraction of beef and noodles," I stammer apologetically.

I may be blind—or at least insensitive—to the pleasures of a plateful of Amish-made noodles swimming in gravy flecked with crumbs of beef, but those with deeper roots in the Hoosier State count the dish as among their favorites at Davis Family Restaurant. "It is a popular item and people come in especially for them," Robin says. "People compliment us on them all the time, so we know they are good."

Robin's U.S. Food Service sales representative, Dave Oetting, understands my cross-cultural predicament. He has sold food products to restaurants in the upper Midwest for several years, and as a result has a firm grasp on regional food traditions and eating habits. He identifies distinct patterns in Indiana, a state which he says is divided both geographically and culturally into north and south. Northern Indiana is home to noodle eaters, but the folks south of Indianapolis tend to prefer dumplings. "I can't give away catfish north of Indianapolis," he explains as another example, "and down south I can't sell Icelandic cod. The only thing they want is catfish—only down south they're fiddlers." Yet despite their differences in food preferences, one thing unites Hoosiers. "We have an old saying in the food industry if you want to move any kind of overstock product in Indiana," Dave says.

"Just put gravy on it."

NEW HAVEN
Rich's Cafe
613 Broadway Street
(260) 749-6073
M–Su 5:30 A.M.–2 P.M.
Jim Symington

In May 2004, Jim Symington cashed in his thirty-year career in various manufacturing industries to become owner of Rich's Cafe, which he had patronized since moving to New Haven from Chicago in 1985. As one of the regulars, Jim recognized that the restaurant was a well-established business in need of a little fine-tuning and polish. Much of its success was due to the experienced staff, all of whom stayed on board during the transition. "The waitresses are like lawyers," Jim explains. "They've been waitressing ten, fifteen years and have their own clientele. The cooks have proven themselves in the kitchen. I have a real hands-off managerial approach. I believe people will be creative if they're given the authority. The best thing I can do is get out of their way."

"Amen," agrees a waitress cleaning a table nearby.

Jim's midlife career switch is less incongruous than you might suppose. His work in manufacturing taught him how to multitask, manage employees, deal with government agencies, control inventory, purchase goods, and rotate stock so products don't go out-of-date before they're used. These business skills merged nicely with the experience he gained watching the restaurant operations from the customer side of the table. Plus, he adds, "I like to eat, and I know good food."

Rest assured you will find it here, where Jim buys in-season fruits and vegetables from local farmers; quality roasts, ground beef, and sausage from New Haven Meats; and dairy products from Schenkel's Dairy in Huntington. He prepares a grocery list every day and does the shopping himself, scouring the ads from the local grocery stores to get the freshest food at the lowest prices. He insists on buying locally because New Haven "businesses all support each other because we're in it together." Nowhere does he skimp on quality, so you will find Land O'Lakes butter on your toast and real blueberries in your blueberry pancakes. "The little kids get Mickey Mouse pancakes with blueberry eyes and a mouth," Jim says. "Kids get so crazy about that."

Rich's Cafe also passes the test in the potato department. "I buy potatoes in fifty-pound bags," Jim says. "We clean them, peel them, boil them, shred them, fry them, and mash them if we have to." In igloo mounds iced with gravy, mashed potatoes make the perfect accompaniment to Wednesday's best-selling meatloaf. "We make a ten-pound loaf that sells out in an hour. They're into comfort foods here." Culinary warm fuzzies also include chicken-fried steak, hand-shaped burgers, roast beef and roast pork, and fried chicken.

For me, comfort food definitely includes pie, not all of which is homemade at Rich's Cafe. "We buy some and make some," Jim says. "I'm still looking for somebody who can make me a good rhubarb pie." Until he or she surfaces, ask your waitress for guidance in selecting homemade over frozen. If it's early summer, you can't go wrong with the strawberry or strawberry banana pie made daily in the rear kitchen.

Jim kept the former owner's menu when he came on board but is constantly at work revising it. He notes, "You can't make any big changes or you'll lose people," yet he also recognizes that an injection of new ideas keeps things fresh and up-to-date. He added a corned beef, sauerkraut, and swiss cheese sandwich ("You'd be surprised how many people didn't know what a Reuben is") and invited Mauricio, his Mexican cook, to make the kinds of foods he makes at home. As a result, the menu now includes authentic chicken quesadillas and burritos. Other additions, like the Sunday roast pork and dressing dinner, come from asking customers what they're hungry for. Jim also honors special requests. "When one lady wanted Egg Beaters, I went down to Kroger and bought some." Another asked for and got raisin bagels and cream cheese. Wisely, Jim's aim is to please each and every customer. "If you upset one of them, you upset ten of them. I know that."

If dessert is your object, be forewarned: the portions at Rich's Cafe are so big they don't leave room for much else. "We get a lot of hard-working blue collar workers, and they're big eaters," Jim explains. He's noticed, however, that many people eat just half a serving and pack the rest as leftovers, so he's recently begun offering smaller portions. Like Goldilocks, I find my cheeseburger just right—and as good as promised—but the two construction workers at the counter next to me are unaware of the standard Papa Bear helpings.

The tall one orders the daily ribs special with two sides, while the short one opts for a sausage and fried potato omelet smothered in sausage gravy. When their waitress levers their heaping plates onto the counter in front of them, they cast surprised, questioning looks at each other.

"I don't know how I'm gonna eat all this," moans Short.

"Well, you won't have to worry about supper," replies Tall.

Twenty minutes later, Tall throws in the towel at four ribs out of six and concedes victory to the takeout box. Though his pace has faltered considerably in the waning minutes of the feat, Short has managed to finish his omelet. As he struggles to rise from his stool, he rubs his belly with pleasure and amazement.

"Now I'm gonna have to find a wayside to take a nap."

OSSIAN
Nel's Cafe
101 South Jefferson Street
(260) 622-7345
M–F 5:30 A.M.–3 P.M.; Sa 5:30 A.M.–2 P.M.; Su closed
Pieternella "Nel" Geurs

After visits to nearly a thousand small town cafes in Wisconsin and Indiana, I have concluded that most owners are pitiful interior decorators. Inspired by the do-it-yourself home building centers, the standard look goes like this: wainscot of cheap wood-look paneling topped by a chair rail or wallpaper border, above which is a wall of neutral color decorated haphazardly with faded framed prints or country-themed decorations. So mundane. And the food usually follows suit.

This is why it is such a pleasure to eat at Nel's Cafe, a place rippling with zip, humor, and lots of cool stuff. The morning I dropped in for breakfast, the temperature was twenty degrees cooler than the night before, carried in on a rainstorm that showed no sign of letting up. A hot cup of coffee and a golden pancake laced with popped batter bubbles was certainly called for. But I was ecstatic to find much more, including a coincidentally phrased poster promoting spay and neuter assistance. "Raining Cats and Dogs?" it asked.

Perched warm and dry in an elevated green vinyl banquette, I feasted on my surroundings. On the wall above me was a framed poster captioned "Café Society" depicting three matronly English ladies wearing black dresses, pearls, and hats. Though they are staid and proper, they have abandoned tea in dainty cups for glasses of foamy-headed Guinness. This is the kind of unexpected whimsy that characterizes Nel's, best epitomized by the circus train running on tracks suspended from the ceiling. If you have kids—and even if you don't!—ask your waitress to flick the switch. With its feeble headlamp lighting the way, the train chugs around the cafe playing circus music. If the cafe is full of locals engaged in friendly wit, as it was when I was there, you'll find yourself wondering if you're seated in the audience of a one-ring circus. Or in the ring itself.

For twenty-two years, the antiques, collectibles, handmade crafts (two biplanes made of Pepsi and Coke cans battle it out over the center tables), and colorful murals by artist Nancy Wagner of nearby Poneto have distinguished Nel's as a cafe apart from all others. Owner Pieternella "Nel" Geurs, a native of the Netherlands who immigrated to Fort Wayne in 1957 as a child, was prompted to open a restaurant by her mother. "I had always cooked at home, and my mom thought I was pretty good," Nel explains. She made offers on several restaurants only to be repeatedly refused. "I was really fuming one day," she recalls, "when I saw the For Sale sign in this building and bought it. My friends came in and said, 'You didn't!'"

But she had, and over the next six months, with the help of friends and family, the former drugstore was converted into Nel's Cafe. She bought secondhand booths, tables and chairs, and kitchen equipment, and relied on her dad's skill at stainless steel work to craft things she couldn't find or afford. Even the tableware and dishes are secondhand, continually picked up at yard sales and flea markets because things regularly disappear.

"I couldn't figure out why I'm always running out of things until the guy with the flower shop closed and brought back a bunch of my glasses," Nel laughs. Glassware may come and go, but the personal coffee mugs brought from home by the regulars generally remain on the lower shelf of the rack behind the counter. Regular Ron Harris carries his own mug with him when he makes his daily morning visit, filling it up himself at the coffee pot. His mug can get pretty dirty, Nel says. "Sometimes the waitresses grab it right out of his hands and wash it."

Nel's original plan for the cafe featured Dutch food, baked goods, and specialty coffees, but she quickly abandoned this idea because her customers "wanted bacon and eggs and burgers and fries." With American pancakes replacing *pannenkoeken* and mashed potatoes and gravy substituting for *hotch potch*, Nel acknowledges her heritage in a culturally safe manner by displaying symbolic tokens such as wooden shoes, windmills and tulips, a panel of handmade lace, and Dutch girl and boy figures leaning forward in a kiss.

With no Dutch specialties on the menu, Hoosier-style plate lunches range from burgers and soup to country-fried steak and roast pork. ("I really outdid myself with the pork yesterday," Nel confides. "The gravy was so good I was eating it by bowlsful.") Other sure bet choices include thick cut, cured bacon made at Ossian Packing Company just down the road, homemade curly fries, apple dumplings, and the day-before-Thanksgiving turkey dinner that Nel has prepared for the past ten years.

"I roast five of the biggest turkeys I can find, one at a time because I have only one oven like you have at home." The event has become so popular that she serves over one hundred people, none of whom leave hungry. "We're not skimpy on the food," she says.

Like her cafe, with its wonderful assortment of stuff, Nel is a woman of delightful surprise, masterfully combining incongruous talents and skills. If you do not find her at the cafe when you stop in, chances are she is on National Guard duty. Since 1984 she has been a member of the Guard, serving ten years as a weapons mechanic and, since 1994, refueling jets and helicopters. When she is away, she relies on her trusted staff—Karen, Lisa, Kathy, and my waitress, Edie, who has been here since the beginning. "We are a real team here. Everything is smooth. They take up the slack when I am away," Nel says.

PORTLAND
Kate's Coffee Shop
244 South Meridian Street
(260) 726-7610
M–F 5 A.M.–2 P.M.; Sa 5 A.M.–10 A.M.; Su closed
Ruth and llen Bruss
There was no cafeteria at the Redkey school when Ruth Bruss was a student, so the kids went home for lunch or walked down to the local cafe.

As one of the waitresses, Ruth got there a bit earlier than the rest in order to be ready for the noon onslaught of patrons. This part-time job launched Ruth into a life of restaurant work that culminated in 1994 when she became owner of Kate's Coffee Shop. With slight disbelief, Ruth thinks back to the waitress work that started it all. "I've been working in restaurants since eleventh grade, but back then I never dreamed I'd be doing this at this stage in my life."

When Kate and Charles Thorn closed the Coffee Shop after fifty years in business, it sat idle and vacant for six months before it was purchased by Ruth and her husband, Allen. During those six months, the regulars drifted off to establish new routines in Portland's other restaurants. People told Ruth she'd never make it, but as the town's businesses closed one by one—the lumber company, the used car lot—Portland's economy entered a slow and steady decline. The restaurants soon followed—all, that is, except Kate's Coffee Shop. Proud of her staying power, Ruth wryly notes, "I'll be here on my cane, that's what I say."

Knowing well enough not to change a good thing, Ruth picked up exactly where Kate left off. From its old wood counter paired with stools of chrome and orange vinyl to its wood-grained Formica tabletops and orange banquettes, the cafe has a vintage 1940s look that evokes not only stability and endurance but also humor and deep roots in the local community. "About the only thing I did was to get a larger table," Ruth says. It's filled every day at five o'clock in the morning and again at eight, noon, and two. Wednesday is the only day that's different. That's because the factory workers talked Ruth into coming in at the wee morning hour of four o'clock so they could gab over coffee before heading off to work. "It's just like home, really," Ruth says about the coffee groups who meet throughout the day. "They sit around and gab, and if we're really busy, they get up and help themselves."

One day merges into another, with the regulars filling up the cafe on a predictable basis. If someone doesn't show up at the usual time without giving advance notice of a doctor's appointment or vacation, Ruth or Lori, her single waitress and lone employee, will call to find out if everything's all right. As Lori jots down my order on her notepad, I comment about a man who comes in through a back door and sticks his head into the kitchen to request a takeout order. "That's typical," Lori laughs. "They come in the back door, the front door. They'd come in the windows if we had any."

I have taken a booth along the side wall so I can get a good look at the cafe. There's a lot to see! The eclectic decorating at Kate's is not a scheme but an appealing conglomeration of everyday stuff. Pinned to the wall near the front entrance are faded and outdated maps of Portland, Jay County, and the states of Indiana and Ohio (Portland is just a few miles from the state line). On the opposite wall is a huge bulletin board loaded with yellowed business cards advertising everything from antique dealers looking for their next big buy to the Thom-Ass Acres donkey farm, hands down the wittiest card of the bunch. Scattered here and there, Ruth's own handwritten posters advertise homemade whole pies, apple butter, and noodles, as well as secondhand paperback books (twenty-five cents each or five for a dollar) piled into cardboard boxes on the end of the counter.

"I've got too much junk," Ruth concedes without apology as she hands me a copy of the joke taped to the wall over my table:

> Senior Citizens
> Are the nation's leading carriers of
> AIDS!
> Hearing AIDS, Band AIDS, Walking AIDS, Government AIDS,
> And most of all
> Monetary AIDS to their children!
> The Golden Years have come at last!
> I cannot see, I cannot pee, I cannot chew, I cannot screw.
> My memory shrinks. My hearing stinks. No sense of smell.
>   I look like hell.
> My body's drooping, got trouble pooping.
> So, the Golden Years have come at last?
> Well, the Golden Years can kiss my ass!

Most of Ruth's customers are between forty and eighty—just the population who find the joke funny because it describes experiences they have had firsthand or will face soon enough. The joke gets so many knowing laughs and understanding smiles that Ruth has a stack of copies ready to give away when people ask. It's also printed inside the menu's front cover, making it the most requested item for takeout in a menu filled cover to cover with no-fail choices.

In order to successfully compete with approximately twenty other area restaurants for business, Ruth concentrates on home-style cooking at affordable prices. To the printed menu filled with standard fare, she adds daily specials and side dishes derived mostly from family recipes. Every weekday has a set special, Ruth points out, "so when I bring leftovers home, my husband knows what day it is." If he has meatloaf or grilled chicken for dinner, Allen knows it's Monday. If he's served chicken and dumplings or salmon patties, it must be a Tuesday, and likewise throughout the week. The daily specials are "tried and true," Ruth explains, time-tested by the regulars who insist on no surprises. Consistent best sellers include beef and noodles, pan-fried chicken, fried fish, and sauerkraut and sausage. "One time I had kraut and wieners," Ruth recalls, "and they said, 'What's this? Where's our sausage?' I never tried that again!"

Every daily special comes with a large choice of sides, so that on any given day you might have to choose from mashed potatoes and gravy, cottage cheese, tossed salad, applesauce, coleslaw, corn on the cob (which Ruth calls a roasting ear), or canned or fresh fruit. The decisions don't get any easier when you're faced with the long list of desserts, including nearly twenty varieties of real homemade fruit and cream pie. If they're listed on the daily specials board, don't bypass the gooseberry, black raspberry, or cherry pie made with berries picked by Ruth herself. That's about as real as pie can get.

Luckily for adventure eaters, Ruth is as frugal as she is insistent on homemade quality. She buys farm fresh brown eggs because she believes they are healthier and because the yolks are deeper yellow and make prettier and tastier noodles. She also frequents farm stands. What she doesn't buy alongside the road is generally supplied by her customers, who bring in rhubarb, beans, tomatoes, and zucchini from their gardens. They also contribute plenty of Golden Delicious apples that Ruth uses to make pie, apple dumplings, and apple butter, all of which are available year-round.

My chicken and dumplings are the Hoosier variety, not the kind I grew up on in Minnesota. Ruth stews chicken until it falls from the bones, then adds rolled dumplings to the hot broth until the stew thickens. Her dumplings are flat, soft, and rather doughy, like giant noodles. The dumplings I grew up on were drop dumplings made with baking powder. Spooned into a simmering chicken soup laden with celery, carrots, green beans, and any other vegetables found while cleaning out the refrigerator, they fluffed up to resemble soft biscuits. In Minnesota, chicken and dumplings is an entire meal. In Indiana, chicken and noodles is often only *part* of a meal. At Kate's Coffee Shop, I watch with amusement as the woman at the next table uses a fist-wrapped fork to shovel together her mashed potatoes (they're the instant variety) and chicken and dumplings, then uses a slice of white bread to gather in the stray gravy. With the exception of the bits of chicken, she lunches on starch, starch, and more starch. The menu cover boasts "Servings like Mom's." I guess deep down I'm still a Minnesotan. After seventeen years in the Hoosier State, I still prefer servings like *my* mom's.

ROANN
Lynn's Restaurant
170 North Chippewa Street
(765) 833-5191
M–Th 6 A.M.–8 P.M.; F–Sa 6 A.M.–9 P.M.; Su 6 A.M.–8 P.M.
Jennifer (Lynn) and Joel Ellis; Robert Lynn III and Kristina Lynn
Jennifer Ellis has fond childhood memories of the restaurant her grandfather Bob Lynn Sr. owned and operated in downtown Roann. They're the flavor of strawberry milkshakes and Choco-Cola bought by the bottle on trips into town, the vision in her mind's eye of the restaurant's counter and stools, and the sound of her grandfather's voice and laughter. This is why, in 2001, Jennifer and her brother, Bob Lynn III, seized the opportunity to reclaim the restaurant in the Lynn family name. "It's always been our dream to buy back Grandpa's restaurant," she explains.

Jennifer was only eight when, in 1971, her grandfather sold the place after more than twenty-five years in business. As a newly returned World War II veteran, Bob had cast around his hometown for a way to support his family without commuting to one of the area's larger cities for work. He converted the telephone company building into a small restaurant and within a few years had achieved enough success that he moved it into the Glitner's Grocery building just down the street. When a disastrous fire broke out on the block, Lynn's Restaurant and the hardware store next door were miraculously saved. They are the only two-story commercial buildings on Roann's two-block main street left from the nineteenth century.

Loss and reclamation are themes that underscore Jennifer's narrative of the family restaurant and the tiny town itself. After her grandfather sold the restaurant, it went through five different ownerships under various names. When the last owner died, the restaurant closed, sending the people of Roann into a tailspin. Where would they eat? Meet? Greet?

"We felt an obligation to the community to reclaim the restaurant," Jennifer explains. "I love my hometown. It's a good community, like Mayberry RFD. You can send your kids uptown to get the mail and know they're going to come back. It's just a nice, safe, family place."

With pride, Jennifer notes that the same sentiment she and Bob share is at work elsewhere in the picturesque Wabash County town, where community identity and spirit are closely tied to the Roann Covered Bridge. Built in 1877 by the Smith Bridge Company of Toledo, Ohio, the Howe truss bridge spanning the Eel River was twice victimized by arsonists. Both times—when the roof burned in 1972 and most recently in 1990 when the entire bridge was a wisp away from being completely destroyed—residents rallied to save the structure, the focal point of the Roann Covered Bridge Festival held every September. Pride in local historic landmarks mixed with civic boosterism also led to the establishment of the Stockdale Mill Foundation, spearheaded by Dwight and Susanne Fouts, Roann natives who had moved away and then moved back. Restoration of the Stockdale Mill, built between 1855 and 1857 just west of town, reached a high point in the summer of 2004, when water rushed through the race and turned the huge roller mills for the first time since 1972.

"People who were kids when Grandpa had the restaurant are grandparents now," Jennifer observes. "The town is kind of recycling itself, and I feel like it's our turn now to contribute to the community as adults."

In order to restore the family business, Jennifer quit her job delivering mail, and Bob quit his job at a factory. Together they talked their mom, Rita Lynn, into retiring from nursing and assuming the role of baker. With the somewhat tepid endorsement of their grandmother Colletta Lynn ("She looked at us and smiled and said, 'I hope you kids know what you're getting into because the restaurant will consume you,'" acknowledges Jennifer), Lynn's Restaurant was back in business after thirty years.

The people of Roann were thrilled. Gradually, the thirty-year gap between Bob Lynn Sr.'s ownership and that of his grandchildren is slowly being closed. Witness the Fishing Pox sign displayed on the wall up front, brought in by one of Bob Sr.'s own customers who found it while cleaning the garage. "Anyone who knew Grandpa knows it describes him perfectly!" Jennifer says.

Lynn's Restaurant
WARNING
FISHING POX
Very Contagious to Adult Males
Symptoms—Continual complaint as to need for fresh air, sunshine and relaxation. Patient has blank expression, sometimes deaf to wife and kids. Has no time for work of any kind. Frequent checking of tackle catalogues. Hangs out in favorite Sporting Goods Store longer than usual. Secret night phone calls to fishing pals. Mumbles to self. Lies to everyone.
NO KNOWN CURE. TREATMENT—Medication is useless. Disease is not fatal. Victim should go fishing as often as possible.
—Bob Lynn, Chief Consultant
Roann, Indiana

Jennifer and Bob III hope to someday make the sign the centerpiece of a display that will depict the history of Lynn's Restaurant. Rita shares with me copies of old black and white photographs that she retrieves from storage. One shows her father-in-law in the restaurant and another shows her husband, Bob Lynn Jr., as a toddler in the restaurant's kitchen. Yet the day-to-day operations of the restaurant have not made it easy to fulfill all the plans the siblings have for it. They dream of "putting it back the way it used to be," complete with a soda fountain, counter, stools, and booths.

Until then, Jennifer and Bob concentrate on the same authentic home cooking that has distinguished the restaurant for years and keeps the regulars coming back once, twice, sometimes three times a day. They never get enough of the prime rib, battered and fried whitefish, breaded pork tenderloins, and daily specials like today's country-fried steak. After seeing an order of whitefish delivered to the lady at the next table, I quickly decide on the same. The batter is lightly seasoned, coating the fish instead of smothering it. My side of canned green beans is just the way I have come to like them: zipped up with bacon and minced onion. Undoctored, canned green beans just aren't worth eating.

A pretty salad bar dominates the central portion of the dining area but, sadly, it is stocked only on weekends. I am at Lynn's on Wednesday, dejectedly listening to Rita and Jennifer describe all the glory I am missing. "Everything is homemade," they assure me, including specialty salads such as chicken, ham, macaroni, potato, and broccoli, as well as coleslaw and fruit salad. In addition, Rita prepares three or four kinds of pudding desserts; don't overlook the Iowa pudding, or vanilla pudding layered with granola.

Every day of the week, Rita experiments with a variety of baked desserts such as cakes, pies, and cheesecake. Strawberry pie and raspberry pie are always available. Unless, that is, the diners at the next table snag the last two pieces to take home, as is my misfortune.

TIPTON
Faye's Northside Restaurant
506 North Main Street
(765) 675-4191
M–F 4:30 A.M.–2 P.M.; Sa 5 A.M.–10 A.M.; Su closed
Theresa Louthen and Faye Stevens
You'll find Faye's Northside Restaurant five blocks north of the courthouse, just shy of the railroad tracks studded with an impressive old Romanesque depot in sorry need of repair. Owned by Faye Stevens and her daughter, Theresa Louthen, Tipton's haven of home cooking is easily identified by the lineup of cars and trucks on the street out front and a rustic barrel filled with a burst of multicolored petunias beneath the front window. The flowers lend a domestic air to the plain red brick building and let you know that the people inside are a nurturing type. They coddle the petunias with water and fertilizer through the killing heat of summer with as much devotion as they tend their customers.

It is just ten o'clock on a Friday morning in July, a little too early for the daily fish special, which is not quite ready. My waitress, Amy—one of two waitresses named Amy, both married to Johns—brings a piece of warm apple pie to tide me over until I have gained conviction enough to select from one of the four daily specials. In the meantime, Theresa Louthen joins me for a chat. "If you really want to see this place, stay here until eleven fifteen, and you won't be able to move," she advises.

Theresa sits opposite me in a booth up front, in the portion of the cafe once occupied by a barbershop. From a gilded frame on the wall, Aunt Hazel peers down at us approvingly. Another portrait shows Theresa's uncle as a little boy sporting knickers and a ruffled white blouse posed in an elaborate wicker chair. A third photo—this one much more recent—depicts the entire Stevens clan.

Family is both a theme at Faye's Northside Restaurant and the glue that has held it together since the door first opened in 1982. "When Mom was sixteen, she came to Tipton from Tennessee to work for an uncle who owned a restaurant uptown," Theresa relates. "Cousins, aunts, uncles, they all lived on the same hill in Tennessee. Mom met Dad at the restaurant, and so she stayed in Tipton. When they went on their own and opened this place, the uncle didn't think they'd make it. The uncle's restaurant has been gone for years, but Mom is still here."

Theresa herself has worked at the restaurant since she was eleven, and after graduating from high school, she joined Faye full time. "I was used to the hard work, and I like it," she explains. "Our customers are just like family. A lot of gentlemen live by themselves and don't have kids nearby. If they don't show up at their typical times, we call and find out why. A lot of them are just like dads to me."

Although Theresa has grown up in Tipton, there is much about the town and its residents that she does not know. She relies on the knowledge and memory of the "Old Timers" circling the Roundtable inside the front door. At this table, day after day, old railroaders who have worked this side of town for years mingle with other retirees. Joining them without fail are Theresa's uncle George Ogden, the mayor of Tipton, and her Aunt Mae, Faye's twin sister. Even Faye herself is there; she joins them in the few quiet minutes before the noon rush. The Old Timers remember that the building used to be the home of Benson's Bakery (although they have forgotten the name of the barber who occupied the front half). When Theresa ponders aloud why fish is always served on Fridays, both George and Faye respond with a brief lesson on the pre-Vatican II Catholic doctrine of abstaining from meat on Friday.

First and second helpings of wisdom—with side dishes of experience, advice, and wit—are dished out at the Roundtable, but there is plenty of eating going on there as well. "If you want a good meal, come here," I'm told.

"This is the only place in town where you can get a good one." Today's choices are a good indication of the variety. With the hour hand creeping toward eleven o'clock, all of the daily specials are hot and ready. I debate over fried whitefish, salmon patties, roast beef, chicken and noodles, and beef Manhattan. Seeking guidance, I look across the former barbershop to Joe and Phyllis, my neighbors at the next booth.

Joe and Phyllis come every day for lunch. "We're regulars," Phyllis says as she points out the others—a lady in pink, Theresa's Uncle George, a small group of older woman sharing a table. Both have favorites among the daily specials that rotate week by week. "Monday is ham and beans," Joe recites from memory. "Tuesday tenderloin and beef and noodles, Wednesday fried chicken and kraut and wieners, Thursday chicken and noodles, and Friday fish. That's on account of the Catholics."

While Joe enjoys the chicken and noodles, Phyllis lunches on the salmon patties—and because she does, I order the same. Made from canned salmon, complete with the crunch of bones and other skeletal bits, the patties are lightly battered and deep fried to a golden brown. A side of green beans and instant mashed potatoes are a suitable ending to a meal begun with homemade apple pie.

While Phyllis and I compare notes on the salmon patties, Joe listens quietly. When I note that chicken and noodles is a special at Faye's Northside on both Thursday *and* Friday, Joe enthusiastically joins the conversation. "They know how to make them here." He ought to know. He makes his own at home. "You have to make your own noodles and cook your own chicken. There's no substitute. The flour from the noodles thickens the broth to make the gravy."

"Do you add vegetables? Carrots, celery, onion?" I ask.

"I don't, but some people do. They don't here. We just love them plain. Nothing fancy."

As Joe's zeal indicates, chicken and noodles is among the favorite dishes at Faye's. Other big sellers are meatloaf, swiss steak, kraut and sausage, Wednesday's kraut with wieners, and Monday's ham and beans. "Monday was washing day, and you put on ham and beans," Theresa explains. "They'd cook all day, and you'd have supper ready at the end of the day. That's why we have beans on Monday." At Faye's Northside, as well as most every other cafe in the Hoosier State.

NEXT BEST BETS

ALEXANDRIA

Rachel's Hi-Way Cafe 🍴

2617 South Park Avenue (State Road 9 North)

(765) 724-2944

Oh, my. Home cooking is served up nearly nonstop in this service-station-turned-eatery at the edge of town. Breakfast demands french toast made from bread baked right here. And the blueberry pie. Blissful!

AVILLA

Harlan's Country Kitchen

108 West Albion Street

(260) 897-2612

I lunched on cavanini, a spiral pasta dish inspired by Pizza Hut. With the exception of spaghetti and Hoosier-style goulash made with hamburger, tomato sauce, and elbow macaroni, pasta isn't common in Indiana cafes.

BRYANT

Jinny's Cafe

305 North Hendricks Street (U.S. Highway 27)

(260) 997-8300

A favorite of truckers and local farmers. Plastered with business cards, auction notices, and announcements—including an open invitation to my waitress's wedding reception—the bulletin board proves that Jinny's is the living newspaper of Bryant.

BUTLER

Fry's Broadway Cafe

136 South Broadway Street

(260) 868-9090

Friday night frog legs jump out as unusual offerings alongside the all-you-can eat fish. The vintage appearance of this main street cafe impresses me more than my bowl of vegetable beef soup overloaded with canned corn.

CAMBRIDGE CITY

Lumpy's Cafe

20 South Foote Street

(765) 478-6510

The guest book on the counter records the visits of interstate travelers fleeing the fast lane in search of a slow-food, small town diner just like Lumpy's where the local after-church crowd chows down on platters of B&G and Sunday-special pan fried chicken.

CENTERVILLE
Blair House Family Restaurant
107 South Morton Avenue
(765) 855-3178
While tourists fill the trendier cafes straddling the National Road, the locals seek refuge here. My short stack of buttermilk pancakes, blessedly served with real butter, was far too tall for me to finish.

CHURUBUSCO
Ramble Inn
601 South Main Street
(260) 693-2053
On your next visit to Turtle Town, ramble in to this local hangout that began life in the mid-1960s as a small lunch counter. The decor and the home cooking have changed scarcely a whit over the years.

CONNERSVILLE
Maggie's Diner
1124 North Eastern Avenue (State Road 1)
(765) 827-8776
Six blocks from downtown, across the street from the Amtrak station and within view of the grain elevators, Maggie's is the local lunch spot of choice. The cherry pie is fetching but not nearly as tempting as the chocolate layer cake with icing sliding down its sides.

DUNKIRK
Dunkirk Family Restaurant
126 East Commerce Street
(765) 768-7133
In Indiana's glass capital, the choice for dining is crystal clear. Best sellers include from-scratch biscuits and gravy, home fries, hand-breaded tenderloins, and the Friday perch special.

FAIRMOUNT
Outpost Restaurant
Corner of State Roads 9 and 26
(765) 948-3722
With Fairmount's main street cafe open and closed, open and closed, the Outpost is the only place to get food worth eating. Some say it is regardless. The cheeseburger and apple pie are A-1.

GENEVA
High Line
404 East Line Street
(260) 368-7623
At seven in the morning, a man paints the curb opposite the High Line a vivid no-parking yellow. Inside, sparks of comparative brilliance come from the wits circling the coffee table.

GREENS FORK
Joann's Cafe
17 East Pearl Street
(765) 886-5762
A crew of Wayne County highway workers refuel on pork chops, MPG, and canned corn before tackling the afternoon's work. My vegetable beef soup needed more brew time—a sure sign of homemade.

KNIGHTSTOWN
Firehouse Cafe
12 East Main Street
(765) 345-2460
Lunch was a tasty tenderloin and a wedge of banana cream pie so fresh that the filling had not yet cooled. Hot bananas are a weird taste sensation, surprisingly sour and slippery! Cigarette smoke nearly forced me to U-turn out the front door.

LEO-CEDARVILLE
Leo Cafe
15024 Leo Road (State Road 1)
(260) 627-5628
A short drive but a million miles away from the franchise restaurants that characterize the dining scene in nearby Fort Wayne. Don't assume that everything is homemade; my cinnamon roll was wrapped in cellophane.

LIBERTY
Liberty Restaurant
7 West Union Street
(765) 458-5223
Across the street from the Union County courthouse, the Liberty boasts nothin' fancy cookin'. Try the homemade pork sausage in milk gravy over biscuits as fluffy as clouds.

MIDDLETOWN
Middletown Diner
1007 West Mill Street
(765) 354-9284

Everyone in the restaurant—every single person!—was eating onion rings, so of course I followed suit. These are no mere rings. These are fourteen-karat gold bracelets. You deserve to be shackled if you leave without having them.

MONROEVILLE
The White Dove Cafe
108 South Street
(260) 623-6000
My fresh fruit cup for breakfast really was fresh. Any cafe owner who cubes honeydew, cantaloupe, and fresh pineapple isn't likely to be taking many short cuts elsewhere.

PARKER CITY
Petro's Country Kitchen
124 South Main Street
(765) 468-6325
After parking his school bus in the lot, an older fellow ordered the waitress to "get me an egg and bacon sandwich on wheat toast" as he made his way to the coffee table. Pass yourself off as an insider by using the side entrance. Those who use the front door (as I did) get stared at.

PENDLETON
The Diner
609 East State Street
(765) 778-1974
Pendleton is "a meat and potatoes town, a rural town that lives on their belly," I'm told. On a Friday morning, my friend Joe asked the gal working the register if The Diner was for sale. "Any place packing 'em in like this has to be a gold mine!"

PORTLAND
Corner Cafe
301 North Meridian Street
(260) 726-8922
A perky and popular hangout featuring fresh sandwiches, daily specials, and baked goods delivered daily from Concannon's Pastry Shop in nearby Muncie.

RUSHVILLE
Corner Restaurant
250 North Main Street
(765) 932-3878
The menu boasts the "best homemade meals in Rushville." The heartbeat of downtown Rushville for many years, this timeworn diner will not be for everyone.

SOUTH WHITLEY
Corner Cafe
202 South State Street
(260) 723-5841
Mainly home cooking under a fine vintage pressed-tin ceiling burnished from years of nicotine. My "br loin" was a stand-in for the daily special beef stew that was long gone by a quarter past one.

SPICELAND
Spiceland Family Restaurant
6641 State Road 3
(765) 987-7101
I am oddly attracted to this smoky highway diner that is a curious combination of small town cafe, pizza place, soft-serve dairy bar, walk-up window, karaoke palace, car wash, and town hall. Think of it as Main Street under one roof.

UNION CITY
KP's Cafe
415 West Chestnut Street
(765) 964-3488
Formerly Cheryl's Restaurant, this highway eatery boasting from-scratch cooking is a time-tested local favorite. Customers ranged from a Little League lad to a ninety-two-year-old gent the Saturday my husband, Mark, and I dined on mushroom steak and barbecued ribs. And pasta salad, deviled eggs, broccoli and cauliflower salad, cukes and onions, pistachio pudding, and butterscotch pie. Oh, heaven.

UNION CITY
Sweet Shoppe
213 North Columbia Street
(765) 964-3366
A genuine antique garbed in 1960s birch paneling, gray crushed-ice Formica, and space age chrome wall fixtures, the Sweet Shoppe opened in 1938 as a combination restaurant and confectionery. You'll find home cooking, old-fashioned ice cream treats (try the chocolate–peanut butter shake), and a variety of ooey gooey desserts.

WINCHESTER
Mrs. Wick's Pies
100 Cherry Street
(765) 584-7437
Not a cafe so much as a restaurant, Mrs. Wick's has an unusual twist that makes it worth a visit: it's an adjunct to the Wick's pie factory with thirty daily varieties of pie. Me? I'll hold out for real homemade.

WINCHESTER
Round the Corner Cafe
130 East Pearl Street
(765) 584-2111
Opened in May 2006, this cafe promises homemade just about everything. My waitress tells me the real mashed potatoes are "just like home. Sometimes they're lumpy, sometimes they're not." Dessert is included with all daily specials.

YORKTOWN
Tigers Hometown Cafe
9413 West Smith Street
(765) 759-4888
Yorktown Tiger pride displayed in a growing collection of high school sports memorabilia, including not-so-recently retired team jerseys in green and gold. Mom's chocolate gravy over homemade biscuits is found only here.

YORKTOWN
Yorktown Cafe
9144 West Smith Street
(765) 759-8368
Not quite so spirited—so Tigerous?—in its interior decor, this downtown diner buzzes with breakfasters before the workday officially begins. The month-at-a-glance menu reminds me of school days.

Central

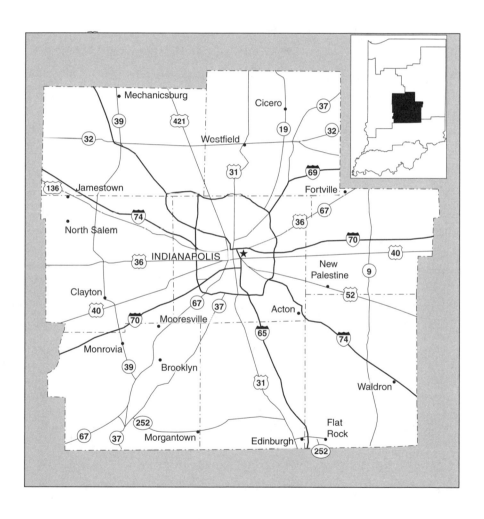

CLAYTON
Clayton Cafe
76 East Kentucky Street
(317) 539-6419
M–Th 6 A.M.–8 P.M.; F 6 A.M.–9 P.M.; Sa 6 A.M.–2 P.M.; Su closed
David and Beth Slingerland

On a Friday night in early October, my husband, Mark, and I approach Clayton from the south. Our first indication of something out of the ordinary is the smell of fried fish hovering in the crisp air. Even with our windows tightly rolled up, the odor—some say the fragrance—is unmistakable.

At six o'clock, cars are parallel parked for several blocks up and down the highway in the vicinity of the Clayton Cafe, located in the old IOOF lodge building. People are standing in line, streaming down the cafe's handicapped ramp and nearly reaching the street corner. In search of a parking spot, Mark turns onto a side street, where we see cars fender to bumper along the curb. A bowlegged man wearing a cap and chewing on a toothpick walks to his car, lurching from side to side as if he has just gotten off a horse, or gorged on way too much catfish. We pull into the spot he vacates.

We take our place in line, behind a young couple who pulled up in a car with a ninety-three Marion County code on the license plate. Her furtive comments indicate that this is their first trip to the Clayton Cafe, inspired, no doubt, by a gushing article that recently appeared in *Indianapolis Monthly*.

The slanted ramp provides a perfect view of diners inside the cafe, including an old guy licking his fingers under a reproduction poster for the 1945 Robert Mitchum film, *West of the Pecos*. A woman several places behind me laughs and points him out, and we all turn our eyes to get a look. An uneasy mother reminds her young son that it is "impolite to stare." But none of us can turn our eyes away from the lucky folks inside gorging on their first, second, some even their third helpings of golden catfish. We're all salivating at the chance to be finger deep in platters of our own.

A kind of festive, anticipatory air settles over the people trapped on the ramp. We talk and laugh sporadically, inching forward until the young Indianapolis couple in front of us bolts from line and boldly claims two seats at the counter. Through the front window, Mark spies additional vacant seats, and we follow them in. Too late, we realize there are not two seats side by side. We are banished back to the waiting line, forced to start again at the end instead of cutting in and reclaiming our former positions. Impatient and restless, Mark opts for a walk around town. Within minutes, a middle-aged man and woman emerge from the cafe, recognize me, and announce that there are now two seats available at the counter. I seize them and quickly order for both of us: two all-you-can-eat catfish fillet dinners with choice of two sides and choice of bread: baked beans and breaded tomatoes for Mark, Hoosier-style green beans and pineapple salad for me, and hush puppies—my waitress writes *pups* on the ticket—for both of us.

On my return visit several months later, David and Beth Slingerland nod knowingly when I share my story. For six years they have carried on the traditions established by David's mother and stepfather, Betty and Stephen Hoop, the cafe's previous owners. David and Beth relocated to Clayton from North Carolina to take over the family business, bringing their son Jacob with them. Now nine, he has since been joined by sister Sierra and brother Trey and countless mothers and fathers, grandmothers and grandfathers, who comprise the cafe's extended family of regulars.

David speaks with the slow, drawn out vowels of the South and sprinkles his side of our conversation with yes ma'ams and no ma'ams. I am not accustomed to being called ma'am, and I find it sweet and slightly flattering. Beth has acquired the Hoosier dialect and speech patterns more easily. Nevertheless, she explains, "When I'm on the phone with my mom, the people here tell me I sound more North Carolinian. But my mom thinks I sound like a Hoosier and teases, 'So you're a Hoosier now?'"

They are both well on their way. David laughs about coming to terms with beloved Hoosier cafe specialties. "I never heard of a breaded tenderloin until I came here! And ham and beans was something I never knew existed." The Slingerlands knew better than to make changes to a cafe that had been running smoothly for years, so they wisely continued with Betty and Stephen's time-tested menu, experienced staff, and well-established routine. They quickly discovered that the cafe regulars tugged them back into line when they veered slightly off course, objecting even to the most minor adjustments. "We thought we'd save time by using preshredded cabbage for the coleslaw," Beth offers by way of example. "You wouldn't believe the uproar over that! They want the chopped cabbage that they're used to."

The Friday night all-you-can-eat catfish special presents the perfect opportunity to see the Clayton Cafe operate at its well-oiled best. It is not unusual for David to prepare up to four hundred pounds of sweet, fleshy catfish—all hand-dusted in seasoned cornmeal, deep fried, and served crunchy hot. "That first Friday, I was just shocked," Beth remembers. "We'd been told what to expect, but we couldn't believe it. You really have to get in the mood. Every night you have to be up."

Back in October, Mark and I sat at the kitchen end of the white counter, perched on lozenge seats of faded brownish-orange vinyl on steel posts. Paper placemats filled with ads for local businesses covered the surface in front of us. To our left, we watched David tending the deep-fat fryer just inside the kitchen. He dropped white-coated fillets and whole, bone-in fiddlers into the vat of oil, and drew out honey brown pieces with long tongs, stacking them in a large stainless steel pan. The pile grew to an impressive mound, quickly disappeared, grew again, and dwindled to nothing—ad infinitum. With catfish constantly frying, David deftly loaded up plates, pulled steaming, foil-wrapped Russet potatoes from the oven, and occasionally stepped out of sight to dredge more fish in the handmade coating mix.

Behind the counter, a young man in a baseball cap and black T-shirt that read "Please . . . fire me" cooked frozen, preformed beef burgers, chicken patties, tenderloins, rib eye steaks, and American fries at a small grill directly in front of us. To his right was a steam table filled with deep stainless-steel tubs containing the night's hot side dishes: mashed potatoes ("They're real but they're frozen," Beth says), macaroni and cheese, baked beans and green beans, and breaded tomatoes. A high school girl portioned out each order, tucking the bill under the catfish before calling out the waitress's name.

The entire Friday fish fry frenzy was staffed by a mere eight people: David at the deep fryer, the grill cook, steam table girl, four waitresses, and one teenage boy busing and clearing tables. He wore a neon green T-shirt for the Cascade High School cross-country team. The slogan on the back—"We kick our butts to kick yours"—perfectly describes the Clayton Cafe on a Friday night.

The all-you-can-eat promise plays out every Monday through Friday between 4 and 8 P.M., just as it has for the past twenty-some years. Monday features shrimp and french fries or chicken livers and a choice of three sides. Tuesday brings spaghetti and meat sauce, chicken-fried steak, or deep-fried fingerling smelt—an oddity in the Hoosier State introduced by Stephen Hoop in 1986. Wednesday is reserved for skillet-fried chicken plus three sides and Thursday for barbecued beef ribs. A waiting line is not common except on Friday.

By no means let it deter you. The catfish at the Clayton Cafe is the best I found in Indiana's small town diners. Perfect accompaniments include the Hoosier-style green beans with bits of ham and enough black pepper to provide a bit of a bite, the crusty cornmeal "pups," barbecue-style baked beans, and yeasty dinner rolls. The Sara Lee peach and blackberry cobblers, served in old Homer Laughlin bowls with turquoise and gray leaves on the rim, nearly passed for homemade.

A quirky delight is the Clayton Cafe's specialty salad made with pine-apple chunks, marshmallow bits, and half-inch squares of American cheese stirred into a sauce of sweetened and thickened pineapple juice. I have to confess that when I found the first square of pale orange cheese, I assumed it had gotten into the salad by mistake. But then I found a second one.

"The cut cheese is a little different," Beth admits. "If I were the one making the salad, I'd probably switch to shredded cheese. But that's another change the customers would go to war over."

By the time Mark and I spooned the last of the cobbler from our bowls, the clock read seven thirty. A few customers inside the door were waiting to claim the empty tables cluttered with dirty dishes, evidence of the deluge of customers the staff had already served. A lull settled over the cafe, and the waitresses, grill cook, steam table girl, and bus boy began to relax. Their voices lost the tense, vibratolike quality of service under fire, and they joked jauntily with each other. I sensed that they saw the end of the evening in sight, that they were hoping they might get out a bit early for a change.

We were paying our bill at the register when the thunderbolt struck, sending waves of alarm rippling throughout the cafe. A whisper echoed from employee to employee.

"A party of eighteen!"

"No way!"

"Did you hear? There's a party of eighteen."

The news electrified the staff. Hope for the downward side of evening disappeared as quickly as David's mound of fried catfish. As we stepped outside, a woman on the concrete ramp out front had a cell phone tucked under her ear.

"There's eighteen of us, but come on down. They're not busy at all."
If only she knew.

EDINBURGH
Christine's Breakfast and Lunch Box
131 East Main Cross
(812) 526-6767
M–Sa 5:30 A.M.–2 P.M.; Su closed
Christine Bryant

The school board minutes on the wall behind the counter of Christine's Breakfast and Lunch Box are a sure indication that the main street cafe is an important community gathering place, where talk covers matters both serious and light hearted. Much of it occurs at the long, white-topped Liars Table in the center of the room. Men gather here in a "constantly rotating set of liars" every morning between five thirty and ten o'clock, owner Christine Bryant says. "They keep it full all morning talking about fishing, coon dogs, hunting, whose biscuit is bigger—all the important topics, you know."

Having opened in 2004, Christine's Breakfast and Lunch Box is a new addition to Edinburgh's beautiful and historic downtown, but its youth belies enduring associations with the community. Housed in a late-nineteenth-century commercial building that has been used for everything from a grocery store and pool hall to an economic development office ("Oh, honey, you name it"), the cafe boasts a recessed entry in a vintage glass storefront and a soaring ceiling of pressed tin. I love the ice cream parlor–style bentwood chairs bought secondhand from a Whiteland bar that give the dining room a mellow, nostalgic character.

As tasteful as it looks, however, Christine's tastes even better. That's because Bertha Wilbur, who owned Bertha's Place, an Edinburgh institution for over forty years, is back where she excels: in the kitchen. Bertha sold her namesake cafe and retired a few years ago, and then discovered she missed both the work and the people. When Christine called and asked her to cook, she happily agreed. "We all love this lady," says Christine, who worked at Bertha's Place for eight years.

With the titles turned, Christine has discovered that running her own restaurant is more work than she expected. ("I figured I worked so hard for others, I thought I'd try it by myself," she says.) Bertha, on the other hand, is enjoying the freedom she's gained by coming in, cooking, and going home when she's tired. "Bertha's in control of the kitchen. She's been doing it so long that she has her own way of doing things," Christine explains. "She taught me how to peel a potato with a knife—not a peeler. 'Honey,' she said, 'this is how you do it.'"

Christine's friend Jo Ann Burton nods in agreement. "She has a certain way of making pea salad. She dices up everything teeny tiny and mixes the dressing in a separate bowl. I helped out once and made the salad, and everyone knew it wasn't Bertha's. 'Oh, honey,' she said, 'you've got to cut up everything very fine.'"

As queen bee in the kitchen, Bertha turns out favorites like meatloaf, lasagna, fried chicken, ham and beans, and swiss steak that keep the locals well fed and happy. "Honey, the whole town of Edinburgh is spoiled, but I doubt that they know it," Christine laughs. They're accustomed to nothing but Bertha's everyday best: real mashed potatoes, homemade salads—in addition to pea, there's homemade macaroni, coleslaw, potato, and kidney bean, plus seasonal salads like cucumbers and onions—even homemade tartar sauce for the Friday fried fish. Another popular item is the breaded tenderloin, made by hand-pressing fresh cut pork loin into beaten eggs, dredging it in seasoned flour, then repeating both steps before dropping it into the deep fryer.

"Honey, you gotta really work those eggs into the meat so you don't get a dry tenderloin," Jo Ann explains.

"Honey?" I echo playfully. I can't resist.

It suddenly dawns on both Christine and Jo Ann that Bertha's pet word has become their own. "Oh, hoooney!" they laugh, mimicking the way Bertha draws out the syllables.

Among Bertha's many gifts, as cherished as "honey," are her large repertoire of pies. Chocolate and coconut cream are perennial favorites, but the best seller is Quick as a Wink pineapple pie, a confection of crushed pineapple, cream cheese, vanilla pudding, and Cool Whip spooned into a graham cracker crust. Variations are made by substituting other fruit for the pineapple. Quick as a Wink peach pie was on the specials board the day I had lunch, but it had long disappeared from the pie case. In fact, my piece of chocolate cream was the orphan in the case, and I called dibs on that even before I ordered my chicken salad. Honey, when it comes to Bertha's pie, it's better to be selfish than sorry. Order pie first.

As word about the good food at Christine's Breakfast and Lunch Box spread among local residents, soldiers at Camp Atterbury, even people from Columbus and beyond, business has steadily increased. "For a small town of five thousand, I'm surprised we have the volume we do," says Christine. "But we're pretty unique in that just about everything we serve is home-made. You don't find that many places anymore. They're the survivors. *We're* the survivors."

A witty Web tribute to survivors of another kind—"all the kids who survived the 1930s, '40s, '50, '60s, and '70s"—is found on the wall behind the register, right next to the school board minutes:

First, we survived being born to mothers who smoked and/or drank while they carried us.

They took aspirin, ate blue cheese dressing, tuna from a can, and didn't get tested for diabetes.

Then after that trauma, our baby cribs were covered with bright-colored, lead-based paints.

We had no childproof lids on medicine bottles, doors or cabinets, and when we rode our bikes, we had no helmets, not to mention, the risks we took hitchhiking.

As children, we would ride in cars without seat belts or air bags.

Riding in the back of a pickup on a warm day was always a special treat.

We drank water from the garden hose and NOT from a bottle.

We shared one soft drink with four friends, from one bottle and NO ONE actually died from this.

We ate cupcakes, white bread and real butter and drank soda pop with sugar in it, but we weren't overweight because WE WERE ALWAYS OUTSIDE PLAYING!

We would leave home in the morning and play all day, as long as we were back when the streetlights came on.

No one was able to reach us all day. And we were O.K.

We would spend hours building our go-carts out of scraps and then ride down the hill, only to find out we forgot the brakes. After running into the bushes a few times, we learned to solve the problem.

We did not have Playstations, Nintendos, X-boxes, no video games at all, no 99 channels on cable, no video tape movies, no surround sound, no cell phones, no personal computers, no Internet or Internet chat rooms.

WE HAD FRIENDS and we went outside and found them!

We fell out of trees, got cut, broke bones and teeth and there were no lawsuits from these accidents.

We ate worms and mud pies made from dirt, and the worms did not live in us forever.

We were given BB guns for our 10th birthdays, made up games with sticks and tennis balls and although we were told it would happen, we did not put out very many eyes.

We rode bikes or walked to a friend's house and knocked on the door or rang the bell, or just walked in and talked to them!

Little League had tryouts and not everyone made the team. Those who didn't had to learn to deal with disappointment. Imagine that!!

The idea of a parent bailing us out if we broke the law was unheard of. They actually sided with the law!

This generation has produced some of the best risk-takers, problem solvers and inventors ever!

The past 50 years have been an explosion of innovation and new ideas.

We had freedom, failure, success and responsibility, and we learned HOW TO DEAL WITH IT ALL!

You might want to share this with others who have had the luck to grow up as kids, before the lawyers and the government regulated our lives for our own good.

And while you are at it, forward it to your kids so they will know how brave their parents were.

Kind of makes you want to run through the house with scissors, doesn't it?!

FLAT ROCK
Flat Rock Cafe
2748 West State Road 252
(812) 587-0155
M–T 6 A.M.–2 P.M.; W 6 A.M.–10 P.M.; Th 6 A.M.–11 P.M.; F–Sa 6 A.M.–
midnight; Su closed
Beth Michaels

"I've been a junker all my life," says Beth Michaels about the whimsical, witty, and altogether wonderful collection of eclectic stuff that fills the Flat Rock Cafe she bought in 1997. "When I got the restaurant, my decorating plan—if that's what you want to call it—was going to be all antiques and racing. Then people started bringing me stuff, and it just kind of took off from there."

By the looks of it, you'd never guess that Beth hasn't spent a lifetime at the cafe located next door to the Flat Rock post office. Built in 1962 as a windshield shop (with a quirky pink and gray tile floor), the place has a layering of time and things that belies Beth's occupancy but speaks volumes of local residents' high regard for her. While you're waiting for your order to come—preferably on the red vinyl–topped chrome counter stools—absorb the contents of the cafe for thirty seconds, then close your eyes and remember what you've seen. I see burlap seed bags; old record album covers; a Mona Lisa print in an oval frame; an inflatable shark on the ceiling-mounted furnace; a print of *Nighthawks,* Edward Hopper's classic diner scene; photo collages of the regulars; Pee-wee Herman on a miniature John Deere tractor—and Woody on a giant chicken; and a mannequin wearing a barbecue apron. Go ahead. You try. Don't forget the huge black and white photo of Bishops Grocery and other historic photos of old-time Flat Rock ("This used to be a big town") or the Starlite Drive-In sign advertising thirty-five-cent burgers affixed to the front of the counter.

"People come in all the time and ask for a thirty-five-cent burger. I say, 'Sure, but it'll be this big,'" Beth laughs, holding out her thumb and forefinger in a circle the size of a quarter.

Beth has found most of the items at flea markets, yard sales, and auctions, including the first-Monday-of-the-month auction held just up the street. She's such a fixture at the local sale barn that the regulars know exactly what she's interested in and courteously stay out of the bidding.

They're confident that whatever Beth buys is likely to wind up on the walls of the cafe. "One night there was this airplane propeller that I wanted so bad," she tells me. "I could just see it hanging on the wall. But the bidding went up to $900, and I had to bail out. The rest of the night I was boo-hoo-ing about how I didn't get my propeller."

Waving her hand at a winged hunk of cast iron circled by Marilyn Monroe posters, she continues. "A friend had this propeller-looking thing in the barn for years. He cleaned it up and brought it in. The funny thing is, that thing has generated more conversation than the propeller ever would have. Here it is about ninety years later, and they're still coming up with ideas about what it is!"

Trinkets, toys, and junk from auction box lots and yard sales end up priced and tagged in Beth's never-ending "garage sale" in the cafe's back corner. Her smallest customers, including babies and toddlers, have a field day pawing through the ever-changing stock of treasures. "They just love coming here," Beth says. "I remember when I was a kid. We'd go to the store and fill brown paper bags with candy from a jar on the counter. That's why I have a candy jar on my counter, and I keep popsicles in the freezer. I want this to be a fun place for kids that they'll remember."

The nostalgic atmosphere at the Flat Rock Cafe extends to the menu as well, with old-fashioned real food served fresh and hot Monday through Saturday. Beth learned to cook as a farm girl by helping her mom and grandma in the kitchen, and by participating in 4-H. "I make everything I can from scratch because that's just the way we always did it at home," she says. You can rely on burgers that are hand-pattied from fresh beef; homemade coleslaw, potato, and vegetable salads; seasonal slow-simmered soups; and daily specials like meatloaf, fried fish, and country-fried steak. Breakfast is often the busiest meal of the day, with the Crushed Rock—eggs, hash browns, and smoked sausage served with a biscuit or toast—and the Flat Rock—one egg, six silver dollar pancakes, and one piece of sausage or bacon—going head to head for best-seller status.

In summer, Beth gathers fresh garden produce and puts it up for winter use. She dices, stews, and freezes tomatoes for chili, and cuts fresh sweet corn off the ears before putting it into the freezer for later use as a side dish. She even makes her own salsa. With no grocery store nearby, it pays to plan ahead and keep the pantry well stocked, but sometimes she miscalculates and runs short. "If I run out of something, I have customers who will bring me things from home," she says. "They're just good people. We all help each other out."

The people of Flat Rock provide Beth with steady day-in and day-out support. But on Wednesday nights, the cafe fills with people from far and beyond hungry for fried chicken and small town camaraderie. I'd been tipped off to the Flat Rock Cafe's midweek fried chicken dinner by two different people—both owners of nearby cafes, in fact. Generally I take the recommendation of cafe owners as a ringing endorsement, but I have to admit that in this case I had my doubts. What could be so special about plain old deep-fried chicken? This is how, on the day we dropped off our son, Pete, at Indiana University to begin his freshman year, Mark and I spent our first night as empty nesters making a seventy-five-mile round-trip to the Flat Rock Cafe.

There was only one unclaimed table, just inside the door, when we arrived at five thirty. The cafe was filled with farmers and their wives, towns-folk, and a party of golfers just off the course. Our waitress apologized that there would be a bit of a wait for the chicken because a new batch had just been dropped into the fryer. So we ordered cans of Miller High Life—the Flat Rock is one of the few cafes in Indiana with a beer and wine license—and rummaged through Beth's garage sale until it arrived, so sizzling hot that juice flowed from the pieces when we broke through their crispy skins. Coated with flour breading—a special recipe of Beth's husband, Dan—it rates among the best deep-fried chicken we have ever eaten. Beth's potato salad, coleslaw, and broccoli salad porked up with bacon bits were equally delicious. Only Mark's instant mashed potatoes were a disappointment, but that didn't prevent him from cleaning his plate.

"Do you like chicken salad?" Beth asks me on my return to the Flat Rock Cafe a few days later. "We sometimes run out of chicken on Wednesday night, but other times we pick it off the bones and use it for chicken and noodles or chicken salad. We don't waste anything here." She brings me a small bowl with a compact mound of chicken and diced celery, hard-boiled eggs, celery, and sweet pickle relish held together with mayonnaise. The deep fryer adds a lovely, rich flavor to the chicken salad. Despite my best intentions, it is so good that I keep eating until it's gone.

Every Friday and Saturday night, the Flat Rock Cafe features live music by area bands and solo musicians on the small corner stage. Among the favorite performers is blind bluegrass fiddler and guitar picker Brian Allen from Scottsburg, who has a standing gig the first Friday of every month.

JAMESTOWN
Dick and Judy's
11 West Main Street
(765) 676-5707
M closed; T–Th 6 A.M.–8 P.M.; F–Sa 6 A.M.–9 P.M.; Su 6 A.M.–2:30 P.M.
Dick and Judy McGee

"I've always been a pretty good food critic," says Dick McGee, owner with his wife, Judy, of Jamestown's family-owned cafe. As a high school graduate in Choctaw, Oklahoma, he took a job at the local burger joint. At first, the burgers were just about the best thing he'd ever tasted, but he grew sick of them quick enough after a daily regimen of eating. He found a partial antidote in the home cooking at Maggie's Cafe in nearby Harrah, "the greatest place to get a plate lunch just heaped up with good food." By the time he was in his thirties, Dick was eating out a lot on the road as a salesman for an educational publishing company. It was a transfer that brought him and his family to Jamestown.

Away from home more often than not, Dick "used to envy people who lived here and worked here." When the company sold out in 1985, he had the chance to fulfill a longtime dream of going into business for himself. It could have been any business, but after considering what Jamestown had to offer, and what it needed, he and Judy opted for a restaurant. "I'd eaten out a lot and figured I was qualified to open a restaurant," Dick explains. They signed a lease on a vacant building that had been a cafe since at least the 1930s and set about reclaiming history. They rolled up their sleeves and remodeled, purchased kitchen equipment and tables and chairs at auctions, and devised a limited menu based on the kinds of food they fixed at home.

They quickly discovered that cooking for the family was a far cry from cooking for the community. It took five years to settle in, during which time Dick often thought about "throwing in the towel. Neither one of us had a clue about how much work it would be." Twenty-two years later, Dick regularly puts in ninety hours a week between the restaurant and his side job painting houses, a necessity because the restaurant income isn't enough to support the family. "I work harder now than I ever have, but I have a lot more freedom to make decisions."

Sitting at a table near the side wall, Dick lights a cigarette and passes time in conversation before heading home for a rest. (Behind him, a Smokefree Indiana poster with the sports schedule for Western Boone High School reads, "The Only Thing I Smoke Is My Opponents.") Today's rain keeps him from painting, but he fills the void with work at the restaurant.

The years have taken their toll. Dick readily admits that he and Judy are "wearing down" and notes that although "so much of our life is in the restaurant," a lot more is missed because of it. "We missed a lot of our kids' activities and now the grandkids' activities are being missed." They think about stepping down, but they know they couldn't sell the restaurant for what it's worth. So they keep on. Keep on getting up before dawn. Keep on offering good food at a good price. Keep on working ninety hours a week.

Dick and Judy's has developed a loyal clientele over the years, with regulars returning time and again from as far away as Brownsburg and Speedway. "People drive a long way for our biscuits and gravy and pork tenderloins because we make it all ourselves." It's not uncommon to go through five gallons of sausage gravy on a weekend morning. Folks eat it over biscuits, spooned over omelets and fried potatoes, and, later in the day, on top of country-fried steak. The pork tenderloins are made fresh to order from butterflied loins prepared at the local IGA. "Ours are real," Dick says proudly. "Most places make fritters, these little bitty things they buy frozen. We pick up ours fresh from the IGA several times a week and bread them with flour and egg. They're about ten to twelve inches long when they come to the table."

As a native Oklahoman, Dick "never heard of pork tenderloins" until he came to Indiana. He also never heard of sugar cream pie. "There's quite a bit of difference in food. Take chicken-fried steak. Here it's called country-fried steak, but it's not really the same. I've tried and tried, but I can't really duplicate the flavor of Oklahoma chicken-fried steak. I tell myself I should go to a small diner and go back in the kitchen and ask. Another thing is ham and beans. We have them in Oklahoma, too, only it's pinto beans. We rarely fix 'em even though we know other places have 'em every Monday."

With two or three specials on the menu every day, Dick and Judy often feel trapped in a rut preparing the same foods over and over. Sometimes they experiment with favorite dishes from their home state, such as black-eyed peas and fried okra. They don't usually attract much interest, Dick concedes. "People who eat here are country people that go for meat and potatoes. They like their roast beef and burgers. Even spaghetti doesn't go over real well."

Boasting "delicious home cooking since 1985," Dick and Judy's menu includes a popular ten-ounce Big Okie burger made from "fresh (*never* frozen) hamburger," and a wide selection of steaks, including a twelve-ounce Black Angus T-bone, bacon-wrapped filet mignon, and fresh cut prime rib. Steaks are the main attraction on Friday and Saturday nights, along with barbecued ribs, fantail shrimp, and fried catfish and cod. These are the nights that Dick and Judy's becomes a destination rather than a local restaurant. "A lot of Friday nights we have people waiting in line," says Dick. "We get a few Jamestown people, but most are from out of town. The locals want to go out to eat, and that means driving out of town. For everybody else, going out means coming here. We got people from Lebanon last week. They say they'll come back."

Sunday is one day the locals stay home for Judy's after church dinner just like Grandma used to make. There's always fried chicken and fish, plus one other entree—maybe roast beef, baked pit ham, swiss steak, or roast pork tenderloin—topped off with dessert, of course. Judy has an experienced hand in making lemon meringue, coconut cream, and sugar cream pies, fruit cobblers, and cakes.

Dick and Judy have made many friends over the years, so many, in fact, that their namesake restaurant has become one of Jamestown's most popular social centers. Others come once but are never forgotten. "Sue Ann Gilmore came here one Friday night," Dick says. "She told me, 'Yeah, I've heard your name around the statehouse several times.' Typical politician! And Dick Wolfsie, that television personality from Channel 8, that guy on early in the morning, did a spot from here a few years back."

Then there are the regulars whose visits range from several times a day to four or five times a week. These are the friends who are so hard to lose. "The thing that bothers us the most is we get pretty close with a lot of our customers," Dick told the local *Daily Sun* in a February 2006 interview. "We've had a lot of 'em pass away. Some of 'em we were extremely close to. We had an older guy in town that used to come in and help us. He used to come in at four in the morning and make biscuits and gravy. He helped us for nineteen years. When we'd hire a new waitress, and Jim would come in here, I'd tell that waitress, 'Now he can do anything he wants to do. As far as you're concerned, this is his place.' He died a couple of years ago; that was tough."

Dick doesn't have a copy of the *Daily Sun* article, so after he departs for home, I walk across the street to the all-volunteer library. After an unsuccessful search, Kathy, the woman at the front desk, offers to take me to the home of Betty Buriss. "She has a copy," she assures me.

Together we walk the few blocks to Betty's trim white house. I never think to ask Betty why the article means so much to her that she has bothered to save it. On our way back to the library, Kathy tells me about Betty's husband, Jim. "He was so bored after he retired that he started going down to Dick and Judy's. Pretty soon he was in the kitchen every morning making biscuits and gravy. That's the kind of thing that can only happen in a small town, don't you think?"

NORTH SALEM
Liz's Country Cafe
7 West Pearl Street
(765) 676-9063
September–April: M–W 5:30 A.M.–2 P.M.; Th–F 5:30 A.M.–2 P.M. and 5 P.M.–8 P.M.; Sa 5:30 A.M.–2 P.M.; Su closed
May–August: M–Sa 5:30 A.M.–2 P.M.; Su closed
Liz Freeland
North Salem is a pretty town, a Mayberry-esque village where Old Fashion Days is celebrated every Labor Day weekend and where a handwritten notice taped on the post office window invites folks to a local man's Friday night funeral. Vintage two-story brick buildings stretch out lazily along Main Street's two-block length. On the newer east end, under the shadow of an old-fashioned blue water tower, you'll find the town hall and the adjunct town hall. The latter is Liz's Country Cafe, which relocated from across the street a few years ago when owner Liz Freeland bought a "former exercise place." I find this quirkily amusing: in the very same building where folks worked out to lose weight they now put it back on with Liz's homemade pretty much everything.

In 1995, Liz made a big decision. She bought the restaurant where she had worked four years as a cook, deciding it's better to work for herself than for someone else. A few years later, she decided she'd be better off with a mortgage than rental payments. While some folks thought she might be getting a little too big for her britches, others hitched up theirs, rolled up their sleeves, and pitched in to help her reshape the gym into a restaurant of her own design. They rightly reasoned that the sooner it was completed, the sooner they'd be back in their old familiar places.

"It was exciting to make the restaurant just what I wanted instead of taking what I got," Liz says. "We wanted to make it feel like you were at home. A few days after we opened, a little girl came in and said, 'We can't eat here. This is somebody's house.' That's when I knew we'd done it right."

The new cafe is fresh and spacious, with enough room between tables for friends and neighbors to pause and pass the news yet not get in the way of the waitresses. Country framed prints, knickknacks, and rustic, hand-painted plaques decorate the soft gray walls. By themselves, they are cute and nice yet rather mundane. But juxtaposed—like the cafe and the exercise place—they become drolly clever, reducing me to stifled giggles. Are they intentionally or unintentionally paired? Does anyone else see their humor, or is just me?

Try this: Tacked to a center post, a small cutout of a pie reads "homemade apple pie." Below it, a larger pie moans "Dieter's Prayer: Help Me God."

And this: On the wall behind the locals-only round table—bought and brought in by one of the regulars, who insisted round was superior to square for the not-to-be-missed daily gatherings—you'll find a sign that says, "Your village called. Their idiot is missing." And next to it, this sign: "You're among friends."

These are just two in the side wall collection of signs whose tongue-in-cheek sayings pretty much sum up the day-to-day experiences of running—and patronizing—a popular local gathering spot. Most are commercially available plastic signs common in cafes throughout Indiana.

Have you seen this one? "Labor Rates. Answers $1. Answers that Require Thought $2. Correct Answers $3. Dumb looks are still free."

Or this one? "I can please only one person at a time. Today is not your day. Tomorrow doesn't look good either."

Liz's sign collection began innocently enough when she hung a small plaque with a chicken and the words "No fowl moods here." Then someone brought in a second—"Hunters, fishermen, and other liars gather here"—and hung it behind the community table. Soon enough, Liz explains, customers started bringing in other signs they "find at yard sales and flea markets and bring back from vacation." Purchased with the cafe crowd in mind and presented with no expectations other than laughter and a place on the wall, the signs are a reliable measure of customers' affection for Liz and the degree to which they consider the cafe theirs as much as hers.

The food, as well as the fun and fellowship, keep them coming back. By one o'clock on a Friday afternoon, they've devoured the last of the beer-battered fish. By default, I opt for the salmon patty with a small bowl of pineapple cheese salad and hand-peeled, hand-mashed real potatoes. I didn't have much difficulty bypassing the rainbow of other side dishes in favor of the salad, a curious combination of chunky pineapple, miniature marshmallows, and cubed cheddar cheese in thickened pineapple juice that I've rarely if ever encountered outside Hendricks and Montgomery counties. Of course, I top off lunch with a piece of banana cream pie made by Liz herself.

Liz's pie is true and honest. Few Hoosier cafe owners go to such lengths, opting instead for partway pies that combine homemade fillings and a frozen or premade crust. Need I admit it? I am a pie snob. The best require a crust mixed and blended, rolled and tucked into a pie plate by the baker's own gentle hands.

I'm known to scrutinize a slice of pie like a scientist over a petri dish. I turn the plate around and examine the back crust and fluted edge before gingerly breaking off a piece and popping it into my mouth. I roll it on my tongue, paying attention to its flavor. Having grown up in suburbia, I never developed a taste for lard, which Liz herself uses, but I appreciate that it is a preferred ingredient for pie makers because it makes a beautifully flaky crust. It's all about how the fat molecules adhere to the gluten molecules.

Liz's and my pie talk swings from crust to filling. Before I can stop myself, I divulge an embarrassing secret: I am an abject failure at making a cream filling that sets up thick and firm. Liz is kindly sympathetic but puzzled at the difficulty of something that for her is, well, as easy as pie. "I don't have any trouble," she explains, rattling off the recipe she knows by heart. "I keep it up here," she says, tapping the side of her head.

"My basic cream filling is made with two cups of 2 percent milk, one and a half cups sugar, a half cup flour, four egg yolks, one teaspoon vanilla, and two tablespoons butter. If I'm making banana cream, I slice bananas into the pie shell before I add the filling. If I'm making coconut cream, I add one cup of coconut. If it's chocolate cream, I add three tablespoons of cocoa."

Real pie, like the other real cooking at Liz's Country Cafe, "is just the way I grew up," Liz says. "We didn't have a lot of money. We had a large garden, so everything was made from scratch. People tell me our food is just like Grandma used to make. I don't think of it as special because but it's just the way I grew up."

Liz's interest in cooking goes back to childhood. "I was about six or seven when I made my own little cookbook. I cut out recipes from magazines and pasted them on notebook paper. I even took the stickers off my school papers and put them on the cover. Then I went to my mom and said, 'Let's go through your recipes.' I still have that cookbook." Liz also credits her experience in 4-H and school home economics classes with making her into the cook she is.

Liz's old-fashioned, down-home cooking covers traditional Hoosier culinary territory, from washday Monday's ham and beans, Tuesday's beef or chicken and homemade noodles, and Wednesday's meatloaf and hand-breaded tenderloins to Thursday's pan-fried chicken and Friday's beer-battered fish and salmon patties. The trusted menu is pretty much the same as that which Liz's late mother relied on in the cafe she ran in nearby Lizton.

"My mom knew how hard it was running your own restaurant, but she was excited for me when I opened. She nominated me for Cook of the Month in the *Hendricks County Flyer* a few years ago. Even when she had bone cancer, she'd be in here every day to eat. She'd always ask, 'Is there anything I can do?' She loved the restaurant and was proud of me."

WALDRON
Mohawk Grill
101 East Washington Street
(765) 525-2233
M–F 6 A.M.–2 P.M. and 5 P.M.–8 P.M.; Sa 6 A.M.–9 P.M.; Su 10 A.M.–2 P.M.
Tracy and Kim Miller
It was Tom Smith at Christine's Breakfast and Lunch Box in Edinburgh who tipped me off to the Mohawk Grill. "They've got good food," he said

with conviction. Without his recommendation, I'd probably never have trekked to Waldron, a small Shelby County town straddling the Central Indiana Railroad. There's good food, that's for sure. But Waldron has something special that sets it apart from most other cafes and most other towns. What Tom didn't tell me is that the Mohawk Grill is a veritable shrine to the Waldron High School basketball team, the 2004 state Class A champions.

In a town with fewer than two thousand residents, Waldron has succeeded in keeping its own elementary school, middle school, and high school—all located on a centralized campus just a few blocks from the three-block commercial area. After blue signs went up following the remarkable state tournament run, the stretch of Washington Street connecting the two was designated Mohawk Trail. Mohawk pride runs both high—the water tower sports the Mohawk mascot—and deep here, where a sign still affixed to a post downtown remembers the winter of 2003–2004 as "A Season to Remember."

"We'd only had the cafe about a year when we realized the team was something special," Tracy says. "Pretty soon we were opening up after the games—even the away games. We even had a special post-game menu. The more they won, the more people would come to get together and talk about the game. Sometimes we didn't get out of here until midnight."

As depicted in *Hoosiers,* the Hollywood version of the Milan Miracle of 1954, Hoosier basketball has the power to coalesce community, gathering in folks from the fringes that might otherwise have little or nothing to do with their neighbors. As the Waldron Mohawks won game after game, finally amassing a perfect unbeaten 21-0 season under first-year coach Jason Delaney, the cafe rivaled only the gymnasium as the pulsing heart of Waldron. "What [the championship] meant to this community, what it meant to these boys, what it meant to me and my staff, I wouldn't trade it for anything," Delaney told *Indianapolis Star* sportswriter Bob Kravitz after the championship trophy had been awarded.

After slamming Fort Wayne Blackhawk Christian 69-54, the Mohawks returned to Waldron as Class A state champs. Residents lined the street to cheer the celebratory parade. Within days, "strangers started coming from all over Indiana, even from out of state," Tracy says with, even yet, a lingering incredulity. "You know, there's some people who seek out towns just like this, restaurants just like ours."

"Before [the championship], people didn't know where Waldron was or even if there was a Waldron," Delaney told Kravitz. "One stoplight, the Mohawk Grill and that's about it. But now people know where Waldron is."

And what the Mohawks achieved. Tracy has made darn sure of that. During that long, amazing season, Tracy became a clipper, a collector, a keeper of the flame. She filled the long, empty side wall of the cafe with photos, newspaper clippings, and magazine articles—even *Sports Illustrated* took notice of Waldron's shining season—followed by T-shirts, a team jersey, a "Believe in Blue" towel, and other Mohawk items. As the Grill's collection kept steady pace with Mohawk mania, its position as a community center and fan clubhouse made it the obvious place to display the official IHSAA state championship banner and medal, both gifts of Waldron High School. After perusing the Grill's Victory Wall, head over to the high school to view the trophy, net, and autographed game ball safely enshrined in a glass case inside the entrance.

"If you really want to know about all this stuff, come in at eight thirty in the morning," Tracy tells me. That's when the gaggle of retired guys known as the Liars Club ("because rarely the truth comes out of them") meets to rehash the plays, the games, the season day after day after day. "I don't really know what they talk about because they never let us get close enough to overhear," she laughs.

Most of the Liars Club members are retired farmers used to getting up early, but with sowing and reaping behind them, they now fill hours out of the day with coffee and talk. Sixteen chairs are arranged around the heavy oak table that one of the men crafted from a bowling alley, yet it's not uncommon for another table to be pulled up to make room for even more. By ten o'clock, the Liars Club has thinned out a bit, but by noon the talk is again thick and flowing among newcomers: active farmers and field hands, a local minister or two, utility workers, delivery men, downtown businessmen. "You can set your watch by them rain, snow, shine," Tracy says. "If somebody doesn't show up without letting us know they're not coming, we make a call or send someone to find out if everything's okay."

The Mohawk Grill serves the noon meal until two o'clock, then closes and reopens a few hours later. Unlike most cafes, the Mohawk Grill has a steady evening business, especially from older people who like to eat early and get home before dark. "We're pretty much filled all the time with people, from senior citizens to kids," Tracy says. Since the school is just blocks away, the Grill has become an after-school hangout for both boys and girls, who order "burgers and burgers and fries and more fries."

"Do they do homework?" I ask.

"Not hardly! I've never seen them open a book!"

On weekdays, evenings, and weekends, area residents keep the Mohawk Grill sizzling. Every Friday and Saturday evening, steaks are cooked on a charcoal grill out back. "And that's every Friday and Saturday year-round," Tracy says. "We've even been out there in three feet of snow!" Another evening special that's a big hit is Monday's breakfast for supper, when anything on the breakfast menu—from pancakes to pork chops—is fair game. Popular once-a-month specials are prime rib on the first Saturday and baked liver and onions on the first Thursday. "We've got real liver lovers here. We can go through fifteen pounds of liver a night." On Sundays, the cafe fills up with after-church crowds several times over. They come for the fried chicken, country-fried steak, and one other daily special that changes according to Tracy's whim.

Every day of the week, best sellers include the fresh burgers and hand-breaded tenderloins made from pork processed at Myers Meats in nearby St. Paul, and, of course, the homemade pies and desserts made by Tracy's mother-in-law, Joyce Miller. "She makes pumpkin and rhubarb all year because people ask for it even though they're supposed to be seasonal pies. She also makes sugar cream, chocolate, coconut, and banana cream. They eat them all, but her chocolate chip–pecan pie is so popular it's hard to keep on hand." It was Joyce's sugar cream pie that lingered in the memory of a Wisconsin woman who lunched at the Mohawk Grill while in the area doing genealogical research. "The pie was outstanding and made my day!" she told me three years later.

"Wisconsin?" Tracy asks incredulously. "I didn't know we had customers from so far away!"

Tracy and Kim were already running the general store down the street when they learned the cafe owner planned to close up shop. "We never really thought about running a restaurant, and then my husband had this idea," Tracy recalls. "We just jumped in and had to learn quick!" With all three of their children working here, the Mohawk Grill—named for the winning entry in a community-wide naming contest—is a true family business. When daughter Rachel started her freshman year at Indiana State in Terre

Haute, "she missed the people so much that she came back every weekend to wait tables." The next year, she transferred to Indiana University–Purdue University Indianapolis so she could live at home and work at the Grill.

"The restaurant is hard work," admits Tracy, "but I love it. It really has surprised me. I love it because Waldron is a close community. Everybody knows about everybody, and it's real caring, not busybody."

●●

Next Best Bets

Acton
Ole McDonald's Cafe
11143 Exchange Street
(317) 862-9648
Opened in 2005, this country vittles kind of place features old hand-hewn barn timbers with mortise and tenon joinery. Governor Mitch Daniel proclaims the beef stew among the best he's ever had.

Brooklyn
Brooklyn Grill
6 North Main Street
(317) 831-5336
Located on Brooklyn's one-block, single-sided Main Street, next to the town hall. Talk tabled there is table talk here. Clean, basic, and worth a drop-in if your belly's a rumblin' along State Road 67.

Cicero
Jackson Street Cafe
40 West Jackson Street
(317) 984-7137
Breakfast is a bonanza here, especially on weekends when Morse Reservoir brings boaters and others by the hundreds to this small town in danger of being subsumed by upper-class suburbia.

Fortville
Broadway Diner
426 East Broadway Street (State Road 67)
(317) 485-6120
You won't find five-star atmosphere at this barlike, beside-the-highway eatery, but you will find hometown favorite daily specials. The "wet" tenderloin smothered in brown gravy tickled my funny bone.

MECHANICSBURG
Sigler's Restaurant
8245 State Road 39 North
(765) 325-2477
After peeling potatoes, baking pies, preparing daily specials, and working the grill—in short, doing everything—for the past forty-seven years, George Sigler is looking to retire. He wonders if he'll be able to sell the restaurant started by his father because "young people don't want to work hard today." You'd best get there before he locks the door.

MONROVIA
Amy's Cafe
242 West Main Street
(317) 996-4192
How have area farmers overcome the challenge of eating Amy's substantial tenderloins? (A) By trimming off the overhang and piling it between the buns. (B) By cutting the loin in half to gain mouth access. (C) By maintaining a two-handed grasp at all times. (D) All of the above.

MOORESVILLE
Biff's Pioneer House
14 East Main Street
(317) 831-3899
Biff's food hardly warrants a road trip. Instead, come for the idiosyncratic bismarks—deep-fried cinnamon rolls topped with cream frosting and ground peanuts—created more than seventy years ago from leftover dough.

MORGANTOWN
Kathy's Cafe 🍴
159 West Washington Street (State Road 252)
(812) 597-2729
"I hope that piece isn't the last one" is a common refrain at Kathy's, where people watch the pie board, the waitresses, and their fellow diners as closely as a Colts game tied up late in the fourth quarter. In autumn, don't miss the persimmon pudding and mincemeat pie made with real pork. There's plenty of good eating on the rest of the menu, too.

NEW PALESTINE
Cafe 52
38 West Main Street
(317) 861-5418
A retro, chrome and vinyl, pseudo-fifties look in a converted service station. The beef and noodles served with a yeasty dinner roll and real dairy butter is a Hoosier delight.

WESTFIELD
Marlow's Cafe
112 East Main Street (State Road 32)
(317) 896-3441
A hummer of a breakfast—if you can get in the door. You'll be torn between the biscuits and gravy and the omelets, accessorized with complimentary toast and potatoes. Lunch is primarily burgers, sandwiches, and other short orders. The homemade coleslaw, potato salad, and tartar sauce are stellar.

South Central

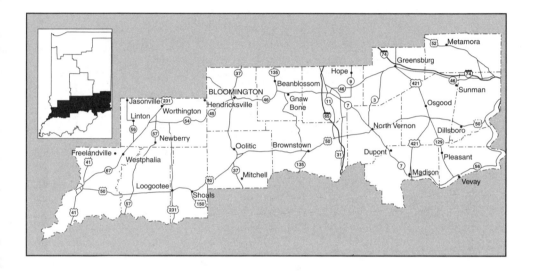

BEANBLOSSOM
Brownie's Bean Blossom Inn
5730 North State Road 135
(812) 988-1147
M–Su 6 A.M.–8 P.M.
Ed "Brownie" and Shirley Brown

Ed Brown, known as Brownie, is a coffee group junkie. "He likes to stop at little restaurants like this and drink coffee," explains his wife, Shirley. "When they close, he gets disturbed because he has to go out and find another one." The last time it happened, Brownie decided the best way to solve the problem was to buy his own restaurant. Closed for several years following the death of its previous owner, the Bean Blossom Inn turned out to be the perfect place to install a permanent coffee group of friends and neighbors.

It wasn't quite that easy. First came months of remodeling, planning, and preparation. "Ed always told me he was going to buy me a restaurant," recalls Shirley, who never took him too seriously. Her only experience with restaurants was eating at them. "I didn't know anything about running one." As just one of many local residents left bereft with the closing of the Bean Blossom Inn, however, Shirley knew the community needed a place for "friendship, visiting, coffee, and talk." To this the Browns added one more requirement: as much food as possible made from scratch. "Ed and I set the standards of home cooking because we know what we like when we go out to eat."

On the first frosty day of fall, I stopped for lunch at the Bean Blossom Inn following my son's cross-country meet in Nashville. After two hours of watching runners wearing little more than shorts and racing singlets, I was the one nearly chilled to the bone. I was glad I'd worn my wool jacket, gloves, and a hat. I opened the door and walked into a roomful of locals abuzz with laughter and talk. When Kimmy came to take my order, I chose the roast pork with dressing special without a second thought. Comfort food, including mashed potatoes and gravy, green beans with bits of bacon, and a warm yeast roll, was just what I needed to warm myself up.

The menu promised that the roast pork would be delicious, and so it was: soft, moist, and well seasoned. The mashed potatoes had just enough lumps to prove they were real. Even the pillowy dinner roll and dressing and gravy, with little transparent puddles of fat, were homemade. Topped off with a piece of chocolate cream pie, the meal transported me back to Sunday dinners at Grandma's house.

Though it is Brownie's restaurant, it's Shirley who runs the place. She does not cook but has been fortunate to find local women with considerable talent and an appreciation for home cooking equal to hers. "They make what they were used to doing at home," Shirley explains matter-of-factly. Pairs of daily specials are rotated throughout the week, so regular customers know which day they should show up for chicken and noodles (Monday), meatloaf (Sunday), salmon patties (Tuesday), or the All-U-Can-Eat catfish feed (Friday) "that brings people in from all over." Other daily specials include lasagna, beans and cornbread, swiss steak, and Sunday's after-church fried chicken.

Perennial top choices off the permanent menu are the hand-breaded tenderloin and beef Manhattan. Tucked into a substantial six-inch bun, the Bean Blossom tenderloin "doesn't hang out all over," says Shirley. The meaty slab of pork that most folks consider undressed without lettuce, tomato, and mayonnaise, handily challenges the pressure-fried tenderloins at the recently closed Food and Fuel in nearby Gnaw Bone praised by *Roadfood* authors Jane and Michael Stern. They're even better with a side of homemade potato chips, something you couldn't find at Food and Fuel. (On the other hand, you won't find gas for your car at the Bean Blossom Inn. Personally, I like to keep my eating and my gassing up separate.)

The Bean Blossom beef Manhattan is a hefty hot sandwich built with seasoned roast beef slow cooked in the oven until it falls away in shreds. "I don't like sliced beef," Shirley asserts, and I have to agree. Two slices of white bread are spread out on a plate, heaped with beef, and topped with two additional slices of bread. Then comes a globe of snowy mashed potatoes and a flood of brown gravy. Shirley is very particular about how to make a perfect Manhattan—and just about everything else—because "I try to do things the way I liked eating it when I went out."

Short cuts are nearly unknown at the Bean Blossom Inn, where even cabbage is chopped by hand for coleslaw. Soups and chili are on the menu year-round, unlike most other Hoosier cafes where they make an appearance only during the winter months. "If chili is off the menu even a few days, they start asking where it is," Shirley says.

It might take a day or two before the regulars start missing the chili, but pie is another story altogether. Keeping the pie case stocked requires making twelve or thirteen pies per week, but even this wasn't quite enough work to keep Wilma Bunch, the Bean Blossom Inn's own pie queen, happily busy. When she passed on her rolling pin to Shirley and the other cooks, they knew they'd have some work to do to match Wilma's magic, especially with the inn's favorite cream pies. They brought in old farm and church cookbooks and experimented with various crust recipes, but "no one's matched Wilma's crust yet," Shirley notes. That isn't to say, however, that the Bean Blossom Inn is bereft of beautiful pies. With its crown of snowy meringue, the single piece of peanut butter cream I see in the glass pie case is as tempting as it is lonely. Somewhere in the kitchen, the daily specials board promises, pecan, chocolate, and fresh strawberry pies are waiting to be cut into pieces and placed in the pie case to keep it company. Other desserts include single-serving chocolate Bundt cake, strawberry rhubarb cobbler, and peach cobbler.

Located on State Road 135 a half mile north of the village of Beanblossom (officially spelled as one word, although the locals prefer it as two), the Browns' cafe is the only one within miles and serves as the local community center. Every morning between seven and eight o'clock, the table closest to the kitchen is filled with coffee drinkers like Brownie—"He's a real cutup," says Shirley—who debate local matters, deplore the cost of health care, and rehash last night's high school ball game. When previous owner Bob Williamson ran the place, a sign reserved the table for the Liars Club between six and eight every morning. The sign came down during the Browns' remodeling, but, Shirley notes, this hasn't kept the Liars from stretching out the morning just the way they were used to. Three other men straggle in every morning at six to jump-start their days with bottomless cups of coffee. "They begged us and begged us to open up at six," Shirley explains. "They drink coffee for an hour before they finally get around to ordering breakfast."

The Browns' extensive remodeling of the Bean Blossom Inn converted the original 1950s-era, side-of-the-road dairy bar into an updated restaurant with knotty pine wainscot and white walls. Outside, gray vinyl siding and a red metal roof gave the old building a much-needed facelift. Inside, new country farm tables mingle with the original Formica tables whose wood-grain tops are worn white in areas by contact with countless elbows and plates. Though it is somewhat plain and eminently practical, the Bean

Blossom Inn is not lacking in humor. On the back wall hangs a sign that reads: "Questions Answered / simple 50¢ / guesses $1.00 / intelligent $2.50 / honest $5.00 / dumb looks are still free." I've seen the same sign in cafes across the state, but it still makes me smile—especially considering its proximity to the Liars Table.

Something I like even better in the Bean Blossom Inn are the wood miniatures of heavy equipment made by local craftsman Donny Alltop, a former patternmaker for the Cummins engine company of Columbus. "They're all pegged—there's no nails—and they all roll," Shirley points out. But there's more: all of the parts that should move do. The steam shovel scoops, the dump truck dumps, the end loader loads, the crane moves up and down. Boys ranging in age from toddlerhood to Liars Club will appreciate Alltop's ingenuity and skill. Take a caterpillar, crane, or semitruck home—they're all for sale—and start your own collection. You'll no doubt be back for more.

BROWNSTOWN
Bessie's Home Cooking
111 East Walnut Street
(812) 358-9000
M–Sa 6 A.M.–7 P.M.; Su 10 A.M.–2 P.M.
Bessie and Bert Stokes
Bessie's Home Cooking is a relatively new cafe with a loyal local following, including the employees of the State Farm office down the street who directed me there. Owner Bessie Stokes operated a tavern here for eleven years before selling the liquor license and leasing the business. When her renter pulled out, she converted the tavern into a restaurant where she could cook to her heart's content. "I got tired of making my living off other people's misery," she says about the tavern business. "I got to the point where I hated to hear the door open."

With its red-framed black and white ceiling and wall panels, red painted concrete floor, and jukebox filled with Fabulous Fifties CDs, the cafe has a pseudo-diner theme. Red and white checked cloths cover the tables, and reproduction advertising tins decorate the walls. The atmosphere is upbeat and energized, like Bessie herself. Try as I will, I can't imagine her as a soured barkeep. She is a mom to everyone who wanders in off the street, including complete strangers like me. As if we have known each other for years, Bessie shares stories, offers me a taste of pickled green tomatoes, and whispers conspiratorially about the matchmaking she has set up between her aunt and a widower. They exchange phone numbers at a table behind me as Bessie watches approvingly from behind the oak counter.

"He said he'll call tonight," her aunt tells Bessie excitedly after the man has left.

As Bessie and I talk, customers and family members flit in and out of the cafe, in and out of our conversation. I am amazed at the demands on Bessie's attention and time. In the forty-five minutes I am in the cafe, an electrician needs her input on the renovation of the back room into a Victorian-themed dining area. Her friend's son seeks advice on setting up a garage sale during the upcoming Watermelon Festival. A Pepsi salesman arrives to take an order. (When he perfunctorily asks Bessie how she is, she replies, "If I was any better, I'd be triplets!") A young woman is looking for her lost wallet and help in making arrangements to pay for and pick up shutters she bought at a yard sale. Fifteen minutes after she leaves, the man who sold her the shutters is asking Bessie's help in finding her! And then there is me, taking notes at the counter until our conversation resumes.

"People call me all the time looking for information, a good deal, the best price for gas, other people. I'm like a community information center," Bessie laughs.

Bessie rules the cafe from behind the oak counter, passing easily between it and the small galley kitchen where she prepares old dishes from memory as well as new dishes from television. "I watch a lot of cooking shows because I like to play with things that are new and different and homemade." She is excited about her plans to add seasoned grits and sauteed shrimp to her new Sunday brunch, where it will compete with chocolate gravy and biscuits, and other more traditional Hoosier favorites. While there are always folks who prefer a fried bologna and egg sandwich, Bessie is confident that her new ideas will be at least moderately well received. "Everybody likes something different, to get away from the humdrum," she says.

With a name like Bessie's Home Cooking, the cafe is guaranteed to please. Count on hand-breaded tenderloins big enough to share, gravy from the roast drippings, even hand-cut, fresh-potato french fries that "never did see a freezer." Other specialties include ham, meatloaf, and country-fried steak.

Sunday dinner features pan-fried chicken and a salad bar stocked with home-made coleslaw, potato salad, macaroni salad, pickled beets, and more.

For breakfast, try Bessie's biscuits and sausage or bacon gravy. The biscuits are not homemade—and for good reason. "I don't know how to do biscuits and yeast rolls," she admits. "Years ago I made a dinner, and everything was beautiful. But a girl bit into a yeast roll and chipped her tooth. My son can testify to that!"

As the lunch rush begins, Bessie and I say our good-byes. On my way back to see what the electricians are up to in the back room, I decide to make a detour to the restroom. As I reach for the door knob, one of the electricians cries out, "Don't go in there!"

"Are you working in here?" I ask uncertainly.

"No, I'm collecting fees. That'll be fifty cents. And if you don't have it, there's a hole right here," he replies, pointing to a drain in the concrete floor.

Immediately I realize I've been punk'd!

BROWNSTOWN
Brock's Family Restaurant
109 North Main Street
(812) 358-3977
M–Sa 5 A.M.–8 P.M.; Su 5 A.M.–3 P.M.
Tom and Gayle (Brock) Gray

At Brock's Family Restaurant, I am surprised to run into Randy Callahan for the second time in less than an hour. I'd been at Bessie's Home Cooking, just around the corner, when he came looking for a young woman who wanted to pay for the shutters she'd set aside at his recent yard sale. "She said she ate breakfast at Bessie's, so that's why I went there," he explains. Apparently, it's not true that everyone knows each other in a small town. On the other hand, there's always someone who knows the people you don't.

Randy's wife, Marge, has worked at Brock's Restaurant for more than thirty years, first for Charles and Leopha Brock, and now for their daughter, Gayle, and her husband, Tom Gray. In 1952, the Brocks opened a little restaurant across from the movie theater and in the 1960s moved to the current location. Today, Brock's Restaurant is somewhat of a southern Indiana institution treasured as much for its history as its enduring commitment to home cooking.

"I've been in and out of the restaurant my whole life," Gayle says as she contemplates a past that has circled around and enclosed her. "I did other jobs—tried to make my own way, you know—but I always came back." As a little girl in the 1950s, she stood on overturned pop cases in order to reach the sink, often washing as many as five or six loads of dishes a day. She also needed help to reach the old-fashioned cash register. "I had to stand on old Pepsi boxes to push the buttons, then I pulled the lever and jumped down so the drawer wouldn't hit me in the chin."

Gayle's most vivid memory of working in the family-owned restaurant may well be Thursdays, the day her dad bought twenty-five chickens from a farm out in the country and prepared them for dinner. "He and Mom would wring their necks in the parking lot behind the restaurant and scald them in boiling water. We'd pick off the feathers, and then they'd singe the chickens over an open flame to get rid of the pin feathers. I hated that so much that I'd hide in the closet, and my dad would have to come and find me."

In addition to preparing fresh chickens for pan frying, Charles and Leopha cut their own steaks and prepared their own tenderloins. "Dad cut the loins," Gayle remembers, "and my job was to pound them flat with a little mallet. I pounded both sides, and then Mom and another lady breaded and stacked them." Today, the tenderloins are made in precisely the same way. And although the chickens are no longer slaughtered and defeathered out back, Tom draws upon his former work as a butcher and continues to buy whole chickens that he cuts himself.

Tom's involvement in the restaurant increased after he retired as an electrician at Cummins engine company in 1999. "For years he told me that when he retired, he wanted to get my mom to teach him how make the pies and yeast rolls," Gayle says. The move from electrician to baker is not as incongruous as it seems. After all, an electrician's schematic and a cook's recipe are both plans for creating something from fundamental parts. Says Tom: "The main thing is the challenge of putting things together and making things happen."

After "kind of a rocky start," Tom conquered the basics of pie making. The hardest thing to master was the crust, especially rolling it out and getting a desirable texture. For a long time, he was limited to only three pies that consistently turned out right, but he gradually expanded his repertoire to forty-nine varieties by building on basic fillings. "I mastered chocolate cream, and then made cherry chocolate by adding maraschino cherries, banana chocolate, and peanut butter chocolate," he explains. A few experiments, like orange cream, a spin-off of his popular pineapple cream, were flat-out rejected by his customers and never appeared again.

Each day, Tom makes between four and eight pies, two of which are always coconut cream and rhubarb. "They're a must-have, seven days a week." More common in southern Indiana than up north, rhubarb has been tops at Brock's Restaurant for many years. "Mom issued a rhubarb pie challenge: if you don't like it, you don't need to pay for it," Gayle says. "There was one man who said he hated rhubarb pie but took the challenge. He scraped his plate clean, and then took three pieces home!" Brock's cherry pie also has many fans. Leopha once received a letter from a South American couple who praised it as the best they ever had; another time, she got a call from the assistant football coach at Michigan State University who hoped she'd tell his wife how to make it over the phone.

Having conquered pie dough and fillings, Tom moved on to yeast rolls and baking powder biscuits, roast pork and baked apples, and other genuine country fare that draws people from near and far. Sunday dinner is no mere meal. It's a destination. Come for baked ham, swiss steak, roast turkey with dressing and gravy from the drippings, pan-fried chicken, and baked sweet potatoes—but be sure to arrive before eleven o'clock. "I think the Presbyterians and Lutherans race to get here," laughs Gayle. "I told them I was going to start staging the amens so they don't get here all at the same time." Those with fried chicken on their mind have no doubt offered a prayer for the pulley bone, or wishbone, and the surrounding pure, moist white meat—what Gayle calls the "fillet of the chicken." As far as she knows, Brock's is the only restaurant in Indiana still serving this choice piece of poultry. In addition to Sundays, pan-fried chicken is also served on Thursdays—as it has been since Gayle plucked feathers as a child.

Brock's celebrates Hoosier farm food by featuring four different specials every day of the week. Try the ham and beans, chicken and noodles, sausage and kraut, and country-fried steak, plus your choice of side dishes from a long lineup that includes real mashed potatoes, homemade salads, noodles, breaded tomatoes, buttered spinach, macaroni and cheese, lima beans, and other vegetables. Breakfast features Tom's homemade biscuits and gravy, omelets, hotcakes, and real-potato American fries. Burgers come two ways: as "regular" ground beef patties (preformed and frozen but with "no fillers," Gayle promises) and "real" patties hand-shaped from fresh ground chuck.

With Brock's Restaurant now into its second half-century, Gayle frequently finds herself contemplating the future. Both of her daughters have careers of their own and are not interested in carrying on the family business. "I have a strong emotional attachment as well as a strong business attachment to the restaurant," she says. "It means a lot to me, and I don't want to let people down. I've been here all my life. There are days I get frustrated and think maybe I'd like to hang up my apron. But I'd also feel guilty. I'd feel that my dad would be disappointed in me."

Gayle is buoyed by the loyalty and friendship of longtime customers— "Our business relies on repeats," she says—including the former owner of the hardware store who used to give her math problems as a young girl, and the late Harold Tormoehlen, who even as a ninety-five-year-old with a walker came every day for lunch. "He'd call if he was going to be gone or if someone else was bringing him dinner," Gayle says. "He'd say, 'Don't worry about me.' On days he couldn't get in, we'd drop something off at his house."

Other valued support comes from loyal, dedicated, longtime employees like Marge Callahan and Mary Sons, who has worked in the kitchen for more than twenty-five years. "We work together. They don't work for me," Gayle points out. Younger employees include high school students like Kourtney Kindred, whose experience led her to culinary school. "She's thinking about going into the bakery business. I told her that since we prepared you to go there, you need to come back and show us a few things." And certainly not least is the praise of customers she has never seen before, like the couple who asked, "Is there any way we could just scoop up this place and bring it to Chicago?"

Running the restaurant day in and day out "can be really frustrating," Gayle admits. "You feel like you're spinning your wheels, and then you hear something like this and think maybe we are doing something special. It warms your heart. I've always thought that when I lose the enthusiasm and sense of accomplishment, I'll know it's time to go."

Note: With great sadness, Gayle reports that her mother, Leopha, passed away on July 18, 2006. The outpouring of sympathy from the community helped ease her grief. "So many people told me stories about how she had helped them in some way, or how they worked their first job for her, and on and on. Of course, at her age and not being at the restaurant for six years, she thought everyone had forgotten about her. Obviously, that was not the case at all."

FREELANDVILLE
Dutchman Cafe
2 South State Road 159
(812) 328-2118
M closed; T–Sa 7 A.M.–2 P.M.; Su 7 A.M.–noon
"Kraut Krew"

Eleven-year-old Clint Pepmeier has never before eaten a Chinese egg roll, but this doesn't prevent him from selecting one from the lunch buffet and placing it on the Oriental plastic plate in his hand, which already holds bright yellow sweet corn, macaroni and cheese, and a piece of good ol' American fried chicken. Clint takes the empty chair next to me at the Roundtable, surrounded by John Clinkenbeard, Gene Williams, Kenny Kixmiller, his father, Bruce Pepmeier, and other men four, five, six, seven times his age.

About ten years ago—no one can remember exactly when—the cafe's owner saw the writing on the brick walls of Freelandville's vacant downtown buildings and decided to throw in the towel. Alarmed by the thought of having no place to loaf and share a meal with friends, a fellow nicknamed Ol' Wag corralled nineteen friends, who put up five hundred dollars each to buy the building and hire a manager.

"Don't remember who they all were to begin with," admits John, one of the nineteen.

"And it went up to a thousand dollars quick enough," remembers Gene Williams, another.

Clint's father, Bruce Pepmeier, who has assumed the share his late father, Herman, put in the cooperative venture, explains, "The cafe is a community project. We just work together to keep it open. It's an informal group. We all just chip in."

The men christened themselves the Kraut Krew in recognition of the community's German heritage, which also explains the cafe's name. That's Dutchman: Dutch as in *Deutsch,* not Dutch as in wooden shoes and tulips. The Dutchman Cafe also commemorates the Freelandville Dutchmen, or

Fighting Dutch, who passed in and out of the neoclassical brick school just a few blocks from downtown until it closed in 1963. After that, the Freelandville kids were sent to the new consolidated school in nearby Edwardsport. Within a few years, the Freelandville school building was torn down.

A member of the Freelandville High School class of 1950, John believes "the closing of the school was the beginning of the town's decline. Then the bank left." With barely a pause to inhale, John rattles off the businesses that made up the Freelandville of his youth. "There were four groceries, four gas stations, three restaurants, two barbershops, a hotel with a continental breakfast, a chicken hatchery, canning factory (tomatoes and pumpkins), two car dealerships, a locally owned bank, feed mill and elevator . . ."

I cannot write fast enough to keep up with his memory.

"What percentage of the town's buildings is vacant?" I ask, attempting to slow him down so I can catch up.

"All of 'em!" replies a man munching fried chicken at the next table. He's wearing a gray shop shirt with a name patch identifying him as Bill.

Retired from Public Service Indiana and now a part-time farmer, John spends four hours almost every morning at the Roundtable. As Freelandville native, free speaker, and a fellow with—apparently—plenty of free time, John both directs and takes a lead role in impromptu Roundtable performances shaped daily by a constantly changing cast of regulars. As men come and go, conversations swing from the local and mundane—weather, crops, grandkids—to the arcane, such as the cost of living in New York City. "My son, a stockbroker, pays twenty-five hundred a month in rent," says John Held. "He pays six hundred dollars a month just for parking!"

It is true that the men of the Roundtable, with its pretty flowered vinyl tablecloth, while away the hours with plenty of idle chatter and friendly banter. But make no mistake. "There is no gossip here," John Clinkenbeard tells me. "It is all the truth. It's all of us concerned about each other."

In the unincorporated town of Freelandville, where the only elected position is that of Widner Township trustee, it is the men of the Roundtable, many of whom sit on the board of the Widner Township Improvement Club, who identify what needs to be done, talk about how it's going to get done, agree on a course of action, raise the necessary funds, roll back their sleeves and contribute hours of hard work, feel satisfaction in the completed project, and then tirelessly repeat the process with what more needs to be done.

"One day we noticed the buildings on the other side of the street falling down," relates John. "We ought to do something about it, we thought. The next day, forty people gave one hundred dollars each, and the buildings were bought for back taxes. We needed a community center and thought it would be a perfect place to build one. We got together with the trustee, who knew the ins and outs of government. We wrote out a grant to build a community center, and our representatives got us Build Indiana funds. We wrote the grant with my daughter's help—she's a grant writer for Vincennes University—and they told us it was the best grant they'd ever seen."

Today, a new community center and fire department occupy the site a block from the Dutchman Cafe. The sheetrock walls are filled with black and white photos of Freelandville graduating classes and sport teams, including the 1941 basketball squad that won the Fighting Dutch their only sectional title. So glorious was that win that it glows in Freelandville even yet. Bruce's dad was a member of that team. "It was one of the highlights of his life," Bruce says. "All those guys. It was one of the bright spots of their lives."

The same civic spirit that keeps the Dutchman Cafe open, built the community center, and preserves and presents the historical past as collective memory is at the root of other impressive achievements. The school site is now occupied by a subsidized housing development and the cooperative Freelandville Community Home offering residential care for seniors. The municipal water system is overseen by a community-owned, not-for-profit organization. Even the insurance company across the street from the Dutchman Cafe is a cooperative business. Says John, "Anything we want to do in this community, we do it. The people who live here are the only ones going to take care of this place."

With the same can-do spirit, the men of the Roundtable placed an ad in the paper and interviewed applicants to replace the cafe's previous manager when she stepped down in late 2005. This is how it happens that the Dutchman Cafe, smack dab in the middle of Hoosier farm country settled by folks of German heritage, is run by two Malaysian sisters, Kene and Kile Wong. This paradoxical pairing of cultures in an otherwise culturally homogeneous small town led to a merging of culinary traditions on the longstanding lunch buffet. Since the Wongs arrived, egg rolls cozy up with mac and cheese, almond cookies with angel food cake, General Tso's chicken with ham and beans and cornbread.

"We lost some business because folks want their German recipes," John explains matter-of-factly. "But we tell the girls what we're hungry for, and then we show them how to make it." He laughs. "Yesterday's fried green tomatoes didn't go over too well."

"Has it been hard learning to cook Hoosier foods?" I ask Kene.

She shakes her head. "American food is much easier than Chinese. I have a few chefs here to help me out! Chinese food takes a lot of time to prepare because it all starts out fresh. American food I can prepare ahead of time and keep it warm. We added Chinese food to the buffet, but all the people here like meat and potatoes."

"That's because they produce it," John points out.

During her time at the Dutchman Cafe, Kene has noted generational differences in taste, with younger people more likely to select Chinese or Mexican food and older ones sticking close to the American food they grew up with, especially burgers, fried chicken, deep-fried chicken livers with milk gravy, meat, potatoes and gravy, and sausage and sauerkraut. ("Do you know what an angry Dutchman is," John asks. "A sour Kraut.")

Next to me at the Roundtable, eleven-year-old Clint has polished off the chicken, corn, and macaroni and cheese he selected from the lunch buffet. Leaning close, I ask if he plans to eat the lone remaining egg roll.

"I didn't know what it was," he explains. He picks up the egg roll, looks at it dubiously, and gamely nibbles at one end. His bite is so tentative that it breaks through only the deep-fried skin.

"I don't like it."

As Bruce and Clint rise from the table, I suddenly realize that not once during my hour- long visit have I seen anyone receive or pay a bill.

"Doesn't anyone get a bill here?" I ask in surprise.

"We just run a tab," Clint tells me, while Bruce shakes his head and shrugs his shoulders.

"How do you know what you owe?"

Bruce smiles.

"Do you have any idea what your two meals cost?"

"No."

I am fumbling for clarity. "How do you know what to pay?"

"I just give her a hundred dollars, and she lets me know when I've run out. I figure they can use the money up front to pay for expenses."

I'm flabbergasted.

The cooperative spirit sure runs wide and deep among these Dutchmen. More power to them.

GREENSBURG

Storie's Restaurant 🍴
109 East Main Street
(812) 663-9948
M–Sa 8 A.M.–7:30 P.M.; Su closed
Don Storie, Chuck Storie, and Beth Storie-Sanders

I came for breakfast and stayed right through lunch, moving from biscuits and gravy to Storie's acclaimed hand-pressed pork tenderloin, coconut custard pie, and scrumptious rhubarb cobbler. Two hours later when I walked out into the hot summer sun, I was toting a whole coconut cream pie in a white pasteboard box. Storie's is an adventure eater's dream. Rarely is a cafe so perfect, an experience so rewarding.

In 1963, Lewis Storie—Don, Chuck, and Beth's father—was tired of work as a supervisor for Colonial Bread and began casting about for a change. With his wife, Katherine, he bought a little restaurant and before long had established a bustling business. He did this three different times before buying out F. H. Keillor, owner of a restaurant on the courthouse square in downtown Greensburg, and settling in for the long haul.

"Dad was Storie's Restaurant," says Don, who took over operation of the family business with Chuck in 1989. "He was a very good people person. He had the kind of personality that drew people in. And Mom was an excellent cook." Together they made Storie's a Greensburg—make that a Hoosier—institution that the brothers are adeptly carrying into the next generation. "It makes us proud to carry on the family business. All we've done is tried not to screw up what our parents left us," Don says.

The secret to Storie's success is really no secret at all: when you've got something good going, change is both foolish and reckless. Continuity is crucial to longevity. Don points out, for example, that all the recipes used in the restaurant "are the same as Mom's." Some are written down and others exist as memories and rhythms passed between Katherine Storie and Bobbette Robbins, who has cooked at Storie's for more than twenty-seven years. Chuck's wife, Jane, has also been a recipient of Katherine's experience.

Jane has been Storie's storied Pie Queen for the past eight or nine years. You can thank her—and believe me, you will!—for the thirty to thirty-five beautiful pies she makes every day. Unless they run out—and believe me, they will!—you can count on peach, apple, and cherry, plus coconut, banana, graham cracker, and butterscotch cream pies. As if this lineup isn't enough, Jane makes a daily "surprise pie" of her choice; it might be chocolate cream, lemon meringue, or today's coconut macaroon—a baked coconut pie "made with a pound of butter and a pound of cream. It's rich, rich, rich," Don says.

As I traveled around the state in search of home cooking in Indiana's small town cafes, people I met gushed, swooned, positively salivated over Storie's pies. For many, a trip down Interstate 74 just isn't bearable without a ramble into Greensburg for pie, regardless of the time of day. People admitted to eating Storie's pie for breakfast ("What's the difference between cherry pie and a cherry Danish?" a Harley rider pointed out), topping off a perfect tenderloin with a wedge of "to die for" graham cracker cream, or stopping midafternoon for pie and coffee for no other reason than a respite from the tedium of an interstate drive.

Don has heard such stories about peripatetic pie eaters many times before. But ask and he'll tell you one of his own, about the day a high school friend flew into the London airport, picked up a copy of *USA Today,* and discovered a front-page column by Craig Wilson about Storie's Restaurant and Jane's "quite spectacular" lemon meringue pie. ("I would've ordered rhubarb but there were strawberries in it," Wilson complained.) You can read the entire column for yourself. Don and Chuck have a framed copy hanging on the front wall.

Storie's Wall of Fame also includes other articles, awards, and recognition, including a travel story from the *Indianapolis Star* (the journey begins with breakfast at Storie's Restaurant); a Reader's Choice Award for Best Tenderloin from the *Electric Consumer*; Best Dessert, Pie, and Tenderloin awards from readers of the *Greensburg Daily News*; and a 2005 Hoosier Hospitality Award for excellence in hospitality and dedication to service and quality presented by Lieutenant Governor Becky Skillman. By all accounts, Storie's Restaurant is one of the finest cafes in the state, and it deserves the compliments. "This is the kind of business you put your heart and soul in," Don says in appreciation for the honors. "It doesn't hurt to get a pat on the back every now and then."

As the awards attest, it would be a severe oversight to bypass what Don humbly calls "regular diner food" in your rush to get to the pie. There are treasures in every part of Storie's menu. Two specials are prepared fresh every day on a rotating schedule to keep the regulars returning for their favorites. Mondays are reserved for meatloaf and smoked sausage and kraut, a fairly recent addition that has gone over very well. On Tuesday, you'll find chicken-fried steak and old-fashioned ham and beans served with hot corn bread. Baked pork tenderloin and dressing shows up on Wednesday along with chicken tenders. Thursday brings baked ham and pan-fried chicken, with the workweek closing out with swiss steak and salmon patties or battered cod. Saturdays always feature barbecued ribs and one other cook's-choice special. Every day of the week, typical side dishes include a choice of two vegetables—"one of which is always green"—homemade salads such as coleslaw, macaroni, potato, and fruited Jell-O, and, of course, mashed potatoes. They're made from instant pearls doctored with milk and real butter. "We tell people the mashed potatoes aren't real, and they frown, but once they taste them, they're sold," says Don.

Among Storie's varied menu, Don counts the pan-fried chicken and pork tenderloin as top tickets. Every Thursday, Don's wife, Annie, coats two hundred fifty to three hundred pounds of fresh chicken pieces with dry breading and drops them in hot oil, hand turning each breast, wing, thigh, and leg until it's golden brown and crispy. "It's a tradition that comes from Mom's day," he explains. That's a lot of chicken, but, amazingly, the amount of tenderloins prepared and sold surpasses it. It requires five hundred pounds of fresh pork loin every week to meet the constant demand. Storie's acclaimed five- to six-ounce tenderloins are hand cut and tenderized, soaked in a mixture of milk and egg, dredged in flour and seasonings, and then dropped into the deep-fat fryer. Each and every one is flattened to order, so you can have yours as thick or as thin as you like. "For some people, the bigger the better," Don says, holding his hands in a circle the size of a dinner plate. "It's the eye appeal thing." Other people—like me—prefer a meaty, moist tenderloin that nestles nicely into a decent sized bun.

From its location in the center of town, just opposite the Decatur County Courthouse—which is famous for the tree that grows from the roof of its tower—Storie's Restaurant is an important community center. Townspeople gather to share the latest news (that new Honda plant!), strengthen friendships, connect with highway travelers and neighbors from the surrounding towns, and conduct business. "Over the years, there's been a lot of businesses and farms sold here," Don notes. The restaurant is also popular with politicians who know where the crowds can be found. Governor Mitch Daniels has dropped in to share coffee and talk, and state legislators Cleo Duncan and Robert Jackman regularly meet here. Duncan also holds town meetings at Storie's to discuss property taxes, economic development, daylight saving time, and other matters of interest and importance to local voters.

Without a doubt, Storie's Restaurant plays many important roles in the Greensburg area community—not the least of which is represented by the row of decorated coffee cans at the register. When you're paying your bill, drop a few extra coins in the cans. You, too, can help elect this year's Little Miss Tree City. I couldn't resist voting for Mollie, whose can was wrapped in purple paper frilled up with glitter and lace and this hand-lettered campaign slogan: "My name is Mollie / Cute as a Dolly / Vote for me, I'll be Jolly."

HOPE
Sugar Shak
310 Jackson Street
(812) 546-2253
M–Sa 6 A.M.–8 P.M.; Su closed
Jackie Miller
Founded by Moravians in 1829, Hope is "A Surprising Little Town" of twenty-five hundred people centered on a grassy public square that is home to a small museum dedicated to rural mail delivery. Peer through the glass windows to get a glimpse of earlier days, when letter carriers such as James Rose of Borden "carried a gun to ward off thugs." Then amble around town and discover the modern—architecture, that is: the 1958 Irwin Union Bank and Trust designed by Harry Weese and the more recent Hope Library and Hope Elementary School. Both are products of the Cummins Engine Foundation, a unique architectural program that connects world-class architects with Bartholomew County public agencies.

Hope is indeed a surprising blend of history and modern day, as is the Sugar Shak on the north side of the public square. In 2002, Jackie Miller and a friend opened a small bakery here, in the same building that had long been occupied by Frank Hall's restaurant. "We called it the greasy spoon," remembers Jackie, a Hope native who grew up in the Moravian church. When it became apparent that a bakery wasn't going to be enough to pay the bills, the Sugar Shak expanded into a full cafe. Jackie carried on alone after her partner departed, claiming the business and the space as her own by filling it with store fixtures and items from the drugstore her parents ran for many years. "Mom and Dad kept everything," Jackie explains, showing me a pressed glass Green River dispenser from the drugstore's soda fountain. A massive oak wall case is filled with other drugstore collectibles, including mortars and pestles, a one-gallon Coke syrup container, a peanut jar, and pieces of hobnail Vaseline glass.

As the daughter of longtime business owners, Jackie is well known in the Hope community, especially among the older residents who have assumed a kind of parental role since the death of her parents. Many of the recipes she uses in the cafe come from "older women around town who swore me to secrecy," Jackie says. "They told me, 'We're giving these to you because we raised you.' And there's a whole lot of people had a hand at raising me."

Other customers and residents help out by scouring flea markets, yard sales, and thrift stores for good used dishes, tableware, cups, and glassware that Jackie uses in the restaurant. "I had one guy who broke a cup, and two days later he brought in two boxes of cups to replace it," Jackie laughs. "One guy started bringing in little bowls. He loved that because he said he finally had a reason to go to all the thrift stores. I always have new things coming in. We don't go for the matching things at all here!"

Though Jackie is the owner of the Sugar Shak, she sometimes wonders if her customers are really running the place. When the regular ten thirty and three o'clock coffee groups began complaining that their table was too small, Jackie had a new one made. Known as the Knowledge Table and the BS Table—"and believe me, sometimes it's so deep around there that you need hip boots!"—the new table has an oak top securely mounted to a vintage cast iron pedestal. Its octagonal shape makes it easy for eight men to pull up a chair, and another eight to fill in the corners. "There's quite a few days they're stacked two deep," Jackie says.

At two o'clock on a steamy midsummer afternoon, the Sugar Shak is in a lull. Lunch is over and the coffee group hasn't yet arrived in full force, although a handful of men are warming up by shooting the breeze over deep glasses of Coke and ice water. When one spots the town hearse drive past out front, he and Jackie debate its destination and the identity of the recently deceased. "I've got a pretty good idea who it is," Jackie confides as she tells me about the two funerals she'll be attending tonight and tomorrow. With a window on main street, the Sugar Shak is the living newspaper of Hope, and Jackie is its editor. "If people want to know something, they ask me. If I don't know, I tell them I'll find out."

A few minutes later, the hearse is again spotted, this time heading in the opposite direction. Jackie sighs with relief. "It's just running an errand," she concludes.

With the help of Carroll "Cookie" Stroup, a navy veteran with thirty-five years of baking and cooking experience, Jackie regularly furnishes pies to Norman Funeral Home across the street, which provides them to family members during visitations. Cookie returned to Hope after retiring from the navy and ran a filling station until he joined Jackie a few years ago. "He got his nickname when he was a boy, kind of like his profession was made for him from the get-go," Jackie says.

In constant demand "because there's no place in town to get home-made," the Sugar Shak's lineup of baked goods includes pie and cake and everything in between: cookies, cheesecake, cobblers, cinnamon rolls, Danish, donuts, and long johns. I swooned over the peanut butter pie, a heavy vanilla custard zipped up with peanut butter nuggets and topped with a meringue made extra buoyant and sweet with the addition of minimarshmallows. Despite my gender, my addiction for pie qualifies me for the three o'clock coffee group, whose members make it a regular part of the ritual. All that is, but Walter, whose doctor has ordered him to have "no more pie."

"Just take me out and shoot me," commiserates a fellow coffee drinker, fork poised over a wedge of cherry pie.

For those like Walter, who settles for a fried egg sandwich, and others who insist on more substantial fare as a preamble to pie, the Sugar Shak delivers daily specials—roast turkey and dressing, meatloaf, country-fried steak, and other Hoosier reliables—that fill up even the hungriest of farmhands. It is a hard-working, working-class kind of cafe built on meat and potatoes daily specials and quality Black Angus burgers hand-pattied from fresh meat in a whopping twenty-one varieties—everything from a plain patty on a bun to the Shak burger piled high with grilled onions, mushrooms, barbecue sauce, and swiss cheese. Other don't-miss items include the homemade biscuits and gravy, made fresh every morning, and the hand-breaded and tenderized tenderloin. You'll get a substantial slab of pork at the Sugar Shak, not a barely there wafer valued more for its diameter than its flavor.

Although the regular menu, repertoire of daily specials, and lineup of baked goods is extensive, Jackie is always open to new suggestions. "If someone has a recipe they want us to try, we'll do it," she says. Often the new is really something old, as in the old-fashioned vinegar pie requested by one woman. "I tested recipe after recipe on her until she finally said, 'This is it.' It was a pie that she grew up with in the Depression days, something you made when you had nothing. And when I tasted it, I was surprised. It wasn't bad. Now we make two vinegar pies for her every year."

Another special request was for old-fashioned jam cake, a recipe for which Jackie "looked and looked. I have cookbooks clear back to the 1700s in a collection begun by my grandmother and mother, and I couldn't throw any of them away. I finally found a couple of recipes for jam cake and made one for this lady who requested it. That cake must have weighed fifteen pounds. She took it for Christmas and everyone loved it. They said it tasted just like Grandma's."

Jackie refers to these special requests as "taste memories," sensual images of the past that cannot be forgotten but are not easily reclaimed. They linger and persist over time because they are closely associated with certain periods of one's life, specific places, a historical event, a dear family member, a holiday or other special occasion. When Jackie accepts the challenge of a request for vinegar pie, jam cake, chess pie, or redeye gravy, she accepts the challenge of restoring history and tradition to those for whom it is most meaningful. By her own admission, she is a saver, a collector, a person who can "never throw anything away."

JASONVILLE
Sharon's Kountry Kitchen
101 East Main Street
(812) 665-4177
M–Tu closed; W–F 11 A.M.–8 P.M.; Sa 7 A.M.–8 P.M.; Su 7 A.M.–2 P.M.
Bill and Sharon Boyd
Update: Sharon and Bill Boyd closed the doors of their Jasonville restaurant in December 2006. "We decided to take life easier and enjoy doing things we never could," Sharon explains. "I cried the day that I locked the door, but I don't regret it one bit." The restaurant is for sale.

At two o'clock on one of the hottest July days on record, Sharon Boyd sits down with a glass of iced tea and reflects on the past years. It was in June 1997 that she and her husband, Bill, packed up their house in Evansville and moved back to Jasonville, her hometown, to take over operation of her brother's Main Street restaurant. She'd dreamed of running a bed and breakfast but when her brother got ill, she turned to Bill and said, "I think I could run that restaurant." Bill agreed, and so they headed north.

Between the two of them, they'd already put in years of work at a variety of jobs. Sharon worked at the AMAX Minnehaha coal mine for eleven years, nearly half of them as a single mother supporting five children by operating an overburden drill. When she married Bill and the mines closed, they moved to Evansville and ran a Snap-on tools franchise. From heavy labor to sales and heavy service, they learned to work hard, work honest, and manage money. Sharon is quick to add three other rules for their current success: "Keep the restaurant clean, serve good quality food, and treat people as friends."

"You know why I like this business?" Bill asks me without pausing for an answer. "It's a challenge. Every day is different. I've worked the mines, Snap-on, and let me tell you. This is the easiest job I've ever had."

Satisfaction comes from a job well done, the proof of which comes from a growing number of loyal customers and recognition by area newspapers, such as the tribute by readers of the *Terre Haute Tribune-Star* hanging on the wall. In April 2005, Sharon's Kountry Kitchen was voted the Wabash Valley's Best Bargain in the restaurant category in recognition of Sharon's coupon for 15 percent off your next meal. The restaurant has also been featured in several Indiana restaurant guidebooks. Sharon carries copies of these books to the table, fans out the pages, and reads excerpts from what has been written about her cafe. She is proud of the renown the Kountry Kitchen has garnered, yet at the same time is slightly amazed. "I just do what I do," she says. "When this book came out, press releases went out all over the state. I'd get people staying at the park from Indianapolis, northern Indiana, Gary. People came from all over. They'd say, 'We saw a little clipping in the paper.' Then one day I got a call from the Terre Haute TV station saying they'd like to come out that afternoon. I said, 'Give me a little time to get myself together. My restaurant is always ready.'

"I tell people, 'If I getcha once, I'll getcha twice.'"

The publicity helped to bring in business the Kountry Kitchen wouldn't otherwise have enjoyed, and that provided a short-lived boom because, Sharon concedes, "we cannot survive on the locals." She admits that running a restaurant—or any business—in a town the size of Jasonville is a difficult prospect. "You have to operate on pennies and keep your bills paid." Out-of-towners are often surprised to discover a good restaurant in a town that, like other small towns throughout the state, has experienced a dramatic decline in recent years.

On the wall above our table hangs a collection of historic photos showing a far more vital Jasonville, with prospering businesses stretched out along Main Street, cars bumper to bumper along the curb. Outside the front window, the view today is considerably bleaker. Buildings stand empty and neglected. A recent downtown revitalization that accompanied the widening of the state highway has left brick sidewalks and pretty reproduction lampposts but has contributed nothing to the local economy.

Sharon sighs. "Jasonville is the Gateway to Shakamak State Park. I'd like to see the downtown buildings filled with shops. People go camping and want something to do, so let's get them to drive into town. If I could only get the other folks on Main Street to see my vision, we could have a little gold mine."

Until then, the town's greatest draw will remain the nearby state park and Sharon's Kountry Kitchen, where darned near everything is made from scratch. Every morning, Sharon prepares two or three noon specials and repeats the feat again each evening. She plans menus months ahead of time, spacing things out so meatloaf and swiss steak don't appear so frequently that the regulars get bored. "I had a much larger menu of specials than I do now," she explains, "but Bill condensed it down to what they want." Eliminating a hundred alternatives made things a bit easier, but it doesn't mean that Sharon has eased up. She remains committed to making her own sauces—spaghetti, barbecue, tartar, shrimp—and coleslaw dressing, as well as soups, chili, gravies, even homemade noodles in batches so big that each one requires ninety-six eggs.

"That's a lot of noodles!" I exclaim. "Why go to such an effort? Why not buy Amish noodles?"

She pooh-poohs my suggestion. "Because mine are a lot better. I use my mother's recipe."

Everything Sharon makes she makes in such quantity that "ninety-six is a magic number, it seems." It takes a lot of food to feed the steady stream of customers who day in and day out demand her best-selling meatloaf, biscuits and gravy, chicken-fried steak with milk gravy, beef barbecue, beans and corn bread, and liver and onions. "I have a call list for liver and onions," she says. "I've got a lot of working men who like that and older people who don't want to make it for just one person." Other favorites include Bill's specially seasoned steaks and pork chops prepared with or without Sharon's secret barbecue sauce, all-you-can-eat fried fish and fried chicken dinners available every day of the week, and homemade tenderloins. Sharon shows me a frozen one waiting to be ordered and dropped into the deep fryer. It is so flat, so big, so pale that it reminds me of a pizza crust. Cooked and served in a bun, it extends past the rim of a plate by at least four inches all around.

Lighter eaters will relish the specialty salads, so rare in small town cafes that they're practically nonexistent. Tuck your napkin under your chin and dive into the grilled Hawaiian chicken breast salad made with pineapple ginger chicken and grilled pineapple, the southwest mesquite chicken salad made with mesquite-seasoned grilled chicken, or the chef salad featuring diced Amish ham. Even the everyday side salad is extraordinary. Sharon layers a mixture of chopped iceberg lettuce and leaf lettuce with green pepper, red onion, carrots, red cabbage, and tomatoes and serves it with your choice of dressing. "People always tell me, 'Gee, this is such a nice salad,'" she notes with pride.

There are a few things that Sharon doesn't make from scratch, it turns out. "I'm not gonna lie and tell you that I did," she admits when she points out that my cabbage roll comes frozen. Pies and desserts are another thing she sidesteps in her pursuit of home-cooked specials. "I started out making pies but couldn't keep up with the demand," she explains without apology. Instead, she stocks the refrigerated glass case with the best bakery pies, cheesecakes, and specialty desserts she can find.

As good as the food is, at Sharon's Kountry Kitchen the gawking may be even better. The yellow pine walls are filled nearly inch to inch with themed collections that reflect Sharon's and Bill's individual lives, their life together, and that of the Jasonville community. Altogether, the decor is a marvel to behold.

"Did you have a plan when you started?" I ask, my eyes roaming over the walls.

"I'm not a planner like that, honey," Sharon laughs. "It just took its natural course!"

She takes me on a tour of the cafe, starting with a series of faded color photographs that show a younger Sharon working the overburden drill at the Minnehaha Mine. Next is a collection of old black and white photographs showing a younger Jasonville: a view of a crowded Main Street looking east, a portrait of "Uncle Billy Buckallew" who christened the town when, way back in 1855, he picked up a paddle, dipped it into a tar bucket, and wrote the words Jason Ville on the side of Jason Rogers's store. In 1958 the town celebrated its centennial, with banners flying up and down Main Street. Look up: one of the blue and white banners is affixed to the ceiling. That same year, Sharon graduated from nearby Midland High School. The vinyl records, album covers, and paper cutouts of musical instruments on the cafe's ceiling were used as decoration for the annual reunion of the Midland High School Class of 1958. "Since we've had one every year for the past three years, I decided to leave them up," Sharon explains matter-of-factly. The next reunion is just weeks away.

Elsewhere in the cafe you'll find Longaberger baskets (a mere fraction of Sharon's collection), old family photos, Snap-on collectibles, "stuff for the classic car guys," "stuff for the fisherman," and stuff for just about anyone else with any specific interest at all. Can you pick out the autographed color photo of Bruce Borders, the former mayor of Jasonville and Elvis impersonator who bills himself as the Mayor of Rock and Roll? He's now a state senator. Sports fans will naturally gravitate to the cheer corner behind the locals-only coffee table, where Xeroxed clippings of old news-paper stories brag about the athletic conquests of the Midland Middies, the Jasonville Yellowjackets (the 1926 football state champs), and the Coalmont Cardinals, teams that, in 1960, consolidated along with their community schools to form the Shakamak Lakers.

Sharon waves her hand over a small collection of Indiana University athletic memorabilia, including a pair of socks slightly soiled from the backs of the coffee drinkers who come and go from the table more regularly than the waitress. Pinned to the wall, the socks hold up the shoulders of a black Boilermakers T-shirt.

"You see this?" Sharon asks. "They're walkin' all over Purdue."

You're in IU country now.

LOOGOOTEE
Hunt's Steamer Cafe
112 West Main Street
(812) 295-4774
M–Sa 5 A.M.–2 P.M.; Su closed
Sandra Sue "Sue" Hunt
Update: Lisa and Carl Wiscaver took over the cafe on April 1, 2007, rechristening it Country Steamer Cafe. Phone number and hours remain the same.
A few years ago, fire destroyed everything but the façade of the building next door to Sue Hunt's Steamer Cafe. The window and door openings are now hollowed out eyes with nothing behind them. Sadly, tragically, the building is a metaphor for Loogootee's historic downtown, now virtually abandoned for the commercial sprawl along U.S. Highway 50/150—Loogootee's new Main Street.

At one o'clock on a Wednesday in late August, just days after Hurricane Katrina submerged New Orleans, Sue stands inside the kitchen and talks with customers through the pass-through window. Her sister Charlotte waits tables. Charlotte is a celebrity of sorts, having been featured in a front-page photograph in the *Indianapolis Star* in early 2005. The picture accompanied an article about the possible closing of the nearby Crane Naval Surface Warfare Center. "That worry is no longer," Charlotte says. "Now the worry is the price of gas. How is anyone going to go out to eat with gas prices the way they are?"

A man stopping by to pick up a takeout order commiserates: "The Sunday afternoon drive? They ain't gonna be anymore."

The price of gas is just the latest in a long line of threats to the Steamer Cafe, a pre–World War II–era diner as perfect and pretty as a calendar picture. Occupying the first floor of a late-nineteenth-century lodge hall, the cafe is easily recognized from the street by the vintage Coca-Cola sign above the front door. It reminds me of the observation of my son, Pete, who as an astute four-year-old accompanying me on my first *Cafe Wisconsin* adventure in 1991, told me, "You know, Mom, it's easy to find a small town cafe. You just go down the main street and look for the pop sign hanging over the sidewalk."

Step inside the deep, narrow cafe, and you'll find one of the finest counters in the state: a long, inviting icon with black-topped stools on pedestals as slender and sexy as a pinup girl's gams. Take a seat and pluck a menu from the classic stainless steel holders clipped to the counter's inside, the kind that also hold the napkin boxes and salt and pepper shakers. Order a malt made with the mint green Myers Bullet Mixer in front of you, all the while taking in the wall-mounted glass pie case, the Kold Milk stainless-steel milk dispenser, and other vintage behind-the-counter accoutrements.

Defying its age, the Steamer Cafe has an almost aseptic appearance due to Sue and Charlotte's daily cleaning, its lack of heavy customer use, and the fire that destroyed the neighboring building, which necessitated extensive cleaning and redecorating. With the exception of a row of stainless-steel coat hooks behind the counter and a Loogootee High School athletic schedule posted near the door, the walls are empty. But before the fire, they were filled with framed photographs that Sharon now keeps in two plastic shopping bags, treasured memories of more than forty years in business.

Sue empties the bags onto the table in front of us and shuffles through the photographs. Here's one of Larry Bird, another of Birch Bayh. Look here: portraits of her beautiful daughters as teenage contestants in local and state Miss 4-H pageants. A picture of her husband, John, as Martin County sheriff, a position he held for ten years. John's parents in their wedding finery. And, oh! A faded black and white photo of Gussie's Diner—a predecessor to the Steamer Cafe—taken during World War II. I study the image and see the same counter, the same stools. Gone are the men in suits and hats, the women employees in white dresses. Gone, too, is the Art Deco–inspired mirrored backbar framed by Coca-Cola advertising pieces. "All that Coca-Cola stuff was here when my sister Iris and I bought the place in 1965," Sue says. "I threw all that old greasy stuff away!" She realizes that today its value would be considerable. If only she'd known. If only she'd kept it.

Over the past forty-two years—two-thirds of Sue's life—she has seen seemingly insignificant items become valuable and once valuable items depreciate significantly. She doesn't mince words. Times are tough in the cafe. "Survival. That's what it is now," she says.

"Do you see the end in sight?" I ask.

"Oh, yes. I see the end coming. People want to buy me out and make a pizza place, but I'd just as soon close it. Nobody else will take it and work forty-two years like I have. My kids can't understand. They tell me, 'Mom, people make seventy-eight thousand dollars a year. Why do you want to work for nothing?'"

"Oh, sure, I'm proud of the Steamer Cafe," she continues. "I'm proud of the people before me. It was probably the same way with them. They probably saw the writing on the wall, and I was the one who saved them!"

Publicity from the *Indianapolis Star* photograph brought new people from across the state to the Steamer Cafe, briefly energizing Sue, Iris, and Charlotte and validating their dedication to both the diner and its regulars. Over the years, there have been other such customers carried in by a serendipitous breeze. They came the first time by chance or by word of mouth and came back by choice. Sue recalls with lingering amazement the day an Australian motorcyclist riding across America dropped in for a bite to eat. He brought his family the next year en route to the Sturgis, South Dakota, motorcycle rally. "Oh, matey," he told Sue, "New York and San Francisco can fall into the ocean. Give me southern Indiana and Tennessee, and I would stay right here."

There's also the Purdue cycling club that spends a week training in the hills of south central Indiana every year, and a professor from Baltimore who came with his wife, a native of India. From near and far, they all fell in love with the Steamer's authentic looks and Sue's equally authentic cooking—what she calls "old-fashioned, home-cooked meals."

Today's specials include pork chops, roast pork, and country-fried steak, all served with a choice of three sides: buttered corn, green beans, macaroni and tomatoes, coleslaw, pickled beets, and mashed potatoes and gravy. "Are the potatoes real?" a woman at the next table asks Charlotte as she stands with order pad in hand. She must be a first-timer if she doesn't know the answer is a resounding yes. The day's desserts include coconut cake and pear cobbler—something I couldn't resist because I'd never before encountered it. (A word from the wise: when faced with choices, anything different is bound to be good.) Made with fresh pears, not canned, and topped with a buttery cakelike mixture, the warm pear cobbler was the perfect follow-up to the pan-fried chicken I'd eaten for lunch just a half hour ago at Velma's Diner in Shoals.

Sue's drop-in customers bolster her spirit, but it's her local regulars that have sustained the Steamer Cafe all these years. Their loyalty is as firmly rooted as her own. "I see the writing on the wall, but I don't want to let people down," she confides. "Where will they eat if they can't come here? The fast food restaurants? Who wants to eat there all the time?"

She attributes the decline of the Steamer Cafe to several sources, not the least of which is the cookie cutter burger barns and chicken huts stretched out along the highway. "Some lady asked today, 'You always used to have fried chicken. When are you going to have fried chicken?' But that was before KFC came in and before Buehler's started selling chicken out of the deli," Sue says. Another change occurred about ten or fifteen years ago when the high school went to a closed campus and kids that used to stream in for lunch were confined to the cafeteria. Then the town's two factories closed, taking a large portion of Sue's remaining lunch crowd—and the before- and after-work crowds—with them.

"What is this town going to do?" Sue asks with a slight shake of her head, as much resigned as discouraged. "I saw the cleaners go, the drugstore go, other businesses go. One day people will wake up and see that for a small town we have a lot to offer. And then they will say, 'I wish we still had that little cafe.'"

MITCHELL
The Chicken Inn
641 West Main Street
(812) 849-9350
Su–W 6 A.M.–6 P.M.; Th–Sa 6 A.M.–8 P.M.

Dave and Rosalie Hardin, owners
Heather Hardin Sorg, manager
Update: Fin Mill's Family Restaurant, owned by Tammie Finnegan, opened
December 9, 2006.

Rosalie Hardin and her husband, Dave, bought the Old Mill Inn in Mitchell's pretty-as-a-picture downtown in May 2005. As longtime owners of the Chicken Inn in Shelbyville, they had been considering a second location when their daughter, Heather, a Cambellsburg resident, learned that the Old Mill Inn was up for sale. "When I first walked in, it felt like home," remembers Rosalie. "It had just the type of environment we're trying to make."

With its impressive neon sign overhanging the sidewalk, the cafe has been a Mitchell landmark since its founding in the 1930s by Bill Cargas, a Greek immigrant. Many of the older folks in town grew up in the local hangout, sharing Cokes and burgers with friends after school, working their first job as grill cook or waitress, or eating dinner on trips into town from the family farm. "There are lots of 'remember when' conversations going on in here. People love to come in and relive history and tradition," Rosalie says.

As recent additions to the community, the Hardins rely on their customers to fill them in about Mitchell's past and present and are actively seeking old photos and other material pieces of the town's past to hang on the wall. Rosalie says, "I went to a yard sale and found a 1954 high school yearbook. I know some people will think I shouldn't have, but I cut out pages and hung them on the wall. Our customers love to look at them, and have started bringing in things from home."

The Hardins plan to make the original cafe—the room with the counter and stools—"into a 1950s-type diner because that's the period most of our customers remember," Rosalie says. "We recently bought a jukebox because there used to be one here. Down in the basement we found some pieces of the original song selection boxes that used to hang in the booths, and we also found some lamp globes. It feels like we bought a treasure box when we bought this place." Other plans include a wall mural to be painted by grill cook and artist Steven Gilbert; it will depict a 1950s diner with a bright neon sign circled by hot rods and classic cars.

The cafe was expanded in the 1970s when the neighboring building was remodeled into a dining room. With the original wood floor exposed and refinished, barn red lower walls and white upper walls, and a growing flock of decorative chickens—framed prints, figures on shelves, chicken clocks, you name it—the Chicken Inn's dining room is a clean, casual blend of country and class. You won't find red and white checked vinyl tablecloths here, but would you have expected white linen pressed under sheets of heavy glass?

Despite the old cafe's new look—or perhaps because of it—it didn't take long for the locals to be convinced of the Hardins' commitment to both the restaurant and the community. "I think they were a bit skeptical at first, but they continued to see us working here every day, and we showed them that we weren't going to make many changes to the way things had been run. They're comfortable with us and have really made us feel like part of the community. It didn't take as long as I thought it would," Rosalie says.

It's a good thing, too, what with Mitchell's Persimmon Festival just a few weeks off. Held the last full week of September since 1946, the festival activities and special events bring thousands of people to historic downtown Mitchell, listed on the National Register of Historic Places in 1999. The queen and princess pageants, Sunday parade, carnival, and athletic and fine arts competitions highlight the festival for some, but for a coterie of local women, the focus of the week is on only one thing: the persimmon pudding contest. For years, the winning recipes have been shared with the public, but one secret is rarely if ever divulged: the location of the persimmon tree that supplied the winner's fruit.

In anticipation of her first Persimmon Festival and the onslaught of customers it will bring, Rosalie and her staff have been "packing away the persimmon pulp for weeks. By the time the festival starts, I think we'll be ready." She is grateful that the cafe's previous owner passed on her recipe—as well as a few others—because persimmon pudding was not made at the Shelbyville Chicken Inn. It's since been added, so that now, Rosalie explains, "there's a part of Shelbyville here and a part of Mitchell there."

The two Chicken Inns—one in the Indianapolis metro area and the other in southern Indiana—provide Rosalie with a regional perspective on what Hoosiers like to eat. While the menu is virtually the same at both locations, her Shelbyville customers eat chicken and noodles without squawking. Her Mitchell customers prefer chicken and dumplings. "They asked for chicken and dumplings," she laughs, "so now we have them both."

As a native Minnesotan unaccustomed to either dish, I'm amused that Hoosiers distinguish so closely between the two. From my upper-midwestern cultural viewpoint, they're darn near the same thing: chicken and broth and bits of simmered dough. A taste test pitting chicken and noodles and chicken and dumplings head to head was surely in order. Imagine the surprise of my teenage waitress when I order a cup of each.

"A cup of chicken and noodles *and* a cup of chicken and dumplings?" she asks.

"A cup of each," I answer resolutely. I explain my mission, but she returns only a polite, vacant smile.

I detect only two significant differences between the two: the shape of the dough and the thickness of the broth. Quite honestly, I could have substituted noodles for dumplings without the slightest hesitation. The matter is resolved (in my mind at least).

I move on to the next course: the Chicken Inn's famous pressure-fried Broaster chicken. Keeping the comfort of my pants in mind, I order a leg and a wing.

"A leg *and* a wing?" my waitress asks, clearly wondering if I'm going to nibble my way through dinner.

"Yes, and a side of coleslaw and some persimmon pudding."

The chicken is moist and meaty with a crispy, well-seasoned skin— "Broasting seals in the juices," Rosalie says—and the coleslaw homemade just as the menu promised. But trumping everything else is the persimmon pudding, in a slab big enough to share with a friend but far too good to share honestly. It lacked only a huge dollop of sweetened real whipped cream to be absolute perfection.

"The Chicken Inn is not a fancy place. We're just a good home-cooking restaurant," says Rosalie. It certainly is. You'll find regular daily specials throughout the week, such as Monday's ham and beans with corn bread and fried potatoes, Wednesday's beef Manhattan, and Friday's fried walleye. Saturdays are generally unscripted—sirloin tips are popular—but Sundays set the stage for preacher's-coming-for-dinner meals like roast pork and dressing. Everyday on-the-menu favorites include the Broasted chicken, available by the piece and by the bucket; barbecued baby back ribs; ribeye and sirloin steaks, and hand-cut, tenderized, and breaded tenderloins. "They're really gaining in popularity because people are learning we make our own,"

Rosalie says. Side yours with sweet potato fries or a bowl of french onion, beef vegetable, or potato soup.

You won't want to skip the fried biscuits and homemade apple butter, a southern Indiana specialty that the Hardins fell in love with at a Nashville restaurant and then added to their own menu. If they don't satisfy your sweet tooth, there's always dessert. Besides persimmon pudding, the Chicken Inn specializes in homemade strawberry pie, strawberry shortcake, and pumpkin pie in season. (Not all the pies are homemade, so ask before you order.) And the old soda fountain from Cargas Cafe is stocked with real ice cream. How about a hot fudge sundae supreme? Kids will love the clown sundae—a scoop of ice cream with a cone hat and M&M eyes.

Breakfast can be a bowl of oatmeal or grits, a helping of biscuits and gravy, or a simple fried egg and toast—or it can be any one of eleven combination options named after the Hardins' grandchildren. The omelets are most popular, with Joey's Meat Lover—stuffed with ham, bacon, and sausage—taking top prize. Among the honorable mentions are Nicholas's Lorraine omelet, made with bacon, onion, and swiss cheese, and Abby's Chicago, a breakfast sandwich that piles sausage, egg, grilled onion, and American cheese on a toasted bagel.

NEWBERRY
Newberry Cafe ☱
103 East Fifth Street
(812) 659-1452
M–Sa 5 A.M.–1:30 P.M.; Su closed
Lanny and Lois Pickett
Lanny Pickett knows the moment I walk in the door of the Newberry Cafe that I'm not from around these parts. The morning lull has left the restaurant empty of customers, and Lanny, his wife, Lois, and the sole waitress are taking advantage of the down time to put the final touches on the daily special before the eleven o'clock crowd floods in. They all come out of the kitchen to see who has broken the rhythm of the morning by arriving at ten fifteen. It is little ol' me. I debate whether to order breakfast or lunch and settle on a simple fried egg with toast. "Do you want that to go?" the waitress asks. I smile at the idea of a humble egg alone in a takeout box and can't help but wonder if she's trying to shoo me on my way.

Spying the daily specials board on the wall behind the counter filled from top to bottom with handwritten offerings, I am convinced that there's some mighty fine cooking going on in the side kitchen.

"No, I'll stay," I say.

Lanny, the Newberry Cafe's self-ascribed PR man, approaches with curiosity. "Where you from?" he asks. I tell him I'm writing a book about Indiana's small town cafes, and he pulls out a chair along with all of the stops. He has stories to tell about the small cafe he and Lois have run since 2004, and his words tumble and roll like the steady flow of the White River north of town. I scribble notes as fast as I can, but I can't keep up. I ease into Lanny's words, focusing less on what he is saying than what he is telling me about the cafe and his hometown of Newberry, an "elderly town" in transition.

Reduced now to a gas station, two churches, the town park (with its new veterans' memorial), the Masonic Hall, and the cafe, Newberry lives in Lanny's memory as a wonderful place to grow up. He ticks off a list of businesses—grocery stores, hardware store, tavern—that once drew people from miles around but have long since disappeared. A highlight of summer was the nights "when we used to go down to see free shows on the side of the Masonic Hall," a concrete block building on the north edge of town. The moving pictures have been replaced with a painted still life, a mural titled "God Blessed Us." The bucolic scene features a white farmhouse, red barn, old-fashioned corn shocks in the field, and a bountiful basket of vegetables and melons.

Lanny himself grew up on a nearby farm, with a mom who was "a very good cook." It was her meals that inspired Lanny's appreciation for and insistence on food made from scratch. For forty-three years he worked as an electrician in the construction trade, traveling all around the country to job sites. Finding satisfactory food on the road became so difficult that he purchased a fifth-wheel trailer with a kitchen so he could cook for himself. After long days stringing wires, he'd spend his evenings perfecting the same yeast rolls and pies now served at the Newberry Cafe.

Lanny and Lois met over the counter of a Kentucky Fried Chicken, about the only restaurant Lanny found worth eating at. He likes fried chicken. "She couldn't cook a lick when we got married and she came down here," Lanny says. "It took twelve years to change her. We used to have baking contests at the house. She made a loaf of bread one time that was so hard she threw it out the back door, and it bent every beak on every bird out there."

Lois smiles as she stands in the kitchen door, tolerantly listening to her husband joke about her troubles in the kitchen. Blessedly, those days are long past. The Newberry Cafe is the dining room for people from near and far who appreciate not merely good but excellent home cooking. This includes the local retired folks and active farmers, as well as others from nearby communities with cafes of their own.

The door opens and a man walks in, lifting his cap and wiping the sweat from his forehead. "I want you to move this restaurant to Odon so I don't have to drive twelve miles," he calls across the room.

"He lives next to the restaurant in Odon and comes here for lunch every day," confides Lanny.

Twelve miles—twenty-four round-trip—isn't much at all for a cafe the likes of the Newberry. Many of the cafe's regulars think nothing of driving from across the state's border or from towns as far away as Spencer and Vincennes. Another loyal contingent comes from the nearby John Deere factory. "They call us the Newberry Country Club," Lanny laughs. "That's a real compliment about our food." Still other customers are those making the trek between Indianapolis and Evansville. Most have been told about the great food by friends who having stopped once always return. The anticipation of breakfast, lunch, or pie at the Newberry Cafe compensates for the tedium of the trip.

As Lanny and I talk, Lois quietly sets down my fried egg and toast. I am astonished at the beauty of the egg. The sunny yolk is lightly set, and the color of its white is flawless and almost perfectly oval, with no customary brown edges that indicate it has been fried on a well-used grill. "Such a pretty egg," I exclaim.

"It's farm fresh. That's why it's so yellow. I fried it in a pan," Lois tells me, pleased that I've noticed. "You'd better eat it before it gets cold."

A few minutes later, she is back. "Do you like yeast rolls?" she asks, inviting me to sample a steaming roll just pulled from the oven. I tear off a bite, juggle it in my fingers to cool it, and then pass it beneath my nose to inhale the aroma of the yeast. Lanny smiles at my antics. "Those are my yeast rolls," he tells me proudly. "It took me years to perfect them." And it is perfect: golden, soft as a down pillow, real.

Lanny's and Lois's commitment to perfection is evident in the entire menu, from simple and standard fare like fried eggs to the more ambitious. Herein lies the dilemma: you can't possibly eat everything they offer. But like me, you will certainly want to! Lanny is proud of the thick, juicy tenderloins that are hand cut and butterflied, tenderized by hand pounding, and then breaded and deep fried. "We're told they're better than the Gnaw Bone tenderloins." Praised by Jane and Michael Stern in *Gourmet* magazine and celebrated on an episode of *Across Indiana,* the tenderloins at the now-closed Gnaw Bone Food and Fuel have absolutely nothing on the thick, meaty sandwiches made by Lanny and Lois. The Picketts' Newberry tenderloins have a clean, clear taste of juicy fresh pork unadulterated by soiled oil. I like mine best topped with plenty of mustard, tart dill pickles, slices of fresh garden tomato, lettuce, and real mayonnaise.

The cafe day begins at five o'clock when the farmers and others heading off to work file in for breakfast. A plate of biscuits and gravy or a bowl of real grits topped with milk and sugar, butter, or scrambled up with eggs fuels them for the morning work. About eleven o'clock they're back for a refill of cheeseburgers, barbecued ribs, pork chops, pan-fried chicken breasts, Wednesday's beans and cornbread, and other blue-ribbon daily specials served with a choice of two sides. Making decisions difficult is a nearly endless list that includes homemade salads; real mashed, fried, and hashed potatoes; and fruits and vegetables, including today's garden-fresh green beans.

"We make everything we can from scratch," Larry says with pride. "It's nothing fancy, just good home cooking."

"See that old coon over there?" he tells me in a voice loud enough for everyone in the cafe to hear. "He's put on fifteen pounds this year."

"That's right," the man playfully shoots back. "I'm working to close down this place."

The noon meal both begins and ends with a slice of Lois's "bodacious pies." Take a cue from the men at the table next to me pausing during a long day of baling hay: order pie first. While they wait for their orders, they down glassfuls of iced tea—"We have the best iced tea in the country, both sweetened and unsweetened," Lanny promises—while protectively guarding wedges of creamy peanut butter and cherry pie made from fruit picked and brought in by one of the Picketts' regular customers. The out-of-the-ordinary crust derives from the fresh lard bought from the Bloomfield Locker. "Nothing makes a flaky crust like fresh lard," Lanny confirms.

Talk of pie inevitably leads to eating pie. "Would you like to sample a piece of peanut butter?" tempts Lois. I have already eaten my egg, a good part of the yeast roll, and at least one-fourth of a pork tenderloin, so I offer a feeble protest. (It's mere show.) "I'll just cut you a sliver," she assures me, holding out her forefinger and thumb to show me how much. Without hesitation, I plunge in, rolling the creamy, salty, sweet pudding on my tongue. It is so good that I want more, but I push away the plate with measured control. One bite is all I need to confirm that Lois does indeed make bodacious pies.

The Newberry Cafe is housed in a cute 1940s-era building that hints at a previous life as a classic roadside motel. It is long and narrow, with a couple of remaining room doors interrupting the expanse of heavy board and batten siding that just may, as Lanny believes, have been removed from the old Newberry covered bridge dismantled and torn down in 1941. It is unusually thick and shows a bit of rot near the pavement, but it has clearly withstood the years far better than anything available today. I'm inclined to think that Lanny may be right about the bridge, even if the man at the corner table has always believed the cafe to have been built from recycled railroad cars. With its creamy butter-colored paint and cherry red trim, the cafe resembles an iconic image from the heyday of America's roadside, complete with red window boxes filled with red and white petunias, and a slightly faded, hand-lettered CAFE sign on the window enticing motorists off the road for ICE CREAM and SOFT DRINKS.

For over sixty years, Newberryites have dined at the Newberry Cafe. When the last owner closed up shop and shut the doors, despair settled on the town like a muggy July night. A year later, after an assault with mop buckets and elbow grease and a full-scale restoration, replacement, and repair both inside and out, Lanny and Lois flipped the Open sign once more. A second sign declares the cafe a nonsmoking zone because when Lanny quit twenty-three years of smoking, he really quit.

PLEASANT

Old School Cafe ☙
State Road 129
(812) 667-7677
M–Sa 7 A.M.–2 P.M.; Su 7 A.M.–11 A.M.
Roger and Dawn Christman

To the three Rs—reading, 'riting, and 'rithmetic—add a fourth: restaurant.

The Old School Cafe is just that: a former school housing grades one through eight that served Pleasant Township families from 1956 to 1981. Located next to the community park, ball field, and water tower, the red brick school with a green metal roof has been converted into a kind of multiuse minimall, with the cafe occupying the former cafeteria, an apartment in two front classrooms, and a meat processing business in the rear. Out front you'll find a piece of vintage playground equipment, a covered front porch with a variety of outdoor tables and chairs, and pots of giant elephant ears.

Both inside and out, owner Roger and Dawn Christman and Roger's mom, Sue, have done little to disguise the fact that the building is a township school. Instead, they celebrate its history with school-themed antiques and collectibles, including the original green chalkboard in the cafeteria that serves as the daily specials board; a cheerleader's megaphone from the old Austin school, long since torn down; and old class photographs ("People love that. They like to see themselves when they were much younger," says Sue). The main hall leading to the classrooms is filled with even more antiques, including a display of items related to tobacco farming, a restored Allis Chalmers tractor, and a pump organ. You'll find the cafe's restrooms—the boys' and girls' lavatories!—in the back hall as well. You can't mistake the boys'. On the door is a picture of an outhouse with this caption: "Welcome to our Library and Music Room. Please remain seated during the entire performance."

Up front, Roger closed off the main entrance hall and made a cozy lobby area complete with fireplace and wicker chairs. He replaced the original cafeteria doors with wood-framed french doors and added an assortment of farm tools as a tribute to the area's agricultural heritage. The cafe's role as a popular gathering place for men—who comprise 85 percent of the customers by Sue's estimate—is designated by a sign that reads:

Pleasant is a community in transition. Like most others of its size, Pleasant struggles to maintain its own cohesiveness and identity, especially since losing its school. The first change to mark the community's slow unraveling came in 1969 when the seventh and eighth grade students were bused to the high school in Vevay. A few years later, a change in the township districts took more of the Pleasant students out of the community, and in 1981, with the closing of the school, all of the students were sent elsewhere. "A lot of people were against consolidation, and the school had a very high rating as far as academics," Sue remembers.

With all Switzerland County students now centralized in two elementary schools and the middle school–high school campus at Vevay, the Pleasant school remains just one of three township schools still standing in the county. Joy Briggs, a retired teacher, notes with sadness the loss of the school buildings that were once found scattered throughout the county. She cheers the rescue and reuse of the Pleasant Township school. "I think it's great. It would really be a shame to destroy it. All of our one-room schoolhouses are gone, and most of the township schools. When a community loses its school, it loses its identity."

More recently, Pleasant has lost other important community centers. The improvement and expansion of State Road 129 required the acquisition of the old general store that had previously closed, while a second general store closed due to the death of its owner. Since then, "the restaurant has become the only place for people to gather," says Sue. "We have a lot of men who come here every day—some several times a day. They talk and talk and talk. For some, we're probably the only connection to the community that they have."

Day in and day out, week after week, the comings and goings of the regulars is so predictable that Roger, the "kitchen ladies," and other employees take notice of unexplained and unexpected absences and call or stop by someone's house to be sure there is no trouble. If someone is ill, Sue brings in a card and has the cafe crowd sign it. Watching over and taking care of other community members occurs in other ways as well, such as sponsoring benefit dinners and raffles for people with devastating illnesses, like a local boy with bone cancer. And when someone does pass away, the death "affects everyone who works here," Sue explains. "One man came in this morning asking about a neighbor who recently died. Her funeral is today. He was concerned that the cemetery hadn't been mowed and offered to take his own mower over to cut the grass. I think this caring has to do with the fact that everyone here knows everyone in the community and feels responsible."

Area residents regularly fill the old school's cafeteria as much for fellowship and support as for the reliably good, real food. "The people here are meat and potato people," Sue says. This translates into plenty of fried chicken, plus roasted beef and pork, ground beef, pork tenderloins, breakfast sausage, and bacon hand cut and smoked by Bob Schwagmeier. With over thirty years of butchering experience, Bob is the owner of Old Pleasant School Custom Processing located in the rear of the school, in the former principal's office and sixth grade classroom. When a supply of pork chops is needed for the next day's special, one of the "kitchen ladies" brings an empty plastic wash tub to Bob, and he fills it up with choice frozen chops.

On-the-menu favorites at the Old School Cafe are the grilled chicken salad with cook Judy May's own homemade dressing, hand-prepared breaded and grilled tenderloins, the mushroom and swiss burger, biscuits and gravy made with Bob's in-demand sausage, and the breakfast special—two eggs, hash browns, a half order of biscuits and gravy, and a drink. "Did I tell you about my favorite *goetta*?" Sue asks. It's a traditional German breakfast sausage made with oats manufactured by Glier's in nearby Covington, Kentucky.

Popular daily specials include homemade seasonal soups, meatloaf, barbecued pork chops, and real mashed potatoes ("with lumps to prove they're real"), with Friday's fried chicken "selling out right away." By all means, leave room for dessert, including homemade pie and cobblers. Sue makes the pumpkin and chocolate cream pie herself, while Judy "makes an excellent peach cobbler. That's something they always ask for. That and brownies. We always have to have brownies."

SHOALS
Velma's Diner
304 Main Street
(812) 247-2041
M–Su 5 A.M.–7 P.M.
Debbie Montgomery

"I've got one for you," a chamber of commerce representative in northwestern Indiana replied when I asked about small town cafes. "When you get to my hometown of Shoals, you've got to go to Velma's Diner. It's been years since I've been back, but I still get hungry for Velma's fried chicken and pie."

Velma's daughter, Debbie Montgomery, laughs when she learns how I came to be sitting in the cafe's kitchen, but she's not surprised. She's heard similar stories before. They help to reassure her that she and her sister, Shannon Tharp, are doing the right thing in carrying on their mother's legacy. In late 2001, Velma was eating strawberries at a stainless steel counter—in the very spot I am now sitting—when she suffered a stroke that put her in a nursing home. After twenty-one years of ownership and several more waiting tables and cooking for the previous owners, Velma was heartbroken to realize she'd never return to the restaurant she loved. "She has a rough time with it," Debbie admits. "It wasn't a choice she made about giving up the restaurant."

Opening the oven door, Debbie pulls out four large meatloaves and sets them aside on a nearby counter. "Mom always said to let them cool before you slice them," she explains. "Mom is famous for her meatloaf. People are always wanting her recipe." She stirs a kettle filled with elbow macaroni and cheese sauce, then pours its contents into a huge baking pan and slides the pan into the oven. On the stovetop she sets three massive cast-iron skillets and adjusts the gas burners underneath to a medium flame.

"I never cooked before," she says, unwrapping three packages of chicken purchased from the Jay C store a block away. "I just watched Mom. I was scared to death I wouldn't be able to do it the way she did." Few of Velma's recipes are written down, so Debbie relies on her memory and a rhythm acquired from years of working alongside her mother to reproduce the diner's well-loved dishes. With Velma just a phone call or visit away, Debbie depends on her to answer questions and solve problems. When the frozen peanut butter pie didn't turn out quite as she remembered it, she took a piece to Velma and asked what she had done wrong. "She told me I left out the cream cheese—but people ate it anyway." Later, when Debbie tackled chicken and dumplings for the first time, she got sick to her stomach because she was so worried she wouldn't be able to do it. "Mom tells me how but forgets things sometimes. She said my dumplings were a bit small but otherwise I did a good job."

With the chicken soaking in cold water—"Mom says to wash it even if comes in a package"—Debbie fills the hot skillets with a mixture of Fry-Melt and lard. It slowly puddles into liquid. Opening a plastic bowl full of Golden-Dipt poultry coating, she dredges the chicken parts one by one.

"I get emotional when I think about my mom," she continues, dropping the chicken into the hot fat. "She was a single mother raising the kids through good and bad. The restaurant has been her whole life. She worked hard seven days a week." After her stroke, Shannon kept the restaurant going and found out just how demanding the day-in and day-out responsibilities were. Three years later she wanted out, and Debbie stepped in. "She didn't want the restaurant, but I did, I guess. I wanted to see it stay in the family."

As the hot fat roils and bubbles, the chicken begins to turn the color of field corn just before harvest. Debbie adjusts the pieces with a long-handled tongs and then tosses salt and pepper over the frying chicken. "My mom always said the main thing is to put a lid on it," she says as she puts a pan over each skillet. "It makes the chicken crispy and not soggy."

Sandwiched between Ethel's Beauty Shop and Queen's Clothing Store, Velma's Diner is just one of many businesses in Shoals struggling to maintain a foothold in today's faltering economy. Like many other Hoosier towns of its age and size, Shoals has suffered as the longtime neglect and vacancy of historic buildings culminates in their abandonment, demolition, and replacement. Most significant is the 1999 decision by the Martin County commissioners to vacate the 1830s courthouse on a hill overlooking the town. Citing lack of space and inaccessibility issues, the commissioners relocated the county offices into a remodeled bank building on Main Street. The beautiful old courthouse is now a struggling history museum.

With forty-five minutes to wait before the noon meal is served, I promise Debbie I will return for her fried chicken and wander across the street to the Alco Dime Store. A nostalgic throwback to the small town variety store, it has been owned since 1989 by Waldo and Hildred Harshaw. The Harshaws are looking to retire and have had the business for sale without any success. "There've been a couple of folks interested, but they don't have the money," confides Waldo. "My realtor has approached Family Dollar and General Dollar about buying us out, but they're not interested. I guess that means they think Shoals isn't a big enough market for them."

Standing on the sidewalk in front of his store, Waldo gestures down Main Street. "We're an old town with old buildings, old business, and old owners." Across the street, next door to Velma's Diner, Charles "Son" Sorrel tends Queen's Clothing Store, a longtime business established by his father-in-law. Increasingly, the only traffic Son sees are friends stopping by for a visit. "He'd like to sell the business," Waldo says, "but there isn't any interest." Across the highway, an empty furniture store has a hefty price tag of nearly a half million dollars. Down the street, the new brick and vinyl Main Street Church of Christ stands where the hotel once stood.

Despite his view from the Alco Dime Store's front display windows, Waldo believes that Shoals could come back, "what with Crane staying and everything that's going on in French Lick and West Baden." Critical to Shoals future, he believes, is capitalizing on its historic character and organizing community support of local businesses. He proposes a kind of cooperative venture that would have business owners investing in buildings and each other, one by one, until Main Street is back on its feet.

A fine place to start would be Velma's Diner, which is, from what I witnessed, the only business in town that attracts an impressive influx of people on a daily basis. Other small towns have proven that a successful cafe can be the root of revitalization. Osseo, Wisconsin, for example, reinvented itself as a popular tourist destination in large part because of the Norske Nook, known nationwide for its magnificent pies. Debbie admits that the old cafe building needs a lot of improvements but wonders just where she'll find the money and time to tackle them with so much of her attention focused on operating the business.

Back at Velma's Diner, I join a dining room full of folks—retired couples, a young mother with a baby, farmers and their Amish hired hands—for the noon meal. Debbie has prepared not only pan-fried chicken, meatloaf, and macaroni and cheese, but also ham and country-fried steak. Additional specials written on a yellow Post-it stuck to the inside of the menu include made-to-order fried catfish and a fried bologna sandwich ("They just love 'em here," Debbie says). Thirteen side dishes cover everything from homemade potato, kidney bean, and macaroni salad to sliced pickled beets, green beans, and breaded okra. My single large chicken breast is moist and meaty, with a crunch of flavor. The fried green tomatoes—made with a local woman's garden surplus—are a seasonal treat. They're sliced thin, coated with seasoned cornmeal, and cooked in the deep fryer. "Now you know why our customers eat these twenty-four seven," my waitress Mary tells me. "They'd eat fried green tomatoes right on through 'til Christmas if we could get 'em. They start asking for them in April because they think we have connections!"

I finish off lunch with a plump piece of coconut cream pie topped with a pompadour of sweet, browned meringue. I was smitten when I'd seen it cooling on the counter earlier, or I would have been hard-pressed to choose between the day's ten dessert offerings of cobblers, cream pies, cheesecake, even german chocolate pie. Everything is homemade except the fruit pies and cobblers.

Despite a much-repeated repertoire of daily specials—typically two every day, plus meatloaf and baked ham—Debbie rarely gets bored because the days have settled into a comfortable routine. Mondays are always set aside for sausage and sauerkraut and ham and beans (either pinto or great northern), cornbread, and fried potatoes because "Mom always had them on the menu." Saturdays are earmarked for Salisbury steak, and Sundays just wouldn't be the same without more pan-fried chicken—so popular "it's usually standing room only after church and Sunday school." Other time-tested standbys include fried whole catfish ("fiddlers" in these parts) and chicken and dumplings.

Every once in a while, Debbie is struck with the impulse to shake things up a bit "because people need a change." She rarely strays too far from the familiar, however. "I added salmon patties one Thursday, and now they're asking for them. Today we're having foot-long Coney dogs because I like them. What we do here is country cookin'—you know, good old home cookin'. We're just a country kind of diner."

NEXT BEST BETS

DILLSBORO
O'Ryan's Restaurant
12933 North Street (State Road 62)
(812) 432-9999
The sign boasts "the best burgers in town," but I only had eyes for the beautiful white layer cake under a glass dome on the counter.

DUPONT
Railroad Cafe
6873 West Main Street
(812) 273-2756
Whistlestop Burgers, Caboose Favorite sandwiches and soup, Boxcar Sides, and the Conductor's Best Homemade Desserts carry out the railroad theme in this lunch spot popular with what seems like everyone within a thirty-mile radius.

GNAW BONE
Cozy Cabin Cafe
4359 East State Road 46
(812) 988-0229
A new restaurant on the rise. The German tenderloin smothered in grilled sauerkraut was A-1: meaty, fresh, and shrouded with a black pepper–laced breading that shook me out of my doldrums. The manageable miniversion is much appreciated.

HENDRICKSVILLE
Rosie's Diner
State Road 43
(812) 876-3181
A favorite of former IU coach Bob Knight, Rosie's dishes out real home cooking and rustic pies (rhubarb is tops). A few years ago, talk around the coffee table turned into community activism that built a brand new fire station, community center, and museum.

LINTON
The Grill
60 A Street Northeast
(812) 847-9010
In continuous operation for over seventy years, this Greene County favorite sports a classic diner look. The beef Manhattan and "home baked" apple pie were a disappointment, and I found myself eyeing my neighbor's meatloaf and crispy American fries with gnawing envy.

MADISON
Cafe Camille
119 East Main Street
(812) 265-5626
Clean, cute, and clever with a menu that offers a few surprises, like broccoli quiche and seasoned, oven-roasted red potatoes.

MADISON
Hammond's Restaurant
221 East Main Street
(821) 265-3237
This hometown favorite is slowly falling apart at the seams, a victim of long delayed maintenance. Nevertheless, true adventure eaters will appreciate the ultra-laid-back atmosphere, especially the gallery of caricatures by local artist Rod Troyer. Nearly all the regulars are depicted in full color and identified by name, profession, or personal interests and habits. My fave: a sketch of an older fellow captioned "I trade everything on eBay. Just wait until Madison finds out their fountain's missing."

METAMORA
Have-a-Bite
19121 U.S. Highway 52
(765) 647-2002
Don't bother looking for the locals in the restaurants in old town Metamora stretched out along the canal. They're not down there. They're up here on top of the hill having hand-pattied Black Angus burgers, country-fried steak, and homemade pie.

NORTH VERNON
White Front Cafe
51 North Madison Avenue
(812) 346-8102
Established in the 1920s, the White Front had been closed for ten years before it was gutted, reincarnated, and reopened in July 2006. The work-in-progress is "more of an emotional thing than a business thing," according to owner Irvin French. The new White Front is classy and sassy, with a menu to match. Remember me to Mary Lou when you visit.

OOLITIC
Corey's Cafe
733 Hoosier Avenue
(812) 279-3181
Home cooking served cafeteria style, with no menu other than what's on the day's steam table. Meats, vegetables, soups, salads, and desserts are all priced separately. Sundays are popular with the after-church crowd, including beehive-hairdoed ladies of fundamentalist persuasion.

OSGOOD
Whistle Stop Cafe
122 Railroad Avenue
(812) 689-1502
The Colonial Bread logo on the wood screen door is a nostalgic relic at this cafe located opposite the old B&O tracks. Five or six tables pushed together in the center of the room ebb and flow with men who have more time on their hands than just about everyone else put together.

SUNMAN
Tha Store Cafe
104 South Meridian Street
(812) 623-2191
A cross between a tavern, cafe, and full restaurant. Unusual breakfast fare (for Hoosiers, that is), includes pancakes with chunks of sweet potato, corned beef hash, and chopped beef on toast. And then there's Cincinnati-made Glier's *goetta*, a sausage of pork, beef, and steel-cut oats of German persuasion. Ya gotta get goetta.

VEVAY
AJ's Diner
122 West Main Street
(812) 427-3540
In need of a vigorous spit and polish, AJ's claims the "Best Breakfast" in Switzerland County. I watched with amusement as three different men pushed meatloaf and MPG onto their forks with a folded slice of bread.

WESTPHALIA
Country Charms Cafe
12864 North First Street (State Road 67)
(812) 694-8474
A diner has been here, in a former Sinclair station, since the 1940s. The service bay is the storeroom and the station a dining room. Good home cooking by Missy and her staff.

WORTHINGTON
Main Street Cafe
114 East Main Street
(812) 875-3000
You'll find enthusiastic and conscientious output from the kitchen in this cracker box cafe pulled together on a shoestring budget. The puckery, ultrasweet, shake-up-style lemonade reminds me of lemon meringue pie on ice.

South

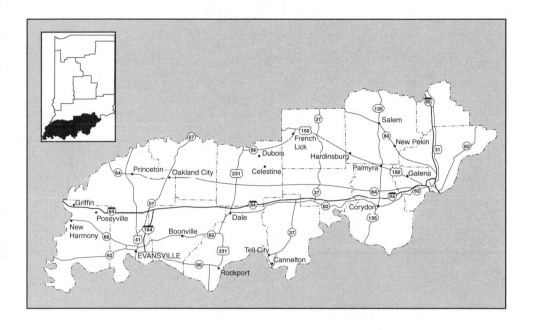

DALE
Windell's Cafe
6 West Medcalf Street
(812) 937-4253
June 1–September 1: M–Sun 6 A.M.–9 P.M.; otherwise M–Sun 6 A.M.–
8 P.M. (Central Time)
Darrel and Betty Jenkins

The Wednesday night menu at Windell's Cafe presents a cross-cultural smorgasbord of good eating. You'll find German-style sauerkraut with pork roast and sausage—a reflection of the area's ethnic heritage—right next to plain old everyday Hoosier fare like Windell's almost-famous fried chicken, sweet corn bread, and navy beans and ham. Plus a whole lot more! A descendant of German immigrants myself, I'm sorely tempted by the daily special of ribs and kraut, but Brittany, my teenage waitress, makes a good case for the buffet. "You'll get to try everything, and besides, you'll get dessert."

I've already spied the pieces of cheesecake, coconut, and chocolate cream pie in the cooler and know that dessert is precisely where my dinner is heading. So I order the buffet, grab a plate, and begin, pausing just long enough at the outset to appraise the bounty: a well-stocked salad bar, kettles of homemade vegetable soup and chili, mashed potatoes and gravy, bright yellow corn, peas and carrots, dinner rolls and corn bread, golden pieces of white and dark chicken, pork and kraut, chopped steak and brown gravy, plus a salad bar with fixings arranged in maroon plastic tubs nestled in ice. Behind the buffet, a refrigerator case stocked with sample-sized slices of pie occupies one of a pair of odd alcoves in the side wall.

"We really did not want to get into the buffet business, but tradition and timing took us that direction," says owner Darrel Jenkins. When he and his wife, Betty, bought Windell's in 1991 it consisted of a small block building seating no more than about forty-five people. Hardly large, it was nonetheless far bigger than the breadbox that served as the original cafe purchased in 1947 by Bob and Margaret Windell. In their capable hands, the business grew in both size and reputation, beloved for its breakfasts, daily plate lunches, sandwiches, and from-scratch pies and other desserts.

As hometown heirs of the Windells' legacy, Darrel and Betty were content to carry on the modest cafe's time-tested traditions. They catered to a local crowd and maintained a pretty low profile. "The main thing we tried to do was keep the same home cooking," Darrel says. In fact, the Windells' own recipes were used (and still are today) to make Margaret's famous coconut and banana cream pie and cheesecake, as well as corn bread and vinegar slaw. And from the kitchen flowed (and still flows today) a steady stream of Hoosier old reliables: fried chicken, chicken and dumplings, roast beef, fiddlers (whole, bone-in catfish), chopped beef, green beans, fried potatoes, and chicken livers.

The tide unexpectedly changed in 1994. That's when a hungry writer for *Midwest Living* magazine in pursuit of great eating along America's interstates received a tip about the virtues of Windell's victuals from a semitruck driver. He came. He ate. From his Des Moines office, he called Darrel and Betty for an interview. "I wasn't too sure about that," Betty recalls, but she gamely answered his questions. And then he wrote, extolling the pleasure of Windell's chicken and dumplings and so-perfect pies. Others wishing to document Windell's magic quickly followed: newspaper reporters from a three-state area, television news crews and WFYI's *Across Indiana*, even the nationally distributed cable Food Network.

"It was in the winter of 2004, and they came down from New York on a Sunday afternoon," Betty remembers. "We were so surprised because it was so cold and snowy; we thought they'd cancel. No one was here because the churches had all canceled their services. They were on a chicken theme and featured our chicken and noodles. The show has been shown several times since then. I'm surprised at how many people say they've seen it. It's been good for business."

Like Duncan Hines before them, the media lit the way through the dining wilderness, inspiring legions of adventure eaters to trek to the Shrine of Home Cooking in little old Dale, Indiana. "It wasn't long before we started getting tour buses," Darrel remembers. "We had single stall bathrooms and would have forty to fifty people standing in line. We knew we had to do something when our employees had to go home to use the bathroom!"

Those odd alcoves behind the all-you-can-eat buffet? They once were the entrances to the original loos!

The dramatic increase in customers necessitated an extensive remodeling. The Jenkinses enlarged the kitchen to more than three times its original size, expanded the dining room across a vacated alley "to justify the cost of the kitchen," and added a public meeting room and two very large restrooms to alleviate those annoying lines. Despite the remodeling—or more likely because of it—the Jenkinses were determined to preserve Windell's most significant and defining original features. Thank goodness. The locals still gather around the lucky horseshoe counter to open their mail, swap stories and news over breakfast, and drink bottomless cups of coffee; the cooks and waitstaff pass through the same swinging kitchen door; and customers sit at vintage chrome-legged, black Formica-topped tables and on padded vinyl banquettes with rear pocket cubbies intended for stowing away customers' hats and other belongings.

"We often wonder why we didn't just tear down the old building and build new," Darrel says. "It would have been a lot easier. But we wanted to save as much of the original cafe as possible, and we would have saved more—we wanted to save the front—if we hadn't had to meet handicap requirements. On the other hand, we could have kept our old building, not remodeled, and stayed out of debt. Or we could have closed. But we saw it as a service to the community to stay in business. It would be a very dark day in Dale if Windell's closed."

Addition of the buffet was another strategic response to the tremendous influx of out-of-area customers. It makes it possible to serve more customers more quickly while providing a greater selection of choices. An additional and unexpected result is that it has also brought in a younger crowd that, Darrel notes, "likes to eat quick and get out." More than fifty years ago, Duncan Hines, America's original Adventure Eater, used the phrase "bolt it and beat it" to describe the same tendency. He considered it a crude and disgusting cultural pattern rather than an age-group phenomenon.

Before the buffet, the average age of Windell's customers was sixty-five and up. Today, due to the patronage of an increasing number of young parents with children, Darrel estimates the average age of his customers to be between fifty and fifty-five. This means that whole new generations are being exposed to old-fashioned, home-style cooking that other cafe owners worry may someday become obsolete.

Thanks to nearby attractions such as Holiday World in the town of Santa Claus, tourism has a significant impact on the community of Dale. "A lot of people come to Dale just to eat," Betty says. A glance at the license plates on cars in Windell's parking lot proves that she's right. In a town of nine-hundred-plus people, Windell's employs about forty-five and contributes $450,000 annually in income, taxes, and contributions to school groups, athletic teams, civic organizations, and area festivals, such as Dale Fest. This year, as in the past, the Jenkinses are sponsoring one of their waitresses as festival queen. "We're a small town," Darrel says matter-of-factly, "so people have to do everything."

As a civic center, Windell's Cafe is central to the social life of an area that covers nearly five counties. The bulletin board in the front entrance shows just how far the communal bonds extend: a poster for Dale Fest is surrounded by others for the Bluff City Pow Wow in Rockport, a euchre tournament "sponsored" by the senior citizens at the St. Meinrad Community Center, a craft fair and flea market at Yellow Banks in Selvin. While the national media attention is certainly appreciated, "the majority of our business comes from the surrounding communities," Darrel says. On Sundays, a waiting line forms as soon as area churches start letting out, with many having standing reservations for congregational tables. The Methodists from Huntingburg sit here, the Methodists from Gentryville there. Assembling at another table are the parishioners from St. Nicholas in Santa Claus. Other congregants—I intend no sin of omission; an exhaustive list would be exhausting—break bread at others. "They all sit by themselves, and after their meal they stand and talk to each other," Betty says.

Windell's is also integral to the social lives of individuals. Consider 101-year-old Ted Roberts, who met his wife at the cafe. She later worked for Bob and Margaret Windell. The couple ate together at Windell's at least once a day, and even celebrated their seventy-fifth anniversary at the cafe. "Every time there was an article in the paper about him turning one hundred, he'd mention Windell's," Betty says. "He's a true friend."

POSEYVILLE
Harold's Restaurant ☻
11 West Main Street
(812) 874-3214
M–Sa 4:30 A.M.–2 P.M.; Su 7 A.M.–2 P.M. (Central Time)
Patti Wilson
Two round mirrors on the glossy red backbar behind the soda fountain at Harold's Restaurant project reverse images of patrons. From a wall booth, I see the fronts and backs, the comings and goings of people in a single glance.

As if by magic, the narrow, boxlike interior of the cafe seems globelike, time oddly circular, and the present is both actual experience and something of a dream. I feel weirdly like a time traveler.

While other cafes affect a nostalgic atmosphere with retro 1950s-influenced style, Harold's Restaurant is the real McCoy—an antique in the modern day. No mere replicas, the backbar, dotted with a pair of vintage Coca-Cola buttons, and the soda fountain have been fixtures for more than half a century. Likewise the blue crinkle Formica countertop, red lozenge-topped stools, dark pine walls, and tufted black vinyl banquettes with red seats. Harold Schweikhart, the cafe's namesake and long ago owner, invested in quality—and now classic—stuff when he decked out the restaurant so many years ago. Blessedly, no subsequent owners ever felt compelled to update and modernize. Or erase his name.

Sitting opposite me in a booth, Patti Wilson, owner of Harold's Restaurant since 1994, ponders the distant past. "Now help me," she says, turning to address the locals gathered at the counter and tables at midmorning. "How long has it been Harold's?"

As long as everyone remembers.

"It's been Harold's so long that people have known it only as Harold's. I would never have called it Patti's—even though they write out their checks to Patti's!—or Main Street Cafe because there's so many of those. It's always been Harold's."

With a love for cooking and years of bakery and restaurant experience, Patti never considered running her own restaurant until friends encouraged her to take over Poseyville's popular cafe. With great respect and reverence for its history, she nonetheless made it her own. "I saw the Coke buttons on the backbar and thought, wouldn't it be cool to decorate in Coca-Cola. I bought a sign at the antique store and hung it on the wall, and then people started bringing in stuff. I've probably bought 15 percent of what's here, with the other 85 percent being gifts from customers. People just keep bringing me stuff!"

From Coke buttons and signs do mighty collections grow! The walls of Harold's Restaurant are filled with Coca-Cola just about everything: vintage and replica, rare and everyday, big and small. Keep the kids entertained while you're waiting for your food by playing I-Spy. Plop them down on the spinning counter stools for a 360-degree vantage point and get them started.

I spy: a biplane made of Diet Coke cans, a set of unused paper dolls, a framed jigsaw puzzle, a wood bottle case, soda straw and napkin dispensers, plastic clock, the trademark polar bear . . .

What? Food's here? Already? Do we haaaaave to eat?

Kids might fuss to continue playing, but one thing they won't fuss about is the food. Even the most finicky eaters will be able to find something on the menu to satisfy them, as they have for fifty years. Many items and recipes have been passed down from Harold to owner after owner. At breakfast, you'll find Harold's Dutch Sandwich—"It goes way back," says Patti—made by layering sausage, egg, and cheese on a bun. Harold's Western Sandwich has a filling of fried bacon and eggs. There's also a bacon, egg, lettuce, and tomato sandwich known as Harold's B.E.L.T. Recipes that originated with Harold include the sweet and sour vinegar slaw, french dressing, and pie dough and pudding fillings.

Every day you'll find two different plate specials, plus grilled ham and chicken tenders, served with a choice of five different sides. Time-tested winners include Monday's chicken and dressing and roast beef; Tuesday's breaded or grilled chicken breast and meatloaf; and Wednesday's pan-fried chicken and hamburger steak with brown gravy. The chicken is so popular that the first plate comes out of the kitchen as early as ten thirty in the morning. (I can't help but note with considerable amusement that the guy who ordered it also asked for two pieces of bread crumbled and covered with gravy—this alongside a helping of MPG). On Thursdays, mainstay Hoosier tenderloin is paired with sauerkraut-smothered real bratwurst from Dewig's Meats in Haubstadt, an award-winning, family-owned butcher shop in business since 1916. "Despite what they say on their advertisements, those Johnsonville brats aren't real brats," says Patti. If you're on the lookout for good brats, depend on the Germans—around these parts they refer to themselves as Dutch—to provide the authentic best.

If you're convinced by Wednesday's pan-fried chicken and ready to return to Harold's for more good eats, the end of the workweek means a full-frontal return to southern-style Hoosier fare, with Friday's catfish fillets and country-fried steak with milk gravy, and on Saturday, barbecued pork and hamburger steak.

Whenever you visit and whatever you eat, be sure to leave room for dessert. Patti pushes back her sleeves, rolls out the pie dough, coaxes it into tins, and fills it with all variety of fruit and pudding fillings. She also makes Hoosier-style cobblers, cakes, and fresh strawberry pie when the fields are bursting with berries. After my dinner of pan-fried chicken, green beans, and whipped potatoes, I splurge on the out-of-the-ordinary banana split pie, so sinfully rich it demands a prolonged penance. I'll finger the rosary beads as soon as I've polished off every last crumb.

From its period looks to its emphasis on from-scratch cooking, Harold's Restaurant is shoulders above most other Hoosier cafes. Patti receives confirmation of this when first-timers return and only-timers dropping in off the nearby I-64 swoon at their chance discovery. Some have a habit of boldly seeking out local eateries on their own, while others are directed by staff at the visitors' center near the Illinois state line. "People come to Poseyville looking for that small town experience," Patti notes. "We have people stop once who make it a point to stop again whenever they're passing through. One year we had an FFA group from New Mexico, and now they come every year and bring us peanuts."

Located just a few miles north of town, the interstate connects Poseyville with the rest of the country, and even the world. The first foreign visitor was a novelty, the second and third a surprise. Soon Patti was keeping a guest book handy near the register for travelers to record their visit and experience. Joanna Sutherland-Young of London, England, praised Harold's Restaurant as "the best cafe in the U.S.A." in July 1998. More common, of course, are American tourists like Whitie and Bonnie Gray, who in September 2002 dropped by for lunch. "We asked three ladies on the street, 'Where is the best place in town to eat?' They said, 'Seek no farther!'" Steve and Melissa Frusella of Amarillo, Texas, wrote, "We love the soda fountain and the spinning stools," while Michael and Jeanie Bragg of Hampton, Virginia, praised Harold's as "a jewel in Indiana. The 'Best' home cooked food we've had for a very long time (other than Mom's, of course)."

Patti had a rare day off to attend a bridal shower when Harold's most famous guest paid a visit. Jerry Seinfeld was on a cross-country road trip when he dropped in for breakfast on the recommendation of an Illinois hotel clerk. "He asked where to eat and was sent here," Patti remembers. "And no one recognized him! He was very quiet and wore a cap. When he got up to pay the bill, his friend said the food was excellent, that it was the best time and the best experience—probably because no one bothered him!"

You'll find a blank guest check signed by Seinfeld and a short news article about his visit hanging on the wall.

The testimony of famous people is impressive, but it's the opinions of area residents that have the most impact. "I drove forty-five miles and passed sixty restaurants just to eat here," an older man confides. Unlike Seinfeld, he'll be back. Again and again and again.

PRINCETON
Emma Lou's Sandwich Shop
129 West Broadway Street
(812) 385-2124
M–F 5 A.M.–2 P.M.; Sa 5 A.M.–11 A.M.; Su closed (Central Time)
Emma Lou Wilson
Update: Lack of parking, the departure of a major downtown bank, and a new business opportunity for Emma Lou led to the Sandwich Shop's closing in 2007 after nearly sixty-three years in business.

Situated on a downtown corner for sixty-one years, the Sandwich Shop resembles a fish bowl with the lure of Home Cooking, Homemade Pies, and Plate Lunches hand-painted on its sides. The cafe's plate glass windows rise up from the sidewalk, nearly filling the front wall and providing from inside a clear view of the Gibson County Courthouse across the street. From outside looking in, they provide me an unobstructed view of a lone man at the vintage counter coddling a cup a hot coffee between his hands.

It's two o'clock and Emma Lou Wilson and her niece, Julie, are just closing up for the day. Though she has been here since five this morning, Emma Lou willingly exchanges an hour at home for one spent chatting with me. In the eighteen years she has operated the Sandwich Shop (and in her ten years as a paid employee before that), she tells me, "No one has ever come in here and been interested in any of this."

Paul McGarrah opened the Sandwich Shop in 1945, and thirty-six years later he fortuitously hired Emma Lou's mother, Jane, to help run the place. "Mom raised three kids on seventy-eight dollars a week plus tips. After everything was paid, she had a dime left," Emma Lou remembers. "She was a hard worker and knew how to save money. We kids always had money to go to the fair."

By the time she was in high school, Emma Lou was working for Paul on weekends and during school breaks. When she graduated, Paul promised her, "As long as I'm here and working, you'll have a full-time job."

Ten years later, "Paul told me he was going to retire and offered it to me," Emma recalls. "He made it to where I could afford it. He never had any children. He was a good man who took a liking to me. It was scary, but I took it. Mom thought my buying the place was a good opportunity and told me, 'We can do it.'"

For two years, Jane and Emma Lou worked side by side under the lovely pressed-tin ceiling, guided and guarded by the happy little cherub in the center plaster medallion. Their shared commitment to success was grounded in the decision to carry on the business exactly as Paul had. "That was a big plus, that the business was up and running." Jane did all the cooking from scratch, including homemade noodles and pies, and for two years things were relatively trouble free. When Jane fell sick in 1990, she prepared for the day she'd no longer be at the restaurant by transferring the recipes from memory to paper. "She wrote down everything she made: pies, vegetable soup, everything," Emma Lou explains. "What I make today is from her recipes."

Continuity and tradition are hallmarks of the Sandwich Shop, where many of the regular customers have been coming for so long they've got both the regular menu and the daily specials memorized. "It's been going on the same way for sixty-one years," Emma laughs. In an effort to spark up the weekly routine, she recently added spaghetti alongside Monday's long-established plate lunch. On Friday she added catfish fillets. The experiments went over reasonably well, but the folks who habitually ordered salmon patties on Friday didn't take the bait. "I cut back to two cans of salmon and ran out. I've got one guy who comes from Oakland City every Friday for salmon patties, and he wasn't about to make a change!"

In the front window, seated at a table whose tan tweed Formica top is worn white in spots from years of use, Emma Lou stretches out her palm. She ticks off her customers' other favorite meals on her fingers. When they're not relishing salmon patties ("You just can't go wrong with them"), more likely than not they're ordering swiss steak, chicken pot pie, and meatloaf. "There are people who won't eat anyone's meatloaf but mine," she says matter-of-factly. Best-selling side dishes include scalloped cabbage, homemade noodles, and, on Wednesdays, rolled dumplings made with flour and real broth. "I have people who tell me, 'These dumplings! They're almost as good as your mother's.' That's a real compliment to me, because Mom was an exceptional cook."

Emma Lou's dumplings perk up the midweek slump and set the regulars salivating for Thursday. That's when Emma Lou features southern-style pan-fried chicken—as far as you can get from the deep-fried or Broaster variety common in cafes throughout the Hoosier State. Slow-cooked, pan-fried chicken is not just another daily special. It's truly special, requiring a watchful eye and a ready hand to lovingly turn the pieces as they slowly brown in a seasoned cast-iron frying pan.

Emma Lou's pan-fried chicken shares its success with her pies, both of which are made with real lard. "That's the best," she believes. "I've got women who come in and want to buy my piecrust. They tell me they can make the filling, but they can't make the crust."

Piecrust is funny like that. It can turn a perfectly competent woman into one crippled by a fear of failure, where one roll of the pin too much means tough, cracked pastry that bakes into a sheet of tasteless cardboard. Of course, we can't all be Aunt Bee, but whoever coined the phrase "easy as pie" didn't know what they were talking about.

There are as many secrets to making a good pie as there are things to fill it. Like Emma Lou, many pie makers put their faith in lard for a tender, parchmentlike crust, but I much prefer shortening. I was not raised on lard and have never gotten accustomed to its rather strong flavor. This said, however, I do have to admit that lard makes the flakiest crust, especially with the addition of a bit of lemon juice or cider vinegar. While Emma Lou makes pie in enough variety to keep even addicts like me content, the regulars can never get enough of her coconut cream or baked raisin. (The Gibson County prosecutor favors peach.) I consider coconut cream to be a real treat, but to me, Hoosier raisin pie is a kind of last-ditch, desperation pie made only when you're out of apples, rhubarb, blackberries, or other fruit.

As steadfast as their fondness for raisin pie, the dedication of the regulars is what has sustained the Sandwich Shop through ups and downs in the economy, the moving in of chain restaurants, and the withering of Princeton's downtown commercial district. Emma Lou notes frankly, "I never took this place on to become rich. I wanted a decent life. It's become much more difficult in the past ten years than it ever used to be."

Among her most nagging worries is the constantly rising cost of food products. "The price of milk has risen three times this year, along with eggs and beef. When I started at this, I used to pay seventy-nine cents a pound for sausage, and now it's over two dollars." Every January, Emma Lou raises her own prices a nickel "almost across the board," an increase that quite honestly doesn't begin to keep pace with her rising costs. Still, she confesses, "I die every time I raise my prices." Most customers understand, but others begrudge the extra five cents for a homemade hot lunch and watch with scrutiny to see that Emma Lou doesn't treat herself to luxuries—a new truck, a vacation—with the pocket change. "It's like living in a glass bowl," she notes wryly.

Less worry than hovering melancholy is the loss of longtime customers who become like family members. "Every year more pass away," says Emma Lou, who after twenty-six years in the business can look back and remember at least three generations of customers. Parents who brought in their children are now grandparents, and their children are now parents. If the cycle continues, Emma Lou's business will be promising for years to come. Yet, if Emma Lou's current customers, who average about fifty-five years of age, are not replaced by younger ones who reject fast food for slow cooking and life on the run for the easy camaraderie of the cafe community, the Sandwich Shop will become a thing of the past.

"I tease my customers, 'What're you going to do when I'm gone?'" Emma Lou confides. Her words reveal that she does indeed contemplate the possibility. Until that time comes, she is warmed by the loyalty, friendships, and support of the regulars like Alvin, Kerry, and the other men who wait in their cars under the glow of the streetlights for the cafe to open. If the minute hand creeps past five and Emma Lou hasn't arrived, they'll call on their cell phones to see if she's on her way. On the other hand, if she's running late, Kerry will be the first to receive the news. He'll unlock the Sandwich Shop with the key Emma Lou has provided for such an emergency. Then he'll get the coffee brewing, turn on the lights, and let in the other men. Together they'll wait for Emma Lou to arrive before draining their cups and departing for work.

What would they do without Emma Lou? What would she do without them? Let's hope it will be many years before they find out.

ROCKPORT
DJ's Main Street Cafe
413 Main Street
(812) 649-9047
M–F 6 A.M.–2 P.M.; Sa 7 A.M.–2 P.M.; Su closed (Central Time)
Donna and Jim Green

Donna Green has big worries. After twenty-one years "off and on" at Rockport's Main Street Cafe, the last eight as owner, she wonders whether she can hold on. Her fate is directly tied to the fate of Rockport, the Spencer County seat perched on the north bluffs of the Ohio River. The 2002 opening of the Natcher Bridge connecting Rockport with Maceo, Kentucky, was trumpeted as a boon to the area, but to Donna, that tune is alarmingly off key. The bridge, she says, "just made it easier for people to pass Rockport by." Now, instead of driving right through downtown Rockport, folks zip along Highway 231 without stopping to shop, buy gas, or eat.

"I do get people from Owensboro, Evansville, and Tell City, and they tell me, 'We didn't even know you were here.' People don't know we're here unless they get lost."

The isolation of Rockport is just one of Donna's concerns. Another is the faltering local economy, hit hard with the October 2004 closing of Peerless Pottery, a Rockport area employer for more than a century. Yet another is the aging of her regular customers, many of whom have made the transition from eating out to staying in to receive Meals on Wheels and other government-subsidized meal programs. As her old-timers settle into the easy chairs, Donna notes she is "not drawing the younger generation. They want to eat fast food and go."

When Donna was sixteen, she came to work for Forrest "Tig" Tigner at the Main Street Cafe, following in the footsteps of her mom, who had worked for Tig for years, supporting six children as a single parent on her wages. Today, even with Donna's husband's second income as a jailer, making a go of the restaurant is a real struggle. There are payments to make on the building, payments for repairs, payments for food and restaurant supplies. "There's no way a woman could raise six children on the restaurant today," she asserts. "Those were different times. Better times."

"I always wanted this restaurant. This was my dream. But now that I've got it, I don't know what to do with it. This place has always been here, and I'd like to see it stay. Things are going to have to change, or we won't make it. But I don't know how to change."

The plastic, glow-in-the-dark skeleton taped to the door seems to share Donna's mixed sentiments. Someone has taped a cutout balloon over his head and used a thick marker to make him say Open and Closed—both at the same time. Inside, the walls are filled with scanned historic photos of Rockport in its heyday, back when the electric railway hummed up and down Main Street, when the city grandstand, racetrack, city park, and Pioneer Village attracted visitors for a day of fun and leisure, when the high school was still located within walking distance of downtown. The high school was relocated to Reo years ago, leaving Rockport to struggle with its lost identity as a self-contained community. The pictures are reminders of what has been lost.

"I decided to get the pictures on the walls because this is home away from home," Donna explains. "Rockport's a nice little town, but I don't know what the future holds for it."

The future of the Main Street Cafe is just as uncertain. With eleven restaurants in a town of only twenty-one hundred residents, Donna is proud that hers is the "only home cooking restaurant here. If they want home cooking," she says, "they have to come here." Yet they don't, despite her best efforts to pull people in. This week she is advertising a $2.99 breakfast special, a true bonanza that includes biscuits and gravy, two eggs, potatoes, and sausage. "I'm not making any money," she concedes. "I'm just hoping they'll come back."

One person that stopped (and has yet to return) is Mitch Daniels. On his RV road trip across Indiana during his campaign for the governor's office, Daniels breakfasted at Donna's Saturday morning buffet. "He liked my french toast sticks," Donna remembers, "and named us 'Best Breakfast' on his Road Map to an Indiana Comeback. But he didn't ask me to sign his RV!"

Despite Daniels's endorsement, Donna hasn't experienced an upswing in business. Sadly, she believes "Mom and Pop places are on their way out. I don't know how they're gonna survive, and that's too bad because where are you gonna find home cooking like mine? About the only thing I don't make is my potatoes."

Monday through Saturday, Donna prepares an all-you-can-eat lunch buffet. "I don't do plate lunches because my customers prefer getting up and helping themselves and having as much as they want to eat." (The buffet also allows her to make do without employees. She runs the place only with the help of her friend Shaney Mayo.) The buffet includes two meat entrees, with Tuesdays reserved for fried chicken, Wednesdays for baked chicken and rolled dumplings. Beyond this, "I never know what I'm fixing until I walk in here. I had a dream last week that I was making liver and dumplings, and the next day, that's what I had!"

The price of the buffet includes a salad bar filled with lettuce and veggies and an assortment of tubs filled with canned fruit, coleslaw, potato salad, and other homemade salads. Dessert is also part of the deal, and if you're lucky enough to find Donna's best-selling coconut cream pie, you'll know Lady Luck has dealt you a winning hand. You'll be far better off than a local preacher and his wife who came in and found chocolate cream pie on the menu.

"I made chocolate pie one day and forgot to put the sugar in it," Donna laughs. "I got busy and just forgot. They said to me, 'Taste the pie. I think you forgot to put something in it.' I took a bite of it, and boy! It made you pucker up!"

Thankfully, sugarless chocolate pie is not standard issue at the Main Street Cafe, but if you're a true seeker of culinary oddities, Donna has one for you. Take a look at the menu, and you will find—neatly typed in unobtrusive little letters, quietly tucked in among burgers and sandwiches—none other than fried brains. It's a queer delicacy found in the Hoosier State only near Evansville, passed down by German immigrants who settled in the Ohio River Valley. Until the fear of mad cow disease led the USDA to ban the sale of brains from cattle older than thirty months, cow brains were the stuff of choice. Now you'll have to settle for pig brains, which most connoisseurs feel is an inferior substitute because it is harder to cook, falls apart easily, and doesn't have as much flavor.

Donna buys frozen pig brains one pound at a time and sets them out to thaw. They're precleaned, meaning she doesn't have to separate the brains from the surrounding membrane. "I can't handle fresh brains," she exclaims. While the brains melt into a gelatinous mass, she mixes a batter of eggs, flour, baking powder, and salt and pepper. The brains are kneaded into the batter, shaped into "slimy" patties ("In other words, they're gross!"), and then fried on the grill until they hold together in a reasonably solid form.

Then into the freezer they go, waiting for the day someone walks through the door with a hankerin' for a fried brain sandwich. Donna rather dreads the moment she reads those words scribbled on Shaney's notepad. It means she'll have to retrieve the frozen brain patty, drop it into the deep fat fryer, and watch it puff up like a blowfish before sandwiching it between two halves of a bun.

I'm told fried brains have the texture and consistency of scrambled eggs and not much of a flavor. Most of the flavor is in the seasoned batter. This might explain why most people douse their fried brains with mustard, ketchup, pickles, and onions. I figure they're either trying to make taste or disguise it.

Years back, it was common to find fried brains served at local fairs and festivals, in taverns, and on the breakfast tables of folks of German heritage, but "it's mostly tavern food nowadays," Donna explains. "This place has always served them, so I left them on the menu. I've got men and women both who eat them. I've got one ninety-six-year-old lady and a little old black lady from Grandview who comes in and eats two!

"Making them makes me sick, but I do it," she continues, pinching her nose with her thumb and forefinger and wrinkling up her brow. "I stand there fixing them and ask anyone watching if they want to try one. If they don't like them, they won't eat them. I don't get any new people giving them a try."

Whew! I'm off the hook. For the time being at least.

TELL CITY
Julie's Tell Street Cafe
922 Tell Street
(812) 547-2579
M–Th 5 A.M.–7 P.M.; F 5 A.M.–8 P.M.; Sa 5 A.M.–2 P.M.; Su closed
(Central Time)
Julie Fischer

Tell City derives its name from the Swiss folk hero William Tell, who shot an apple off his son's head with an arrow. To this day, the high school sports teams are known as the Marksmen and the junior high teams as the Archers. In 1857, Swiss immigrants living in Cincinnati bought land along the north banks of the Ohio River and established a planned city with wide, straight streets where they could raise their families, educate their children, work, and worship as they had in their homeland.

The optimism and spirit of the early settlers are shared by Julie Fischer, who, in 1998, took a leap of faith by cashing in the paychecks she received as a restaurant employee for the opportunity to write checks herself. She'd always dreamed of running her own restaurant. When she turned forty, she thought, "It's now or never" and took the chance.

"When you work for someone else, you work on a set schedule and don't take the business home with you," Julie says about life before and after buying the cafe. "Even though there is a lot of stress sometimes, I love working for myself."

After the former owners turned over the keys, Julie closed the restaurant for a month for some overdue remodeling. The building still had the cavernous, fluorescent feel of the neighborhood grocery it once was, so Julie reduced the open space by adding rustic wood partitions and booths where people can eat in semiprivacy. Filled with tables, the center of the cafe is popular with the regulars because it's easy for friends to lean across the back of a chair to exchange hellos or share a bit of gossip.

Throughout the remodeling, Julie left the doors of the cafe open so people could check on her progress. "They'd stick their heads in the door and ask, 'Is there any coffee?'" Julie laughs. When she set out a few chickens as decorations, they responded by bringing in a few of their own to add to the collection. A few became more, and more became a lot—but, as Julie points out, a lot is never *too* many. You'll find pullets and bantams, chicks and cockerels on shelves, on top of the milk dispenser, on the hood of the salad bar, stretched out along the front windowsill and inside the glass case under the register. With all of those roosters strutting about, there's bound to be competition for king of the farmyard. My choice is the cocky red sentinel inside the front door, a painted chainsaw carving by a local artist who has also left a small menagerie of other animals you can buy and take home with you. The king rooster, however, is not for sale.

The transformation of the neighborhood grocery into a cafe is just one of the many changes that Tell City has experienced in recent years. The closing of the century-old Tell City Furniture Company and the General Electric plant, once the community's leading employers, was a terrible blow. "We could really feel it," Julie says. The Tell City economy has improved significantly with the recent arrival of Waupaca Foundry and Webb Wheel, so that "things are now pretty much getting back to normal." The upswing is also marked by the arrival of a new Super Wal-Mart and an increasing number of franchise restaurants that string out along the commercial strip in a blaze of primary colors and corporate emblems.

"I was worried that the fast food and other restaurants would hurt," Julie says. "When Ponderosa opened, people went there and tried it out. And then they came back."

One visit told them what they wanted to know: there's a big difference between Julie's good home cooking and the imposter offerings at the national chains, acceptable to folks who know nothing but preprocessed food, value quantity over quality, or consider eating less an aesthetic pleasure than a mere bodily function. If that's not you, you'd best head over to Julie's Tell Street Cafe where the crew of devoted regulars is happy to rub elbows with a pretty steady itinerant trade—people sent by area motels and gas stations—as well as political candidates in search of a productive meet and greet. In 2004, both Mitch Daniels and Joe Kernan stopped while on the campaign trail to the governor's office.

The regulars know Julie's repertoire so well that a menu is superfluous, but first timers picking one up for a quick study often get a shock when they discover what may be the Hoosier State's quirkiest eats. I smugly thought I'd escaped them at Rockport, only to have them turn up again here.

"They get so tickled at the brain sandwiches," Julie chuckles. Down here along the Ohio River east of Evansville, fried brain sandwiches are a delicacy for some (and an abhorrence for others), a tidbit of heritage passed down from the areas' German and Swiss settlers who found a use for every last morsel of the cattle they raised.

After mad cow disease was discovered in the United States in late 2003, cow brains were replaced with ground pork brains, which Julie buys fresh in one-pound squares. She holds out her hand with the palm facing upward and makes picking motions with her thumb and forefinger. "The first thing I have to do is clean the brains by picking out the membranes." She wiggles her shoulders in a mock shudder. "I can hardly stand making them!"

"Why do you?" I ask.

"Because I have a group of women who meet here once a week, and they have to have their brain sandwiches."

I confess that I do not have the stomach for such a delicacy! Deep inside I am a culinary coward. Outwardly, however, I save face by using the plate of unfinished meatloaf on my table as my excuse. (The slab my waitress brought out was so sizeable it could have been mistaken for an Ohio River barge.) I have already eaten my fill, and a piece of pie still waits in the wings, so it really would be quite unreasonable for me to eat any more. Don't you agree?

Holding its own amidst the flock of chickens and roosters is a wood sign mounted on the wall that promises Home Cookin'. Even considering the brain sandwiches, it does not mislead. Julie's cook, Deanna Titus, knows her way around a kitchen and turns out meals worth squawking about. Three specials are offered every day with a choice of three sides from an extensive list that covers everything from corn bread and slaw to applesauce and lima beans. The day of my visit, meatloaf shared the daily menu board with country-fried steak and baked ham with pineapple glaze. Country-fried steak is one of Julie's top sellers, as is the chicken and dumplings generally served every Thursday ("They got mad at me last week because I had them on Friday") and the Friday night buffet. The end-of-the-workweek extravaganza features barbecued ribs and fried fiddlers—whole, bone-in catfish to Hoosiers living in the north. "We go through sixty pounds easily," Julie notes. "They just devour them!"

The buffet also includes an assortment of tempting cakes, bars, pies, and other desserts loaded on a table between the two food bars. Most are made from scratch by Deanna in the rear kitchen, but scattered in here and there are purchased gourmet pies and cheesecakes. Even a pie snob on a par with me will have a hard time discerning which is which. My Derby pie, a sweet, sugary custard pie filled with chocolate chips and walnuts, is not homemade, but I would never have known it if Julie hadn't told me.

Although the addition of seasonal specials such as summer salads, autumn pumpkin rolls, and winter soups and chili adds variety to Julie's large menu, she confesses that making the same thing week after week often gets monotonous. She and Deanna and the rest of her staff of fifteen are always looking through cookbooks and magazines for something new to try. If something grabs their attention, they'll offer it as a daily special to test customer reactions. In this way, new things are added to the menu, but never as replacements for the tried and true. "If we don't have meatloaf, chicken and dumplings, or their other comfort foods every week, we'll certainly hear about it," says Julie.

Comfort is derived as much from food as from regular routines. Beginning with the restaurant's official opening at five in the morning and at well-established times throughout the day, shifts of coffee drinkers circle the B.S. Table like ancient Greeks at an oracle. Day in and day out, they entertain Julie and her employees with nonstop conversation, jokes, and pranks. Most are men, but "there's one woman who can go with the best of them," laughs Julie, who gets to know the regulars on a "name to name basis." She is often among the first to learn of an accident, death, or health concern that disrupts the steady and predictable pattern of daily visits to the cafe that make the regulars feel like part owners.

Older men who have retired adopt the cafe as a home away from home. It is a good replacement for the social world of work and helps redefine lives whose meaning has changed. The cafe's official opener, Bernie Herman, is a retiree from General Electric. At three thirty every morning, he uses his own key to let himself in, and in the semidark he makes coffee and iced tea, lays the rugs on the floor, and does other small jobs to help get the day underway. At four thirty, he turns on the restaurant lights, and at five o'clock he turns the lock in the door and lets in the men waiting in cars and trucks along the curb. "It makes him feel important," Julie says, "and it's a great help to me to be able to focus on work in the kitchen. We're like a real family here. We take care of each other."

· ·

NEXT BEST BETS

BOONVILLE
Locust Street Cafe
118 West Locust Street
(812) 897-4724
In late August, Thanksgiving dinner with all the trimmings was unreasonably unseasonable to the out-of-town salesman at the next table, who opted for a breaded pork tenderloin. But the pie. Oh! The pie! He schedules client calls around the cafe's hours so as not to miss it.

CANNELTON
Edie's Country Kitchen
218 South Seventh Street (State Road 66)
(812) 547-5065
Not pretty, but pretty decent country cooking (including evening fiddlers) if you're rambling the river roads.

CELESTINE
Schulz Country Cafe
6762 East State Road 164
(812) 634-1323
The humble hen lays golden eggs in Dubois County, where tanker trucks of processed eggs depart daily for Sara Lee and other corporate bakeries. At Schulz's, a family-oriented cafe with a side tavern—you're in Indiana's German country now, where beer is its own food group—chickens of all shapes and sizes roost on shelves and counters. Fried chicken is a no-brainer, but go Deutsch with the pork and sauerkraut, brats and sauerkraut, or other regional fare.

CORYDON
Frederick's Cafe
112 North Elm Street
(812) 738-3733
The move from New Middletown brought country home cooking—and breakfast all day—to the city. Cream pies to drive for.

CORYDON
Yesterday's Cafe
100 East Chestnut Street
(812) 738-3231
This newish cafe replaces Jock's Lunch, a Corydon institution for half a century. It may take fifty years before Jock's is truly replaced. If that's even possible.

DUBOIS
Mathies Cafe
5416 Main Street
(812) 678-2772
Established in 1945 by Tony and Irene Mathies and now operated by their four children, Mathies is a combination cafe and tavern—an important community tradition in German-Catholic Dubois County. Clean as a whistle and bright as a summer day, Mathies is known far and wide for its fried chicken, hand-breaded tenderloin, German fried potatoes (seasoned with onion), and fiddler dinners. A page in the history book is about to turn, however. A For Sale sign hangs in the front window.

FRENCH LICK
T'Berry's Cafe
8271 West College Street
(812) 936-4220
Look for this local hangout, formerly John Henry's Restaurant, behind the schools complex and next door to the Twin City Feed Mill. The large photo collage freeze-frames the regulars in living color.

GALENA
Country Kitchen
7160 U.S. Highway 150
(812) 923-1109
Save U'r Gas Eat Here. A restaurant with this sign out front doesn't take itself too seriously!

GRIFFIN
Depot Diner
220 South Street
(812) 851-3051
This combination diner, gas station, convenience store, and local museum really is located in Griffin's old depot. Look for the lighted railroad crossing sign in the parking lot. Old photos show the aftereffects of the 1925 tornado—the deadliest in United States history—that destroyed Griffin. Nonsmokers will want to avoid the Depot, where clean air is as obsolete as the passenger train.

HARDINSBURG
Mary's Breakfast Nook
261 West Cheshire Lane
(812) 472-9207
A tuckaway little cafe on a side street where you're sure to be greeted with curiosity. The Nook is more local than the zip code.

NEW HARMONY
Main Cafe
520 North Main Street
(812) 682-3370
Beautiful vintage pressed tin covers the upper walls and ceiling of this century-old cafe featuring plain good cooking. I was kindly offered the last piece of coconut cream pie, rated a "must eat" by Jane and Michael Stern of *Roadfood* fame.

NEW PEKIN
Sandy's Family Restaurant
125 East State Road 60
(812) 967-4802
Hungry? How about the Hamburger with Attitude topped with a slice of baked ham or the Whistle Pig, a deep-fried hot dog stuffed with cheese and wrapped in bacon? A breakfast oddity is the Peppermint Patty Pancake created by one of the regulars. The town is officially known as New Pekin—it's listed that way on the state road map—but common usage, and the name of the post office, is simply Pekin.

OAKLAND CITY
Cozy Cove Cafe
331 South Main Street
(812) 749-3114
Vehicles surround this diminutive diner in a former service station like cowboys circled round a campfire. I had to park nearly a block away—a minor inconvenience that can't keep me away from the Cove's sweet custardy pies, golden onion rings, and daily specials. The knotty pine paneling and vintage linoleum are equally genuine.

PALMYRA
Frannie's Diner
850 Main Street Northeast
(812) 364-4058
Try as I would, I just couldn't finish the stack of buttermilk pancakes placed in front of me. And they were so good. A vending machine near the restrooms exchanges real collectible coins for quarters. Imagine that!

SALEM
Dinner Bell
305 South Main Street
(812) 883-5744
This retro-refurbished red, white, and black diner would impress even HGTV's *Design on a Dime* team. The Dinner Bell's got it all: age, beauty, trademark burgers, pies, and even grilled donuts for breakfast.

SALEM
Kathy's Main Street Cafe
105 South Main Street
(812) 883-9920
"Are you having fish? They've got good fish here," a wizened fellow advised me on Friday at noon. I opted for the BLT, made with too few tomatoes and more bacon than I knew what to do with. The entirely-from-scratch chocolate cream pie would have been a dream if it hadn't been a few days past fresh.

TELL CITY
The Freezer
626 Main Street
(812) 547-8814
This downtown fixture, originally an ice cream parlor, has one foot in the grave and another on a banana peel but is still known for its plate lunches and home-made pies and cobblers.

TELL CITY
Vivien's Place
510 Main Street
(812) 547-7234
Another choice in Tell City with a loyal local clientele and tried-and-true Hoosier tenderloins, fried chicken, and other beloveds.

Epilogue

Looking Back

When I first conceived the idea for a book on small town cafes, I envisioned a directory to good home-cooking spots that could be found within a single state. I planned to concentrate only on food, but soon after my first cross-country trip was underway it became apparent that cafes are more than places to grab a quick sandwich or hot meal. They are social hubs of small communities, where people gather to learn about election results, buy chances on the ladies' auxiliary quilt raffle, and share talk and laughter over a cup of coffee. That first book, *Cafe Wisconsin*, diverged from its original emphasis and developed into an examination of ways in which food is used to bring about social interaction. *Cafe Indiana* follows suit.

Yet *Cafe Indiana* is no mere copycat. The cross-cultural perspective provided by *Cafe Wisconsin* pushes *Cafe Indiana* into a new and interesting direction. As if it had a life of its own, *Cafe Indiana* restores my original emphasis on food, a valuable lens though which to examine Indiana's cultural heritage.

Cultural Influences on Indiana Cafe Food

Indiana is a state of contrasts. Geographically, it is divided across its middle by flat, sweeping prairies in the north and unglaciated hills and deep ravines— *hollers* in the vernacular Hoosier dialect—in the south. Culturally, it is just as diverse, owing to the migration and settlement of several distinct cultural groups: Yankees and European immigrants in the north, Appalachian mountaineers and others from the eastern uplands in the south, and Germans and German-speaking peoples statewide. Indiana's geographical and cultural fault line falls approximately along U.S. 40, the National Road, making a convenient division between its two rather distinct halves.

The state's cultural heritage heavily influences cafe food. As I ate my way around the state, I noticed preferences and patterns that reveal much about the state's culinary traditions. Some are regional and local specialties, a few are idiosyncrasies known only in specific cafes, but most are familiar statewide.

Southern Indiana

The most popular cafe foods in southern Indiana reflect the Anglo Irish and Appalachian heritage of the earliest white settlers, who crossed the Ohio River and pushed north in search of farmland and economic opportunity. They brought with them favorite and traditional dishes, such as ham and beans and biscuits and sausage gravy, both best sellers in cafes today. Ham and beans is typically served with corn bread and fried potatoes and frequently on Monday, the day traditionally set aside for doing laundry. Women commonly set a kettle of dry Great Northern, navy, or pinto beans to soak on Sunday night. The next morning, they'd add a piece of salt pork or ham and let the beans simmer slowly throughout the day as they tended to the wash. By the time the clothes were clean, dry, folded, and put away, Mother needed only to bake a pan of corn bread and fry some potatoes to complete the evening meal.

Split baking powder biscuits make the perfect foil for milk gravy spiced up with pork sausage. The duo is a mainstay in Hoosier cafes, as certain to be on the menu as breaded pork tenderloin. Sausage gravy is especially versatile and used as a topping for American fries, omelets, mashed potatoes, and chicken-fried steak. Sans sausage, milk gravy makes an excellent base for chipped beef or bacon—both served over biscuits. Mixed with pan drippings, it also becomes a tasty gravy for chicken.

Other familiar cafe foods with an old-stock American influence include hominy, grits, mustard and turnip greens, Hoosier-style green beans porked up with bacon or ham and diced onion, bone-in catfish (known as fiddlers in southern Indiana) or fillets, country-fried steak, pan-fried chicken, and chicken and rolled dumplings.

The first German and German-speaking immigrants, among them Moravians and Quakers, began arriving in Indiana prior to statehood. Vevay in Switzerland County was settled by the Swiss in 1796, with New Harmony established by German Anabaptists, the Rappites, in 1814. The second wave of immigration occurred during the 1830s and 1840s, with Germans establishing settlements in Dubois, Posey, Vanderburgh, and Franklin counties. Concurrently, Moravians of German descent migrated from North Carolina to Bartholomew County and founded the village of Hope, and German-speaking Swiss Mennonites established settlements in Adams County. In the 1850s, Swiss immigrants moved westward out of Cincinnati along the

Ohio River and established Tell City. In the 1860s, German-speaking Amish of Swiss descent began settling Daviess County from their former homes in northern Indiana, Pennsylvania, and Ohio.

Germans are the largest immigrant group in Indiana, yet traditional German foods have largely faded away, leaving only a few local specialties in small town cafes. True adventure eaters will want to sample the turtle soup and the mock turtle soup made with chicken, available at small restaurants and taverns in Dubois County. (I recommend Ferdy Flyer and Fleig's Cafe in Ferdinand and the Headquarters on Main Street in Jasper, although they are not featured in *Cafe Indiana*.) I lacked the nerve, but adventure eaters with a stoic bent may want to hold out for the fried brain sandwiches at DJ's Main Street Cafe in Rockport and at Julie's Tell Street Cafe in Tell City. (More on these later.) Much more to my taste is rouladen, a unique offering among others served at the now-closed Gundi's Restaurant in Mount Vernon, and bratwurst, sausage, and baked pork ribs, loins, and chops served with sauerkraut, which frequently appear as daily specials in cafes throughout southwestern Indiana.[1]

Northern Indiana

The culinary picture between the Michigan border and the National Road is noticeably different from that of southern Indiana. Here, for example, chicken and dumplings is replaced by chicken and noodles, a dish that nearly every cafe owner names as the most popular item on the menu. Beef and noodles is a not-too-distant second. An affinity for beef in all its varied forms and textures—chopped and baked beef, meatloaf, pot roast, beef Manhattan—is more prevalent and seems to align northern Indiana more closely with the midwestern farm belt than the mountain south.[2]

The greater ethnic diversity of northern Indiana leads to relatively more varied menus. The influence of Eastern European immigrants who settled in the greater Chicago area, including Gary and Hammond, is seen in dishes such as the stuffed cabbage rolls (or *golumbki*) served at the Town Square Restaurant in Howe. In Knox, at the Family Cafe, the owner's Eastern European heritage and Chicago upbringing play out in such daily specials as roast pork, *pierogi*, dumplings, and sauerkraut. The Greeks are another immigrant group whose culinary traditions linger in some northern Indiana restaurants and cafes; at the Cedar Lake Kitchen in Cedar Lake, you'll find lemon rice soup, salads and omelets, gyros, and other Greek specialties. The presence of the Mennonites, who emigrated directly from Switzerland to Adams County, and of the Amish, who moved into Elkhart and LaGrange County from Pennsylvania and Ohio, is also seen in northern Indiana's cafes. At the Palmer House in Berne, you'll find *Schweizer* salad, *heisse Kartoffelsalat* (hot potato salad), and *roesti* (potato pancakes). Farther north, the Village Inn in Middlebury offers headcheese, souse, and fried mush with tomato gravy—all Pennsylvania Dutch specialties associated with the Amish.

Cafe owners who are more recent immigrants to northern Indiana are also diversifying menus by introducing specialties from their own cuisines. For example, Jozef and Maria Turbak, their daughter-in-law, Agnes, and Maria's sister, Terese, sell more Polish food than American at the Country Cafe in Chesterton. Maria and Terese bake traditional Polish pastries such as *paczki, kolaczki,* and *chrusciki,* along with a variety of cakes and breads to supplement a variety of Polish main and side dishes, including homemade sausage, *golumbki,* and fifteen varieties of *pierogi.* At Daniel's Ligonier Cafe in Ligonier, Daniel Alemu prepares standard Hoosier food throughout the week but reserves Friday nights for dishes from his native Ethiopia. Knives and forks are replaced by *injera,* a traditional flatbread made from teff used to pick up food; barbecued beef is replaced with *wot*; and pink lentils substitute for navy and pinto beans. In Whiting, *chorizo,* tortillas, beans and rice, and other traditional Mexican food shared menu space with Coney dogs, spaghetti, and Oreo pancakes at the Whiting House of Pancakes, which sadly is now closed.

In preparing and serving traditional ethnic and heritage foods, cafe owners act as "ritual specialists" expressing their own, their family's, and their immediate social group's cultural identity through edible symbols of heritage. Most ethnic selections tend to be cautious and familiar—sweet pastries and cakes, pork roast and dumplings, rice and beans—and therefore a safe and easy way of emphasizing ethnicity. Their peaceful coexistence with regional and local specialties and conservative Hoosier meat-and-potatoes fare underscores the fact that Hoosier cafe food, like American food in general, is culturally diverse yet unified.[3]

Legendary, Regional, and Local Foods

Despite dissimilarities in cafe food between northern and southern Indiana, a homogeneity (some might say monotony) in Hoosier food prevails. This is perhaps most evident in the statewide craving for Indiana's foremost iconic cafe dish: the pork tenderloin. Hoosiers everywhere—north and south, east and west, big city and small town—love these pounded, breaded, and deep-fried orbs of pork sandwiched into a bun. To Jane and Michael Stern, America's pop culture food gurus, the tenderloin is "an emblematic regional passion." In their article "Love Me Tenderloin," in *Gourmet* magazine of all places, the Sterns credit street vendor Nick Franstein of Huntington with inventing the tenderloin in 1904. Four years later Franstein discontinued his cart and opened Nick's Kitchen, one of the Sterns' top three pounded pork palaces in the Hoosier State. The other two are Mr. Dave's in Manchester and the former Gnaw Bone Food and Fuel in Gnaw Bone. I do not dispute their choices, but I must add three others: Newberry Cafe in Newberry, Storie's Restaurant in Greensburg, and the new Cozy Cabin Cafe in Gnaw Bone. The Newberry tenderloin is a thick, meaty slab of juicy fresh pork with a clear, clean flavor. Pounded to order—as thick or as flat, as small or as large as you like—Storie's tenderloin has been named best by readers of both the *Greensburg Daily News* and the statewide *Electric Consumer*. And the peppered and breaded German tenderloin topped with sauerkraut at the Cozy Cabin Cafe, a mere twenty-five miles from my Martinsville home, continually lures me back.[4]

If the iconic Hoosier diner meal starts with pork tenderloin, it must rightfully conclude with sugar cream pie, Indiana's second contribution to legendary American regional food. So closely is sugar cream pie associated with Indiana that Ken Haedrich, author of *Pie*, has declared it the "unofficial Hoosier State Pie." Known as a "poor man's pie," "Depression pie," or "desperation pie," because it can be made when the pantry is nearly empty, Hoosier sugar cream pie consists of little more than a pastry crust filled with an eggless cream pudding cooked on a stovetop, baked in the oven, or both. The pie appears to be at least as old as the state itself; a contributor to the *Hoosier Cookbook* (1976) notes that her recipe for sugar cream pie is over 160 years old.[5]

Ironically, despite being synonymous with the Hoosier State, sugar cream pie is something I rarely encountered in small town cafes. In fact,

I sampled homemade sugar cream pie just once; sadly, it was flawed with floury lumps and a wiggly under-doneness. I suspect that most of the other sugar cream pies I saw being eaten by customers or sitting on cafe counters or in refrigerators were mass-produced by Wick's Pies of Winchester. With their perfectly molded crust in a disposable aluminum pie pan, pale filling dusted with nutmeg, and shallow depth, they are easy to recognize. Wick's mass-produces about twelve thousand pies in an eight-hour shift, and although it boasts thirty different varieties, it is best known for its traditional sugar cream pie made from a nineteenth-century family recipe, considered by many folks I met on the road to be the ultimate in Hoosier sugar cream pie.[6]

Persimmon pudding and fried biscuits with apple butter are two more foods considered unique to Indiana, but they are more accurately representative of southern Indiana than the state as a whole. Made from the fruit of the native persimmon tree that grows wild over the Hoosier hills, persimmon pudding is an autumn ritual traditionally made from cherished family recipes passed down from one generation to the next. You'll find it on the menu at Fin Mill's Family Restaurant, formerly the Chicken Inn in Mitchell, which celebrates its role as the state's persimmon capital with the Persimmon Festival held every October. In Morgantown, at Kathy's Cafe, persimmon pudding appears as a dessert special during October and November.[7]

Fried biscuits with apple butter are believed to have originated at the Nashville House restaurant in Nashville. A simple yeast dough is brought to rise and then shaped into biscuits and dropped into the deep fryer. Served browned and hot with homemade apple butter amply laced with cinnamon, the delicious duo straddles the line between bread and dessert. After Dave and Rosalie Hardin, owners of the Chicken Inn, fell in love with this Nashville House specialty, they added fried biscuits with apple butter to their own menu. At Chambers Smorgasbord in Spencer, the combo is a must-have, don't-dare-to-run-out attraction on the daily food bar.[8]

Another menu item that's a regional favorite in small town Hoosier cafes is the fried bologna and egg sandwich. (That's pan fried or grill fried, not deep fried.) I repeatedly found these on breakfast menus in the south central part of the state, in a narrow band stretching from approximately Shoals to Madison. At the now closed Manville General Store and

Restaurant, located in the tiny village of Manville in Jefferson County, fried bologna—playfully dubbed "Hoosier steak"—evoked childhood memories of growing up during the Depression for Lucille Brinson. Back then, bologna was a cheap, everyday part of a town family's diet, but for farm kids bored with eating the family's own chickens and hogs, it was a store-bought treat enjoyed only during trips to town. At the Dinner Bell in Salem, fried bologna is only slightly more popular for breakfast than sliced and fried hotdogs. (Another Dinner Bell breakfast favorite—an idiosyncrasy rather than localized cultural pattern—is grilled yeast donuts.) In Brownstown at Brock's Family Restaurant, fried hotdog slices are layered between slices of bread and served with tomato soup.[9]

The title of quirkiest regional cafe food in Indiana without a doubt goes to the brain sandwich, an unusual specialty of Swiss and German origins found along the Ohio River east of Evansville. More common as tavern food, they are patties of fresh pork brain, coated with egg and seasoned flour, plunged into a deep fryer until they puff up, and served on a bun. Historically, the brains of young calves were used, but since mad cow disease showed up in late 2003, pork brains have been substituted. I'm told fried brain has a very mild flavor and the texture of scrambled eggs, but I can't verify that. I couldn't bring myself to eat it! You can find out for yourself by ordering a fried brain sandwich at DJ's Main Street Cafe in Rockport and Julie's Tell Street Cafe in Tell City. "Making them makes me sick, but I do it," says Donna Green, owner of DJ's. "I stand there fixing them and ask anyone watching if they want to try one. If they don't like them, they won't eat them. I don't get any new people giving them a try."[10]

Diehard adventure eaters will revel in the regional, local, and downright kooky foods found in Indiana's small town cafes. Those who are more cautious will happily settle for the average and ordinary prepared in-house and from scratch. The most common cafe foods throughout the state probably won't be a surprise to native Hoosiers, but they did catch me unawares. I moved to Indiana from Wisconsin, where the most popular items on cafe menus are the Friday night fish fry and the hot beef sandwich—a beef Manhattan in Hoosier lingo. In Indiana, cafe owners told me time and again that their best sellers are breaded, deep-fried pork tenderloin, biscuits and gravy, ham and beans, chicken and noodles, beef and noodles, chicken-fried steak, and fried chicken (either pan fried, deep fried, or Broasted), pretty much in that order. Other top-of-the-list menu items are mashed pota-toes and gravy, seasonal soup and chili, kidney bean salad, coleslaw, and pie.

FOODS I CRAVE BUT RARELY FOUND

I might just as well admit it. When it comes to pie, I'm a real snob. I prefer my pie made by skilled hands, starting with the bottom crust and moving right through the filling on up to the top crust, streusel topping, or pouf of foamy meringue. That's why I am disappointed with the state of pie in Indiana's small town cafes. There are far too few cafe owners baking pies made entirely from scratch, and among those that are, a good number shouldn't be. They'd do best to abandon their boastful claims of homemade and follow the state-wide trend of "partway" pies made by filling extruded, factory-made, frozen crusts with homemade cream fillings. In addition, real egg white meringue is far too frequently abandoned for a commercial bouffantlike marshmallow product that doesn't shrink or weep like the real thing. Some clever cafe own-ers even make partway fruit pies by removing a thawed factory crust from its foil pan, flattening it out, and trimming off the molded ribbonlike edge to make a top crust. Pie connoisseurs like me have to be constantly vigilant to detect such coy chicanery and dodge the tempting promises of "fresh-baked" and "home-baked" pies on daily specials boards.[11]

Whether they're made entirely from scratch or partway, the most popular pies in Hoosier cafes are cream pies, also known as pudding pies or meringue pies because of their topping (although some are topless or covered with a nondairy whipped topping like Cool Whip). Cream pies come in a variety of basic flavors—vanilla, chocolate, coconut, peanut but-ter—that can be creatively blended to expand the repertoire. At Brock's Family Restaurant in Brownstown, for example, Tom Gray makes forty-nine varieties of honest-to-goodness homemade pie, including chocolate peanut butter, banana chocolate, cherry chocolate, and pineapple cream. His fiftieth variety, orange cream, didn't make it out of the starting block. Only one piece was sold. At Brock's, and seemingly statewide, coconut cream is the most popular pie. So much for the Indiana icon, sugar cream. As far as fruit pies go, Hoosiers everywhere are awfully fond of old-fashioned, down-home-on-the-farm rhubarb thickened with flour. Vying for second place in the popularity poll is probably seasonal strawberry made with fresh berries loosely glued together with a light glaze.[12]

Pie made entirely from scratch is scarce in Indiana cafes, but baked goods are even more so. Baking is pretty much limited to biscuits, yeast rolls, and corn bread. I occasionally found cinnamon rolls but never other types of sweet rolls, such as caramel or caramel pecan rolls; neither did I find doughnuts or coffee cake—other than a strawberry buckle variety at Friends Cafe in New Paris. With a few exceptions, cafe owners are not baking yeast bread, dinner rolls, or buns; nor are they preparing quick breads, like banana and pumpkin, or muffins. Deserving recognition are those who do: Marsha Thomas at the Corner Cafe in Nappanee, Tom and Cindy Hackett at the Town Square Restaurant in Howe, Lanny and Lois Pickett at the Newberry Cafe in Newberry, Ruth Herschberger at Herschberger Essen Haus in Converse, and Maria Turbak and her sister, Terese, at the Country Cafe in Chesterton. Homemade cookies and bars, other than brownies, are also rarely found. Pastries are virtually nonexistent save for the *paczki, kolaczki, chrusciki,* and other Polish specialties at the Turbak family's Country Cafe. In fact, more baking is done at the Country Cafe, and in far greater variety, than at any other cafe in the state.

Like real baked goods, real dairy products—especially butter, whipped cream, cheese, and half-and-half and cream for coffee—are also noticeably missing in Indiana cafes. I was served real butter no more than a half a dozen times in visits to over four hundred cafes, and when I sometimes requested it, I was told it was unavailable. Almost universally, Cool Whip or other nondairy whipped toppings substitute for real whipped cream. I like Cool Whip as much as the next midwesterner—more of it is sold in the Midwest than in any other region in the United States—but nothing tops persimmon pudding, a hot fudge sundae, or a slab of pumpkin pie like real dairy whipped cream. Likewise, real cheese is an absolute must for grilled cheese sandwiches, burgers, and omelets. The rubbery, processed variety, which melts into a slick smoothness, is acceptable only for soup. But then, I am a transplant from the Dairy State.[13]

Food Events and Food Places

Much more than places to grab a quick sandwich or hot meal, cafes are a vital social hub of small communities. Folklorists Charles Camp, Lin T. Humphrey, and others have long promoted the study of American food and food customs—foodways—in social context. Food should be studied not by itself but as part of the total event or festive gathering in which it plays a part, such as the family birthday party, community festival, or church supper. Humphrey suggests that the study of foodways includes "places where people get together to eat, drink, and have a good time." Places like Janet's Kitchen in Rensselaer, the Highway 341 Country Cafe in Wallace, and Harold's Restaurant in Poseyville. Places like Cafe Indiana.[14]

The study of food leads to cookbooks and such restaurant guides as Duncan Hines's *Adventures in Good Eating* and Jane and Michael Stern's *Roadfood*. The addition of social context—food events and food places—leads to *Cafe Indiana*.[15] During my search, I explored the various roles cafes play in Indiana's small towns and in the lives of individuals both historically and today. I treated cafes as texts that, like written materials, could be read for social information. Seemingly small details became important. In cornmeal mush and headcheese, I read cultural heritage; in retired men's coffee groups, the renegotiation of individual identities and social roles; in tourist brochures tucked into display racks, the promotion of the local area to outsiders. Certainly cafes play many roles, but in considering decor and architecture, oral and written words, social gatherings and performances, cafes function, most importantly, as heritage centers, senior centers, and chambers of commerce.[16]

CAFES AS HISTORICAL MUSEUMS
Local History: Photos, Artifacts, and Oral Histories
As historical museums, cafes allow communities to review and reshape their past and present it for public consumption as they wish it to be remembered. Walls are often decorated with black and white photographs depicting a town's history: street scenes with boardwalks and horse-drawn wagons, interiors of stores and other businesses, families gathering for reunion picnics. Typically lent or donated from the private collections of regular customers, historic photos are especially popular with older members of the community, who enjoy studying the photos, hoping to find a relative or old friend they recall from childhood. Natives who have moved away and return for visits are also pleased to find images of the past hanging on the walls, images that recall long-forgotten memories and inspire reminiscences and anecdotes. For a community's young residents and newcomers, on the other hand, these photographs establish the past as a knowable time and place.

Physical artifacts also tell the history of local areas. Among other things, you'll find cafes decorated with school memorabilia, railroad collectibles, and items celebrating the achievements of high school athletic teams. In the Old School Cafe in Pleasant, located in the former cafeteria of the township grade school, you'll find old class photographs, a slate chalkboard used as the daily specials board, a cheerleader's megaphone, and little red schoolhouses and red apples. The Gosport Diner in Gosport, once an important station on the Monon and Pennsylvania railroads, has a railroad crossing sign on its front awning and a mural of the town depot painted on an inside wall. In Lapel, Julie Terry's Bulldog Corner celebrates the athletic achievements of the Lapel High School Bulldogs—especially in the 1940 and 2005 state basketball championships—with photographs, pennants, and framed newspaper articles. The Mohawk Grill in Waldron has a similar shrine to the 2004 Class A basketball state champions, the Waldron Mohawks. Distant titles are also not forgotten. Until it tragically burned in June 2005, the Spartan Inn in Wingate had an entire dining room dedicated to local school history, particularly the "Gymless Wonders" who won the 1913 and 1914 state basketball title with no gym of their own in which to practice. Irreplaceable memorabilia and artifacts were destroyed in the fire. Like the mythical Phoenix that arose from the ashes, the Spartan Inn was rebuilt and reopened in the summer of 2007.

Physical objects often stimulate oral histories in the form of personal reminiscences, anecdotes about local characters and events, jokes and riddles, and retellings of practical jokes. At the Spartan Inn, the men around the community coffee table, including two members of the Spartan Club that bought the building so the town could have a cafe, told me about the town's history. I learned about native sons Homer Stonebraker, the first high school basketball superstar, and Raymond "Gaumey" Neal, the DePauw University football coach who in 1933 had an undefeated, untied, and unscored-upon season. The men became Wingate tour guides when they pointed out the tiny brick calaboose across the street; the livery-stable-turned-high-school-gym next to the town's post office; the Japanese pagoda built by John Wingate as a retreat for his wife (located one block west of the Spartan Inn at 108 Main Cross); and, out in the country, the stone marker commemorating the formation of the National Horse Thief Association, the forerunner to the Indiana State Police (Spartan Club member Dallie Jones drove into it during the Blizzard of 1977), and the old Coal Creek School, now home to a small business. For a small town, Wingate has historic treasures galore, and the loss of the Spartan Inn was tragic indeed.

Cafes Then and Now

In interpreting individual cafes as museums, the heritage of specific towns and their surrounding areas is pulled into focus. But if we step outside the individual frame and consider all cafes at once, a history of Hoosier cafes comes into view. Unfortunately, the cafes that remain reveal very little about the earliest years. The story must begin in the 1930s, when restaurants were located primarily downtown on the main business street. As Americans became more enraptured with and dependent on the automobile, drive-ins, grills, root beer stands, burger boxes, and motel and filling station eateries began appearing at town edges.[17]

Perhaps in response to this centripetal pull, by the 1940s and 1950s many new cafes were built and many older cafes were updated with attractive neon signs (one of the best vintage signs belongs to the Chicken Inn in Mitchell), durable stainless steel, chrome, and Formica, and soda fountains and jukeboxes. During this period the cafe became the local teen hangout, where high school kids consumed burgers and malts after school and before and after ball games. Many received or gave their first kiss in the privacy of a booth. The Steamer Cafe in Loogootee dates to this era, as does Janet's Kitchen in Rensselaer, built in a Swiss style to reflect the town's heritage, and Harold's Restaurant in Poseyville. These cafes still look a lot as they did when they opened. Harold's glossy red backbar with round mirrors and vintage Coca-Cola buttons, stainless-steel soda fountain, blue Formica counter and lozenge-top stools, and tufted black and red vinyl banquettes make it the best-preserved 1950s-era eatery in the state.

Another popular mid-twentieth-century restaurant type, evolved from turn-of-the-century horse-drawn food wagons, is the streamlined, stainless steel diner. There are eight authentic examples in Indiana, all located in urban areas, with the exception of Alexander's Sit-N-Bull outside of Clarks Hill. It is a 1950s Mountain View diner resplendent in pink and chrome. While Alexander's Sit-N-Bull is the real thing, two other cafes nostalgically revive the diner mystique in clever simulations. In Garrett, Ozia Clancy and Steve Frappier's Dinky Diner is a porcelain-coated steel diner, a prebuilt, modular type of restaurant placed on site in 1938. A previous owner hung sheets of silver paper behind the service counter to resemble a quilted stainless steel backsplash and decorated in a Coca-Cola theme, all of which Ozia and Steve have retained. At the Dinner Bell in Salem, a clever makeover includes sheets of aluminum affixed to the counter front and lower walls, a countertop of black and white ceramic tiles, and a checkerboard floor laid in red, black, and white vinyl squares.[18]

Many cafe owners go for a 1950s rock-and-roll feel on a leaner budget, relying on replicas of Coca-Cola advertising signs and other pieces, photos of classic cars (Peggy Sue's Diner in Chesterton, where a fifties-themed cafe was an obvious choice for owner Peggy Sue Wellsand), and turquoise and silver metallic vinyl chairs with pink piping and chrome legs (Baby Boomers II in Hamilton).

The 1960s are primarily represented in Hoosier cafe interiors by the continued use of stainless steel and chrome; Formica in boomerang, crushed ice, and tweed patterns; and colors of turquoise, orange, and bright earth tones. Pale birch cabinets, counter fronts, and storage and display cases also appear. The 1970s linger in colors like avocado, harvest gold, and browns of varying shades, as well as faux wood paneling and cabinet doors. The period's most significant—and lasting—impact on Indiana cafes, however, is the advent of the do-it-yourself movement that inspired owners and their husbands to pick up hammer and saw and refashion cafes according to popular, easy, and relatively inexpensive trends. Paneling and wallpaper went up over old plaster walls, carpet went down over cracked and chipped linoleum, and heavy mansard overhangs above front windows replaced tattered canvas awnings. Unfortunately, in far too many cases, these cheap cover-ups substituted for much-needed repairs in century-old main street buildings.[19]

The 1960s and 1970s are also distinguished by a change in service format, namely the introduction of the smorgasbord or buffet. This help-your-self, all-you-can-eat method of dining appears to have been influenced by a Hoosier trend toward cafeteria-style restaurants and the opening of national buffet chains during the same period. When William Miller bought the Home Cafe in New Carlisle in 1959, for example, it was already experimenting with a small food bar. In the 1960s, Miller enlarged the restaurant and expanded the buffet, which now takes up about one-third of the side dining area. Buffets "were a lot more unique back then. Now there's one on every corner," his son Bill Miller says. Down in the Owen County seat of Spencer, Chambers Restaurant became Chambers Smorgasbord in about 1981, after Robert Spencer conceived it as a gimmick to pull in customers. Other notable buffets and smorgasbords in Hoosier cafes are those at the Palmer House in Berne, Windell's Cafe in Dale, and Teel's Family Restaurant in Mentone.[20]

The do-it-yourself remodeling and redecorating of the 1980s is characterized by a love for all things country that popularized wainscoted lower walls and painted or papered upper walls—usually accented with a complementary border. The addition of dropped ceiling panels, inexpensive metal stack chairs, wood-grain-look dining tables and booths, and carpeted floors completes the uninspired, limited-budget interior of a majority of today's cafes.

Sadly, today many cafes suffer from years of delayed maintenance and neglect. Others, like Peppin's Cafe—now The Lovely Cafe—in Remington, have undergone extensive repairs and redecorating so that they are almost entirely new again. When Jane and Michael Stern visited the former Remington Cafe in the mid-1970s, they noted that it had been recently remodeled, with the walls covered with a "plastic wood" paneling. When Ron and Jerri Peppin purchased it thirty years later, repairs required nearly a complete gutting of the building. Across the state, such periodic cleansing and rebuilding has occurred, with small town economy and practicality leading to the recycling of countless retail and private buildings for use as cafes. Today, it is possible to eat in an old school (Old School Cafe in Pleasant), a service station (Country Charms Cafe in Westphalia), even a former jail (Gosport Diner in Gosport). As buildings were transformed, living quarters were typically added upstairs or off the back, so that owners were not only operators but also residents.[21]

CAFE OWNERSHIP

Like a community glue, cafes link the past and present, age and youth. Many are second-generation family businesses. Some children take to them eagerly, like Bill and George Miller, who took over Miller's Restaurant in New Carlisle, a business established by their father, William Miller, in 1959. Other children leave home looking for new opportunities before returning to restaurant life, as did Phil Wolpert at the West End Restaurant in Decatur. Others, like Debbie Montgomery and her sister, Shannon Tharp, at Velma's Diner in Shoals, take over a family business after a parent's failing health makes it impossible to continue. Whether they deliberately choose restaurant work or simply fall into it, these children are proud that their cafes are family businesses—an unbroken thread running from the past to the present. "It makes us proud to carry on the family business. All we've done is tried not to screw up what our parents left us," says Don Storie of Storie's Restaurant in Greensburg. While some hope their own children will continue the family tradition, others urge theirs into an easier, more lucrative life. Still others know that tradition will end with them; their children have families and careers of their own that preclude taking over the family restaurant.

Sometimes family ownership jumps a generation. In Roann, siblings Jennifer (Lynn) Ellis and Bob Lynn III have fulfilled a longtime dream of buying back the restaurant their grandfather Bob Lynn Sr. owned and oper ated for thirty years. They long to restore the restaurant's soda fountain and counter and have plans to create a historical display centered on their grandfather. Jennifer notes that efforts like theirs are "recycling" Roann. "I feel like it's our turn now to contribute to the community as adults," she says.

Family heritage is further emphasized by displaying family portraits, heirlooms, and other personal belongings and by using family recipes and cooking methods. Vicky Pingle at Vicky's Restaurant in Winamac displays her great-uncle's marble collection and framed photographs of her family. At Velma's Diner, Debbie Montgomery relies on the instructions of her mother, Velma, who has been in a nursing home since she suffered a stroke, to prepare the foods her customers have long loved. She refers to the cafe's meatloaf as "my mom's" and the method for making macaroni and cheese as "the way my mom always made it." When her customers let her know the frozen peanut butter pie wasn't up to snuff, Debbie took a piece to Velma, who identified a missing ingredient. Family foodways, like portraits and heirlooms, link generations by making the past an important part of the present.

Because of Debbie's desire to keep Velma's Diner in the family, as it has been for over twenty-five years, the Shoals restaurant has escaped the fate of so many others that have closed or changed hands. While the cafes featured in *Cafe Indiana* have largely stood the test of time, the average length of cafe ownership is only about five years. Many turn over even more quickly than that. Within five years of the publication of Wendell Trogdon's *Main Street Diners* (2000), for example, just over half of the 125 featured cafes remained in business under the same owner, and twenty-five cafes had closed for good. In the three years that I ate my way across Indiana, several featured and many Next Best Bet cafes also shut their doors. The ownership of many others changed. What accounts for such a significant attrition rate?[22]

I am constantly amazed at the number of cafe owners who enter the business on a lark, with little or no experience. Many report that they have always loved to cook, or always wanted to run their own business, and a restaurant just happened to come along. They buy the business or sign a lease and soon realize that (1) they're in over the heads, (2) the fun they expected hasn't materialized, (3) there is much more work than they bargained for, (4) they're just not a people person, (5) the business isn't turning a profit. So the doors are shut and the cafe goes back on the market.

Other cafes close because of aging buildings—and historic downtowns—that are victims of delayed maintenance or downright neglect. After fifty or more years of owners making do or doing nothing, it's often an impossible burden for today's proprietors to make the necessary repairs to structures, interiors, and kitchen equipment. New owners typically invest every cent they have to buy the restaurant and get it up and running. There's rarely extra money to do more than hang new panel board or slap on yet another coat of paint in the name of fixing up. In other cases, an owner's divorce, failing health, increasing age, or death force a cafe to close. Many other operators discover they cannot work with their co-owners and partners; forced to go it alone or quit, they too often choose the latter.

Within a period of five years, 35 percent of the cafes that Trogdon documented had new owners. Amazingly, despite the difficulties in running a cafe, there is always someone else itching to give it a try. While many owners are neophytes, quite a few bring food service experience with them. Children take over the family business, and employees step up to become owners, as did JoAnn Phillips at the former Spartan Inn in Wingate and Sharon LeFever and Saundra Minger at the Palmer House in Berne. Others, like Ann Cain at the Wolcott Theatre Cafe in Wolcott, expand a catering business into a full-time restaurant, or, like Ozia Clancy at the Dinky Diner in Garrett, finally seize the opportunity to put culinary degrees to work.

Still others, like Vicky Pingle at Vicky's Restaurant in Winamac and Ron and the late Jerri Peppin of the former Peppin's Restaurant in Remington, have been in the restaurant business once, gotten out, and then returned to the business they love.

Several others, like Jim Symington, move into restaurant ownership from entirely unrelated jobs. Jim cashed in his thirty-year career in various manufacturing industries to become owner of Rich's Cafe in New Haven, which he had patronized since moving to the area from Chicago in 1985. At Brock's Restaurant in Brownstown, retired Cummins electrician Tom Gray, son-in-law to the cafe's founders, turned an interest in baking into a second career. The same thing occurred at the Newberry Cafe in Newberry when Lanny Pickett traded in his contractor's tool belt to follow his passion for old-fashioned, from-scratch cooking.

What are the keys to a cafe's success? Foremost is an owner or owners with staying power. These are the ones who are in the business for the long haul rather than the short term. Forty years after she bought the Steamer Cafe with her sister, Iris, Sue Hunt looked back on her tenure—the longest period of single ownership in the state—and was amazed that so many years have flown by. Now tired and wanting to retire, Sue would rather close the little restaurant down than see it transformed into a pizza place. She is certain that no one will work as hard or as long as she did, or be as committed to all home cooking, or be as loyal to her customers as she has been. No doubt she is right.

As Sue so strongly believes, a cafe's success depends on the quality of its food and the relationship between owner and customer. It also depends on the upkeep and cleanliness of the building, and its physical appearance. I personally am turned off by cafes with walls stained brown with nicotine and airborne grease from the grill, dirt-imbedded carpets, and sticky tabletops and menus. The personalities of the owner and employees are also important. People who are shy, poor conversationalists, unable to take a joke or fling back a response, crumble under criticism, or lack a passion for their work are probably doomed from the start. Successful owners must have good a business sense (or have a family member or loyal employee who does), have the ability to manage the help, and be motherly enough to care for elderly customers, young employees, and small children who dine with their parents and grandparents. Lastly, success seems always to be related to a large amount of family support. Owners whose spouses, siblings, children, grandchildren, and other extensions of the family are willing to roll up their sleeves and help out stand a much greater chance of making it through the trying first five years. Ask Ruth Herschberger at Hershberger Essen Haus in Converse about this. She has the support of her husband, daughters, sisters-in-law, and other family members who help with the day-to-day work at the cafe.

Cafes as Community Centers
Men's Coffee Groups: Reviewing, Reshaping, and Renegotiating Lives
In cafes throughout Indiana, retired men gather at preset hours to pass the time over coffee, talk, and practical jokes. Often they begin showing up before a cafe is actually open, walking into a dark room through the front or back door. (If the owner hasn't yet arrived to unlock the door, they use their cell phones to wake her up and hurry her along.) They turn on the coffee pot, sweep and straighten the rugs, and help the owner prepare for the day. Often they help themselves to coffee and leave money in a mug or bowl. Naming themselves Bullshippers, Bull Shipping Department, Liars Club, or Gosport University, these coffee klatches are a daily social ritual in which lives are reviewed and reshaped and identities renegotiated after retirement. The members are predominantly men, although from time to time a wife or other woman will sit in with the group. In such case, however, women generally tend to be observers rather than active participants. While it is not unheard of for a woman to be a dominant member of a coffee group, many tend to gather in their own groups—usually church groups, exercise groups, or widows sharing a meal.

Ironically, although women are traditionally associated with coffee parties and gossiping, in small town cafes, men are by far the more notorious coffee klatchers. For retired men, these groups replace the daily social interaction they enjoyed when they were employed. Signs, like the ship with a bull placed front and center on the coffee table at Chambers Smorgasbord in Spencer, declare who they have become—Bullshippers. Similarly, personalized coffee mugs emphasize the hobbies—fishing, golfing, eating out—that now keep them busy. At the local cafe, men are remade.

While they work out new, comfortable identities, the retired men review the past with reminiscences about the work they have done, the things they have experienced, the people they have known. "I remember when" stories are popular entertainments, and local raconteurs spin out tales about football and basketball games played years ago in high school, their military service during World War II, and the cost of medical care a half-century ago. Through their eyes, the past is superior to the present, a time when life was happier and more secure and the young still had respect for their elders.

Review of the past leads to commentary about the present, and coffee klatches "solve all the problems of the world." The most common general topics of discussion between 2004 and 2006 were local politics, the proposed I-69, the increase in property taxes, and hurricanes Katrina and Wilma (and, of course, the resulting rise in gas prices). Less significant topics are also discussed and debated, such as the price of a cup of coffee, the ideal amount of water to drink each day, Medicare payments, golfing, fishing, farming, and the best freeways and approaches to major cities. Talk about current conditions—on international, national, and personal levels—shapes and orders the present and provides the men with a sense of involvement in external events that are unpredictable and beyond their control.[23]

Men's Coffee Groups: Not Just Fun and Games

The smaller, intimate world that coffee groups enclose often requires daily doses of suspense and excitement. In Wisconsin, games of chance (dice, number guessing, and coin flipping) and games of skill (cribbage, euchre, sheepshead, gin) fit the bill. Common tavern pastimes carried over into cafes, games such as these are nonexistent in Indiana. Hoosier men seem content to merely drink coffee and talk, although many shake up the daily ritual by participating in football, horse racing, and NASCAR betting pools. While euchre may well be the Hoosier card game of choice, I never saw it played in small town cafes.

Other common forms of entertainment include sharing jokes and e-mailed and photocopied humor, which then accumulates on owners' walls. A popular complaint transmitted via the Internet that has made the rounds of Hoosier cafes is this one taped to the wall of Kate's Coffee Shop in Portland owned by Ruth and Allen Bruss:

Senior Citizens
Are the nation's leading carriers of
AIDS!
Hearing AIDS, Band AIDS, Walking AIDS, Government AIDS,
And most of all
Monetary AIDS to their children!
The Golden Years have come at last!
I cannot see, I cannot pee, I cannot chew, I cannot screw.
My memory shrinks. My hearing stinks. No sense of smell.
     I look like hell.
My body's drooping, got trouble pooping.
So, the Golden Years have come at last?
Well, the Golden Years can kiss my ass!

Although it debuted more than fifteen years ago and circulated largely by photocopies, the menu for the fictional Roadkill Cafe still circulates throughout the state and includes some of Indiana's Finest Entrees, like Center Line Bovine ("tastes real good straight from the hood"), Slab of Lab, and Guess That Mess. All the rage for a couple of years, the roadkill theme all but faded away—only to reappear now and again in places like the Pleasant Lake Cafe in Pleasant Lake.[24]

Handmade signs and manufactured novelty signs are another form of cafe humor. At the former Spartan Inn in Wingate, this gem hung on the wall behind the glass pie case:

FOR SALE
Used tractor
Missing seat and steering wheel
Perfect for the farmer who's
Lost his ass and
Don't know which way to turn. . . .

Also common are mass-produced plastic and tin novelty signs like this one: "This is not Burger King. You don't get it your way. You take it my way or you don't get the damn thing." Jokes such as these help to alleviate the stress and hardships of growing old, running a farm, and operating a cafe, by sharing and airing complaints in a way that is both entertaining and publicly acceptable.

Despite their joking around, it would be a mistake to assume that coffee group members are just wasting time. There is plenty of serious business being schemed and implemented around Liars Tables statewide. At the Family Cafe in Knox, owner Rich Neuberg is one of a core group of dreamers and doers who gather at the Roundtable "to carry out visions through objectives that can be met." In 2003, the group raised $20,000 in a pledge drive and fund-raising walk for the Starke County Hospice, which itself originated as conversation at the Roundtable. Other fund-raising projects brewed, blended, and baked at the Family Cafe include a radio show and auction for the domestic violence shelter, a drive for Toys for Tots, and a gospel fest that benefited the food pantry, Habitat for Humanity, and efforts to organize a Starke County Boys and Girls Club. Other inspiring community activism resulted in a new community center and fire station in Hendricksville, courtesy of the coffee drinkers at Rosie's Diner, and the Wavestock concerts dreamed up and put on by the folks at Brenda's Kitchen in Waveland to raise funds for town revitalization. At the Dutchman Cafe in Freelandville, members of the Kraut Krew and other coffee drinkers not only cooperatively own the cafe, they also succeeded in building a new community center and fire station. Says Kraut Krew member John Clinkenbeard, "Anything we want to do in this community, we do it. The people who live here are the only ones going to take care of this place."

CAFES AS "COMMUNITY HEALTH WATCH"

Many coffee klatchers, as well as other elderly men and women customers, are so regular in their visits to local cafes that owners know it is nine o'clock when the Bullshippers arrive, or two thirty when John drops in for an afternoon chat and a cup (or two or four) of coffee. Some customers' visits are so regular and their eating habits so predictable that owners or their employees can have orders ready and waiting when they arrive. And when such customers fail to arrive without prior notice of their absence, cafe owners often worry that they may have had an accident and call or visit to check up on the missing persons. Because they are perhaps the only business in town that sees people on a regular, daily basis, cafes function as the "Community Health Watch," a name provided by the daughter of a Wisconsin cafe owner.

From their vantage point behind the counter, cafe owners, their families, and employees supervise the comings and goings of regular customers while keeping tabs on special health concerns and problems. They are often the first nonfamily members to know of heart attacks, strokes, accidents, or a doctor's order to restrict the diet. For customers who are supposed to be watching their cholesterol, owners supervise breakfast orders, ready to intercept the forbidden bacon or sausage. They scold diabetics who scorn sugar-free pies, heart patients who cannot pass up the biscuits and gravy, and dieters who lack the resolve to deny themselves dessert.

Regular customers who have met with an accident or other temporary disability often receive home deliveries from small town cafes. They may choose to phone in their orders or automatically receive whatever is the daily special. If they're able to get out, cafe owners or employees sometimes pick them up at home and bring them back to the cafe for a meal or an afternoon of coffee and conversation.

Until the Lapel Family Restaurant in Lapel was destroyed by fire in early 2005, owners Josie and Larry Montgomery served senior meals through their county's program on aging. Working with a professional nutritionist, they planned balanced meals suitable to the dietary needs of the elderly, especially widows and widowers, who no longer could or did cook for themselves. Although cafe owners often jokingly refer to themselves as "babysitters" and their businesses as "homes away from home," they appreciate and respect the caretaking role they play in the lives of community members, especially those who are elderly or alone.[25]

CAFES AS CHAMBERS OF COMMERCE
Promoting Small Town Life and Tourism
In their role as chambers of commerce, cafes intercede with outsiders on behalf of the local and area community. On any given weekend during the summer—and especially during the fall color season—adventure eaters and other tourists seek out Indiana's small town cafes, where they hope to experience (for an hour or less) small town culture. Bicyclists and motorcyclists all over the state make weekend pie rides to their favorite cafes,

as do Lafayette riders to Ann Cain's Wolcott Theatre Cafe in Wolcott. Fans on their way to or from Indiana University football and basketball games drop in at Kathy's Cafe in Morgantown for Saturday's pan-fried chicken and a piece of pie. To outsiders, the small town cafe is the most accessible of public spaces, a microcosm of an alternative way of life that is appealing because it appears more vital and authentic: slower, intimate, and community based. To locals, visits such as these elevate the everyday nature of the cafe and its clientele. Ann Cain observes that they sit "a little straighter, a little prouder. One of the greatest aspects of the small town cafe is the locals' sense of ownership."

At cafe counters and booths, many outsiders experience small town life through a process similar to osmosis: a kind of absorption through a semipermeable screen of self-protection and privacy rather than direct involvement and participation. At many cafes, tourists and travelers tuck themselves into booths along the wall and occupy themselves with private conversations and intense menu reading. They rarely join the locals at the counter, folks who tend not to have the time or the interest to take part in the social activities going on around them. With their backs toward other diners, waitresses, and coffee groups gathered for laughter and gossip, counter sitters read newspapers, books, and business papers, spreading out the contents of briefcases. The counter is where extra space can be appropriated for private use, unlike square tables set up with two or four chairs that invite company.

However, counter sitting is entirely different for strangers because they are so obvious, so exposed to the questioning stares of the regulars. Counter sitting puts strangers in the midst of the social activity and carries with it an obligation for conversation, especially about yourself: where you're from, what you do, why you're there. Perched on a counter stool, you can easily chat with owners and waitresses, swivel around to joke with the coffee crowd, and covertly evaluate food carried from the kitchen and baked goods sitting behind the counter. For these reasons, I prefer sitting at counters.

In cafes, out-of-towners and local residents come together. Cafes, therefore, make excellent tourist information bureaus. They supply maps and brochures for local attractions, locations of motels, and directions to destinations off the main routes. In Montezuma in Parke County, Janet's Family Restaurant regularly caters to tourists and provides copies of county guidebooks, maps to the area's covered bridges and historic sites, and color pamphlets for the area's tourist attractions. In Syracuse, locals share fishing tips with weekend boaters and lake home dwellers over omelets at the Syracuse Cafe. At the Corner Cafe in Nappanee, owner Marsha Thomas and her staff answer questions about the area's Amish people from curious visitors, who often demonstrate a profound degree of ignorance and naivety.

Cafes act as intercessors for visitors yet also provide refuge to the locals from seasonal swarms of sightseers. On a hot August afternoon in northern Indiana's Amish country, tourists flocked to the 1,100-seat Das Dutchman Essen Haus outside Middlebury, but the Village Inn on Main Street was quiet and cozy with a few tables of Amish and non-Amish people sharing talk over pie and coffee and iced tea. In Shipshewana, the locals' hideaway is the Country Corral Restaurant; in Metamora, they're at the Have-a-Bite Diner up on the highway. At still other cafes, such as Baby Boomers II in Hamilton, the locals tend to gather early on Saturday mornings to avoid the tourists and summer residents who fill the tiny restaurant between breakfast and lunch and force them to either abandon or adjust their regular daily visits.

Integrating the Community

The community bonds in the small town cafe. During locals-only hours, in daily coffee klatches and early morning breakfast groups, native, year-round, and seasonal residents come together for coffee and conversation, discovering commonalities upon which friendships develop and deepen.

Community members integrate in other ways as well. Natives who have moved away often make the cafe one of their first stops during visits home. Over coconut cream pie and coffee, they catch up on news and gossip with family members and old friends. So and so moved away. This person divorced. That person died. Talk brings them temporarily back into the community, connecting them to people and places they left long ago.

In small town cafes, others who have never left establish and solidify relationships with members of the community whom they have known slightly or not at all. Retirees come together in coffee klatches and at breakfast and lunch to reminisce about the years they spent farming, stringing telephone lines, or selling automobiles; though their past lives are different, retirement is something they have in common. Coffee groups especially bring together people who would otherwise have little to do with each other: retirees with working men, laborers with professionals, old men with young men, even adults with children. Eleven-year-old Clint Pepmeier, for example, shares a lunch table with men in their fifties, sixties, and seventies at the Dutchman Cafe in Freelandville

Once the local teen hangout, small town cafes are foreign territories to many of today's teenagers. Most cafe owners note that the largest percentage of their regular customers continues to be those of middle and advanced age. Although each year brings a certain number of deaths, the average age remains fairly stable at about fifty-five to sixty. New people are added to the mix as they retire or undergo life-changes that make possible daily—and many times three or four times daily!—or, at the least, semi-weekly visits to the cafe.

I saw few children in all of the cafes I visited, so few, in fact, that when I did see them, I noticed them. At the Gosport Diner in Gosport, a boy about ten years old lunched with the male scholars under the Gosport University sign. At the Hilltop Restaurant in Lakeville, members of the high school football team gathered for breakfasts of omelets, biscuits and gravy, and steak and eggs, a tradition started several years ago by one player's older brother. Janet Delaney, owner of Janet's Kitchen in Rensselaer, reports that students frequently take advantage of their off-campus permits to lunch on burgers, fries, and Coke, just as she and her friends did in the 1950s. Or rather, the boys eat burgers, fries, and Cokes. The girls tend to eat only fries and Diet Coke. Other people integrate into the community as well. From Howe in the north to Tell City in the south, widows network for friendship and support. At other cafes, divorcees and stay-at-home mothers with kids grown and gone enter the social world of paid employment, and those who otherwise live alone are pulled back into the community. At the Old School Cafe in Pleasant, a man and his son regularly show up for breakfast or lunch. Sue Christman, mother of owner Roger Christman, notes this is about the only contact they have with others in the community. In Jamestown, at Dick and Judy's, the late Jim Buriss filled nineteen post-retirement years by coming in at four in the morning to make biscuits and gravy. Hundreds of miles away, retiree Bernie Herman opens Julie Fischer's Tell Street Cafe in Tell City with his own key at three thirty every morning. By the time she arrives, he has laid out the rugs, started the coffee, and turned on the lights. "It makes him feel important," Julie says, "and it's a great help to me to be able to focus on work in the kitchen. We're like a real family here. We take care of each other."

Supporting the Community: "Living Newspapers," Fundraisers, Festivals, and Investment

As the social hubs of small towns, cafes are "living newspapers." All the news that's worth knowing is channeled through the men perched at the counter or crowded around the Liars Table. At the small town cafe, you'll hear the social column and learn about yesterday's funeral that brought in thirty cars. On the news page you'll learn who was elected county commissioner or school board member. On the editorial page you'll hear various opinions on topics ranging from politics to road construction. On the foods page, you'll digest dishes like Graveyard Leftovers and "Ghoulash" prepared by Donna and Floyd Friend at the Gosport Diner in Gosport for special customer Sammy Terry, Indiana's favorite television ghoul. On the sports page, you'll hear replays from last night's Colts or Pacers game, a shot-by-shot analysis of the local men's golf outing, or a brief introduction to coon hunting.

In the classifieds—the bulletin board near the front door—you can find yourself a drywall contractor, a sidewalk layer, and—at the Old School Cafe in Pleasant—a cemetery restoration professional. At many cafes, the bulletin board is also the entertainment section. There you'll find advertisements for the garden tractor pull in Denver, Friday night's demolition derby in Spencer, and cowboy church in Hartford City. The minutes from the town board meeting are there, too. The ballpark is in need of regrading and reliming, the community center needs 150 new folding chairs, and so-and-so's dog is still running loose. All the news—and then some—that's fit to print.

In addition to providing local news, cafes act as clearinghouses for local information and assistance. At the former Spartan Inn in Wingate, owner Jo Ann Phillips said that "people call here all the time for help. 'I've had my dog hit,' they say. 'Can someone there help me move it?'" At other cafes around the state, callers want to know the score of last night's high school football game, the price of gas in a neighboring town, if rain is on the way, or whether one of the regulars has been released from the hospital.

Another important function of cafes is their owners' support of local benefits, fundraisers, and organizations. Drop the change you receive after paying your bill into one of the many decorated cans next to cash registers. You, too, can contribute to hurricane relief, cancer benefits, the county humane society, or historical museum. At Storie's Restaurant in Greensburg, your vote can help elect this year's Little Miss Tree City. (I couldn't resist voting for Mollie, whose can was hand-lettered with this campaign slogan: "My name is Mollie / Cute as a Dolly / Vote for me, I'll be Jolly.") At Windell's Cafe in Dale, Darrel and Betty Jenkins regularly donate to civic organizations, youth sports teams, clubs at the high school, and area festivals, and sponsor a queen candidate for the annual Dale Fest. "We're a small town," Darrel says matter-of-factly, "so people have to do everything."

Like Windell's, many cafes sponsor league bowling and softball teams, as well as youth T-ball, baseball, soccer, and peewee football teams. Their owners proudly display trophies, plaques, and other awards on shelves and walls and in display cases. Some cafe owners also support civic organizations like the Jaycees, Kiwanis, and Lions by providing meeting rooms and banquet facilities during or after the regular business day. You'll find club banners at the Chicken Inn in Mitchell, Brock's Family Restaurant in Brownstown, the Main Cafe in New Harmony, and at other cafes throughout the state.

Involvement in community festivals is another way cafe owners contribute to their communities. In Wingate, Jo Ann Phillips, who has served as president of the Sweet Corn Festival and chairwoman of the food committee, closed the Spartan Inn during the daylong festival so as not to compete with food booths at the festival. After all, money made on the festival is money made for the community of approximately 325 residents. Each year the festival committee offers cash scholarships to the top two graduating seniors and donates a percentage of festival profits to churches. Other money goes to the fire department. Despite the potential for great business during the weekend of Gosport's Lazy Days festival, Donna and Floyd Friend hold to their regular Monday through Friday schedule. They, too, refuse to compete with the fundraiser breakfast at the Masonic Hall, the hog roast, fish fry, chicken smorgasbord, or the community picnic in the park. In a similar way, cafe owners often support other local businesses by refusing to replicate menus and services. When she first opened the

Wolcott Theatre Cafe in Wolcott, for example, Ann Cain left tenderloins off her menu because the tavern across the street served them.

The Wolcott Theatre Cafe is an excellent example of how cafe owners like Ann invest in their community by reclaiming a vacant building, opening a new business, and giving the local economy a boost. In nearby Remington, Ron and his late wife Jerri Peppin achieved a similar success when they gutted the old Remington Cafe and brought it back to new life, restoring not only a business but an important downtown building. While the most successful cafes have the capacity to rejuvenate communities, many others boost their local and area economies in a more modest way by purchasing locally produced foods and supplies. At Nel's Cafe in Ossian, owner Nel Geurs purchases fresh bacon from Ossian Packing Company. At Sonny's in Hartford City, owner Sonny Melton makes the rounds of local grocery stores for meats and fresh produce every day. At Kate's Coffee Shop in Portland, Ruth Bruss buys fresh garden vegetables and seasonal fruits from local farm stands and brown eggs from a farm. She prefers fresh foods over the canned or frozen variety, but just as importantly, she recognizes the value of mutual support. "The farmers, me, the businesses down the street, we're all in this together," she says.

We are indeed—pie riders, adventure eaters, cafe owners, farmers, food suppliers, Bullshippers, Indiana residents, and curious visitors. We're all in "it" together, and much of "it" can be found in *Cafe Indiana*.

NOTES

1. You can learn more about German immigrants who made Indiana home from Giles Hoyt, "Germans," *Peopling Indiana: The Ethnic Experience*, ed. Robert M. Taylor and Connie A. McBirney (Indianapolis: Indiana Historical Society, 1996), 146–81. As a graduate student at Indiana University in the 1970s, folklorist Simon J. Bronner documented the turtle soup traditions in Catholic parishes in rural Dubois County. See his *Grasping Things: Folk Material Culture and Mass Society in America* (Lexington: University Press of Kentucky, 1986), 160–78.

2. "We find it difficult to be charmed by plain roast beef, but to Midwesterners it seems to be a never-ending source of eating pleasure," Jane and Michael Stern note in *Roadfood* (New York: Random House, 1977), 268.

3. For more on how cafe owners and cooks act as ritual specialists, see Joanne Raetz Stuttgen, *Cafe Wisconsin: A Guide to Wisconsin's Down-Home Cafes* (Madison: University of Wisconsin Press, 2004), 275–78. The conservative nature of Hoosier cafe food is perhaps a result of the compromise between conflicting ethnic and regional food habits, as Margaret Mead suggests of American food in general. Susan Kalčik explores Mead's observations on the "cultural standardization" of American food in "Ethnic

Foodways in America: Symbol and the Performance of Identity," in *Ethnic and Regional Foodways in the United States: The Performance of Group Identity,* ed. Linda Keller Brown and Kay Mussell (Knoxville: University of Tennessee Press, 1984), 37–65. For more on the diverse but unified nature of American food, see Waverly Lewis Root and Richard de Rochemont, *Eating in America: A History* (New York: William Morrow, 1976), 276–312.

4. Jane and Michael Stern, "Love Me Tenderloin," *Gourmet,* January 2003, 22–23.

5. Food historian and cookbook author Linda Stradley supposess that Hoosier sugar cream pie originated in Indiana with the Shaker community in the 1850s. This is very unlikely, as Indiana's only Shaker community—West Union, established at Busro, near Vincennes, in 1810—was plagued with troubles and strife and disbanded in 1827. It's possible that Hoosier sugar cream pie originated with Indiana pioneers, or with the Amish, who make a similar eggless baked cream pie. Linda Stradley, *I'll Have What They're Having: Legendary Local Cuisine* (Guilford, CT: Three Forks, 2000), 185. Also, www.whatscookingamerica.net. To learn about the West Union Shaker community, see Stephen J. Stein, *The Shaker Experience in America* (New Haven: Yale University Press, 1992). Stein is professor emeritus of religious studies at Indiana University. For a recipe for Amish Cream Pie, see Joanne Raetz Stuttgen and Terese Allen, *Cafe Wisconsin Cookbook* (Madison: University of Wisconsin Press, 2007), 152.

6. To learn more about Wick's Pies, see *BizVoice,* the bimonthly magazine of the Indiana Chamber of Commerce, September–October 2005, 50–51, and www.wickspies.com.

7. Linda Stradley identifies persimmon pudding as one of Indiana's "legendary local cuisines" (the other is sugar cream pie) in *I'll Have What They're Having,* 201. *New York Times* food writer Raymond Sokolov has written about Hoosiers' fondness for persimmons in *Fading Feast* (New York: Farrar Straus Giroux, 1981), 23–29, and *Why We Eat What We Eat* (New York: Summit Books, 1991), 163–64.

8. Longtime Hoosier restaurant critic Reid Duffy credits Andrew Jackson Rogers, proprietor of the Nashville House, with creating fried biscuits with apple butter in the 1940s (*Indiana's Favorite Restaurants* [Bloomington: Indiana University Press, 2001], 45–46).

9. The distribution of fried bologna sandwiches appears to be fairly widespread, with West Virginia, Ohio, and southeastern Indiana being the heart of the fried bologna and egg variety. You can follow an entertaining discussion about fried bologna sandwiches on the forums section of www.roadfood.com. No recipe is needed if you want to make your own, but David Letterman's "favorite lunch," Fried Baloney Sandwich, is found in Dorothy Mengering, *Home Cookin' with Dave's Mom* (New York: Atria, 1996), 81. Remember to slit your slice or it'll hump up like an inverted bowl—which, on page 132, Dorothy recommends filling with scrambled eggs for a fun breakfast.

10. Crave a second helping? Stories from CNN, NPR, and MSNBC appear at the following Web sites: www.cnn.com/2004/HEALTH/01/16/brain.sandwich.ap; www.npr.org/templates/story/story.php?storyId=1592227; www.msnbc.msn.com/id/3969530/tory.php?storyId=1592227. These stories cover the impact of mad cow disease on an unusual Hoosier food tradition.

11. Michael Stern describes Indiana as "one of the most piecentric states in the nation" in his review of Gray Brothers Cafeteria in Mooresville at www.roadfood.com. Sadly, Grays, with its commercial marshmallow cream-type meringue, is partly to blame for the worrisome drift toward partway pies. That perfect, pretty dome of fake meringue has become not only enviable but desirable, and some cafe owners have adopted it with relish. I prefer mine made with real egg whites and with beads of sugary sweat.

12. Indiana University folklorist Sandy Dolby, a native of Huntington, credits Azar's Big Boy, a Fort Wayne–based franchise of the national restaurant chain, with introducing Hoosiers to fresh strawberry pie in the mid-1950s. Since then, we've been enraptured. I highly recommend the strawberry pie at Janet's Family Restaurant in Montezuma, available year-round, for a satisfying fix.

13. Terese Allen and I debate the pros and cons of real whipped cream versus Cool Whip in *Cafe Wisconsin Cookbook*, 153–55. See also Jane and Michael Stern, *Blue Plate Specials and Blue Ribbon Chefs* (New York: Lebhar-Friedman Books, 2001), 59–60.

14. See Charles Camp, *American Foodways: What, When, Why, and How We Eat in America* (Little Rock, AR: August House, 1989), and Lin T. Humphrey, "Small Group Festive Gatherings," *Journal of the Folklore Institute* (1979): 190–201.

15. Recent ethnographic culinary quests that use food as a lens for bringing everyday life into clearer focus include Pascale Le Draoulec, *American Pie: Slices of Life (and Pie) from America's Back Roads* (New York: Harper Collins, 2002), and four little books by John T. Edge: *Apple Pie: An American Story* (2004), *Donuts: An American Passion* (2006), *Fried Chicken: An American Story* (2004), and *Hamburgers and Fries: An American Story* (2005), all published by G. P. Putnam, New York.

16. In *The Great Good Place: Cafes, Coffee Shops, Bookstores, Bars, Hair Salons, and Other Hangouts at the Heart of a Community* (New York: Marlowe, 1999), sociologist Ray Oldenburg examines similar informal public gathering places, which he refers to as "'third places' (after home, first, and workplace, second)," and their myriad functions. My thanks to Ann Cain, owner of the Wolcott Theatre Cafe in Wolcott, for my copy of this work. See also Oldenburg's *Celebrating the Third Place: Inspiring Stories about the "Great Good Places" at the Heart of Our Communities* (New York: Marlowe, 2002). For a concise social-oriented examination of the small town cafe as a "food place," where feminist politics are served along with from-scratch cooking, see the chapter "On the Town: The Emma Chase" in William Least Heat-Moon, *PrairyErth* (Boston: Houghton Mifflin, 1991), 122–30.

17. An understanding of the missing periods in Indiana cafe history, architecture, and interior style might be found in my exploration of Wisconsin cafes in *Cafe Wisconsin*, 278–82.

18. Diner devotees will enjoy John Baeder, *Diners* (New York: H. N. Abrams, 1978); Richard J. S. Gutman and Elliott Kaufman, *American Diner* (New York: Harper and Row, 1979); and Gerd Kittel, *Diners: People and Places* (New York: Thames and Hudson, 1990).

19. The do-it-yourself movement received great impetus from publications and retail businesses that encouraged Americans to get personally involved with the construction and maintenance of their homes. Among the most influential publications was Stewart Brand's *Whole Earth Catalog*. Major home improvement retailers include Menards, founded in 1972, Home Depot in 1978, and Lowe's in 1946. The do-it-yourself ideology also inspired owners to build their own cafes. A good example is Rosie's Diner in Hendricksville, built of concrete block by the owner's husband in 1999.

20. According to Sam Stall, *Tray Chic* (Indianapolis: Guild Press–Emmis Publishing, 2004), the modern cafeteria era in Indiana began with Poe's (Martinsville) in 1954, MCL in 1950, Laughner's in 1964, Gray Brothers (Mooresville) in 1969, and Jonathon Byrd's in 1988. Stall distinguishes between Hoosier cafeterias and buffets, which lack "the civilizing presence of the serving line." He denigrates buffets as "hog troughs" and ridicules the food as home cooking "dragged down to the lowest common denominator." This may be true of the national chains, but it's an insult to the owners of many small town cafes who spend several days preparing truly from-scratch foods for their buffets and

smorgasbords. What cafeterias and buffets/smorgasbords share in common is a lack of off-the-menu ordering, food prepared in quantity, and its en masse presentation to the consumer. Featured in *Tray Chic*, Marian's home cooking cafeteria, opened in Oolitic in 1988, is now Corey's Cafe. It is a Next Best Bet in my South Central chapter.

21. For a nostalgic pictorial history of American restaurants, as well as a few Indiana roadside sites, see John Baeder, *Gas, Food, and Lodging* (New York: Abbeville Press, 1982). See also John F. Mariani, *America Eats Out* (New York: William Morrow, 1991). A basic history is Richard Pillsbury, *From Boarding House to Bistro* (Boston: Unwin Hyman, 1990).

22. Reid Duffy cites statistics that validate my observations: 85 to 90 percent of restaurants in the United States close or change ownership within five years of opening their doors (*Indiana's Favorite Restaurants,* vii).

23. Folklorist Simon Bronner explores another traditional way that older men in Dubois County, Indiana, deal with the problems of retirement in *The Carver's Art: Crafting Meaning from Wood* (Lexington: University Press of Kentucky, 1996).

24. See also B. R. "Buck" Peterson, *The Original Roadkill Cookbook* (Berkeley, CA: Ten Speed Press, 1987), and Richard Marco, *How to Cook Roadkill* (Bradford, UK: M.C.B. Publications, 1993). For more popular examples of photocopier lore, don't miss Alan Dundes and Carl R. Pagter, *Work Hard and You Shall Be Rewarded* (Detroit: Wayne State University Press, 1992), and *When You're Up to Your Ass in Alligators* (Detroit: Wayne State University Press, 1987).

25. Other small town businesses often take on the role of "babysitter" for marginalized populations. In *Grand Opening* (1987), novelist Jon Hassler's portrait of small town Minnesota life in the 1940s, the Foster family owns a grocery and deposits a rather senile grandfather at the pool hall across the street, where he drinks coffee and passes the afternoon in idle talk.

Index

By Town

By Cafe